CHRIST
THE FIRST
2000
YEARS

"Christology is a veritable spiritual and intellectual briar patch of tangled interpretations, offered over the centuries by theologians, mystics, and devotional writers. Now, at last, the general reader has a lucid and readable guide to Christian reflections on the nature and work of Christ. An essential book for the thinking believer."

Derek Wilson, historian and author of many books, including *Mrs Luther and her Sisters* (Lion) and *The First Horseman, The Traitor's Mark*, and *The Devil's Chalice*.

"This book is like a whirlwind tour of the history of Western civilization, showing how ideas about Christ have both influenced and reflected changing social attitudes for the last 2,000 years. Drawing from ancient sources as well as their own experience and insights, the authors present a fascinating account that will enlighten even the most well-informed reader."

John Drane, theologian and author of many books, including *The World of the Bible, Introduction to the Old Testament*, and *Introduction to the New Testament* (Lion)

"This is a very impressive book. It is extraordinarily wide-ranging in its scope and deals with a great number of complex issues. Yet, at the same time, it is throughout well-written, attractively presented, and lucidly argued. It is well-informed in all the different areas it covers, and provides an eminently readable and reliable account of all of these. Above all, it shows why the figure of Jesus Christ was so important for the Christian movement from the very beginning, why and how he has been variously understood and portrayed throughout the last 2,000 years –and in all parts of the world – and why he remains so central a figure for Christianity right up to the present day. This is a book that both Christians and non-Christians can read and gain much from."

Dr Andrew Chester, Reader in New Testament Studies, Selwyn College, Cambridge

CHRIST
THE FIRST
2000
YEARS

FROM HOLY MAN TO GLOBAL
BRAND: HOW OUR VIEW OF
CHRIST HAS CHANGED ACROSS
TIME AND CULTURES

Martyn Whittock
and Esther Whittock

LION

Published by Lion Books
an imprint of
Lion Hudson plc
Wilkinson House, Jordan Hill Road,
Oxford OX2 8DR, England
www.lionhudson.com/lion

ISBN 978 0 7459 7045 5
e-ISBN 978 0 7459 7046 2

First edition 2016

Acknowledgments
Scripture quotations taken from The New Revised Standard Version (Anglicized Edition) of the Bible copyright © 1989 by the Division of Christian Education of the National Council of Churches in the USA. Used by permission. All rights reserved.

Quotes from The Qur'an, translated by Professor M. A. S. Abdel Haleem, copyright © 2008, used by permission of Oxford University Press. All rights reserved.

The publisher has no responsibility for the persistence or accuracy of URLs for external or third-party internet websites referred to in this book, and does not guarantee that any content on such websites is, or will remain, accurate or appropriate.

A catalogue record for this book is available from the British Library

Printed and bound in the UK, February 2016, LH26

This book is dedicated in memory of Revd Dr John Hughes (1978–2014), Chaplain and Dean of Jesus College, Cambridge, and greatly valued mentor. His wise words, phenomenal biblical knowledge, and abounding kindness truly inspired me to be the theologian, teacher, and now writer that I am today. This book is just a small token of appreciation for everything that John did for myself, the Cambridge Theology department, and Jesus College. He was a true light and inspiration; his gentle character, thirst for knowledge, and love of God shall be forever remembered by all who knew him.

Esther Whittock

Author Biographies

Martyn Whittock is a Licensed Lay Minister in the Church of England and is also qualified as a Lay Preacher within the Methodist Church. A secondary school teacher for over thirty years, he is currently the Curriculum Leader for Spiritual, Moral, Social and Cultural education at a Wiltshire secondary school, Kingdown School in Warminster. He is the author or co-author of forty-one books, aimed at making historical and cultural themes accessible to the general reader. Recent books include: *A Brief History of Life in the Middle Ages* (2009), *A Brief History of the Third Reich* (2011), *The Viking Blitzkrieg* (2013), *A Brief Guide to Celtic Myths and Legends* (2013), and *The Anglo-Saxon Avon Valley Frontier* (2014). He is currently co-writing a book entitled: *1016 and 1066: Why the Vikings Caused the Norman Conquest* (due for publication in 2016).

Esther Whittock read Theology and Religious Studies at Jesus College, University of Cambridge, where she graduated with a first-class degree. She specialized in Christianity and biblical studies, and also studied modules in Islam, New Testament Greek, and sociology of religion. Her specialisms in her third year were Christology in the New Testament, the theology and composition of the Gospel of John, and the way that Christ and the Bible are understood in Indian and African cultures. She is currently a teacher of Religious Education at an inner-city secondary school, Waverley School in Birmingham.

Contents

Acknowledgments

We are grateful for the assistance provided by a number of people while writing this book. John Worth, Tom Morgan, Hannah Whittock, and Chris Scorer read and commented on the text. Their suggestions and insights were very valuable. We also wish to thank Sabaa Batool and Melissa Nathans for their invaluable explanations and clarifications of how Christ is understood in Islam and Judaism. We also wish to thank Robert Dudley, our agent, and Ali Hull at Lion Hudson for all their encouragement and support. It goes without saying that all errors are our own.

Martyn and Esther Whittock

Introduction

As we were in the process of writing this book, five specific and contrasting approaches to Christ made a *particular* impression on us...

Firstly, when preparing to show a film clip of the life of Christ to a class of predominantly Muslim children, in an inner-city secondary school, one exclaimed: "It's forbidden (*haram*) to see pictures of Prophet *Isa!*" There then followed a discussion centred on the fact that this film clip was part of a unit of work on Christianity and that Christians have no concerns about visually representing Jesus. Here is a glimpse of Jesus, son of Mary, the Christ – or *Isa ibn Maryam, al-Masih* – as understood in Islam.

Secondly, on Highway 4 from San Francisco to the Sierra Nevada mountains, there is a striking image on a billboard beside the road at Farmington. Set against the background of the stars and stripes flag and an American eagle are the words: "JESUS SAVES". Here is Jesus Christ invoked in the context of a very striking form of US patriotism.

Thirdly, in the Sir John Ritblat Treasures of the British Library Gallery, Christ gazes out from the pages of a seventeenth-century Ethiopian gospel book, with skin a delicate shade of brown and almond-shaped eyes. Here is Christ of the Middle East and of Africa.

Fourthly, in the same gallery, the initial page of the Gospel of Matthew, from the early eighth-century *Lindisfarne Gospels*, is a masterpiece of Celtic spirals and Anglo-Saxon interlaced animal patterns. Its illuminated Latin script begins with the words that modern translations communicate as: "An account of the genealogy of Jesus the Messiah [Greek: Christ], the son of David, the son of Abraham."[1] Here is Christ and his Jewish roots as presented by an Anglo-Saxon craftsman in a newly converted barbarian kingdom on the fringes of western Europe.

Fifthly, in a Wiltshire parish church, a mid-nineteenth-century stained glass window depicts Christ crucified on the cross and then, above this image of suffering, he is depicted on a throne as ruler of creation. Here is Christ crucified and then raised and glorified: God's triumphant Son.

Five different understandings and presentations, yet each a reminder of the impact of Christ over 2,000 years. But who is the figure who can give rise to such a rich array of understanding, debate, art, and controversy? Exploring that question is the theme of this book.

CHAPTER 1

What is a Christ?

Today the two words "Jesus Christ" are so familiar to so many people that it can almost seem as if "Christ" was the surname of "Jesus". In fact, Jesus (which is a Latin form of a Greek version of the Aramaic name *Yeshua*) is a personal-name. Jesus/*Yeshua* was a first-century version of the older Hebrew name, Joshua. "Christ", on the other hand, is a title. In Hebrew the word was *mashiach* and meant "the anointed one", a person chosen by God. This word gives us the modern term: "messiah". In Jewish history kings and high priests had sacred oil (olive oil) poured on their heads. In this way they were "anointed" and identified as chosen by God and therefore special. It was this meaning that lay behind the word *mashiach*. The Greek-speaking members of the early church translated this meaning into Greek, which was *christos* and from this we get: Christ. In the gospels (see chapter 3) the writers – writing in Greek – often make it clear that it is a title by using the words "*the* Christ" to describe Jesus.

With regard to language: in the lifetime of Jesus the day-to-day language in the towns and villages of Galilee (such as Nazareth or Capernaum) where he did most of his teaching would have been *Aramaic*; in the Jerusalem Temple and in the synagogues the official language of the holy books of what Christians now call the Old Testament was *Hebrew*; the government language of the Roman empire was *Latin*; but in the eastern Mediterranean the international language, which operated alongside Latin, was *Greek*. This is why the first Christian writings were produced in Greek and it explains why many words such as "Jesus" and "Christ" are Greek versions of Aramaic or Hebrew originals.

All of this means that Jesus is the man and Christ is the verdict on him and his significance. Clearly, not everyone in the first century thought that Jesus was the Christ. The same is true today. Few people today seriously question the reality of a first-century Jewish teacher and preacher named Jesus, because the evidence for his existence is overwhelming. But whether he was "the Christ" is quite a different matter. Today, as then, this question divides people. To a humanist and atheist such as Philip Pullman, the man Jesus has been distorted and misrepresented by the later Christian church. Hence the title of his 2010 novel: *The Good Man Jesus and the Scoundrel Christ*. Pullman knew that he was rejecting all that Christians believe about the nature and importance of Jesus. He sought to sharply divide "Jesus" from "Christ". To Christians, on the other hand, nothing could be further from the truth because they, in stark contrast, believe that the man Jesus was and is "the Christ": the one sent by God to save the world. Even more radical than this, they believe that in this Christian definition of the Christ he was and is, in some way (see chapter 4), the same as God. For Christians, faith in Christ coincides with faith in God. This is very controversial. The battle-lines meet at the word "Christ".

The focus of this book

This great debate about Christ is what this book is all about. It is an overview of the changing ways in which Christ and his nature have been understood and presented up to the early twenty-first century. The study of Christ's nature is known as Christology. This book is not a history of Christianity, as that would be far too large a subject. Instead, it is an overview of the changing understanding and presentation of Christianity's central character. It is as its title explains, *Christ: The First 2,000 Years*. That focus, by its very nature, touches on 2,000 years of history and belief. The study of people's beliefs about who Jesus was and is and his significance can often appear arcane and impenetrable but this book will examine why this does not have to be so and why it is so important.

Of the current world population of about 7 billion, about 2.2 billion are Christians. They are named and defined by that Greek title (Christ) that has been applied to the Jewish teacher, Jesus. Their ideas about Jesus have had a massive impact on the world over the last 2,000 years and continue to do so. In the New Testament we see the beginning of this exploration of the significance of Jesus; but this exploration, this great debate among believers and non-believers, has continued ever since. As a result of this influence, the importance of Christ extends far beyond the Christian faith community and far beyond the religious turmoil of the first century in the eastern regions of the Roman empire. Jesus features in the pages of the Islamic Qur'an and his image can be found in Hindu temples. Christian (and non-Christian) concepts concerning him influence art, literature, and history in all parts of the globe. Across the world in the twenty-first century men, women, and children will live – and some will die – as a direct consequence of what they believe about Christ.

Some key questions

Before we explore any further, there are some important questions that need consideration:

- How was the Hebrew version of the title "Christ" (*mashiach*) used at the time of Jesus? What was its backstory? How did it resonate with first-century Jewish religion and politics?
- Did Jesus ever use it of himself?
- How was the term understood by the Greek-speaking men and women who rapidly became the majority members of what had started as a sect of Judaism, but soon became a separate religion called Christianity?

Getting some answers to these questions will help us understand the foundations for what has occurred since in the way Christ has been understood over 2,000 years.

"Christ" in the first century

Long before the title "the anointed one" was taken on by the Christians, the word and idea was Jewish. And it still is. It is found in the Jewish Bible, which in Judaism is called the *Tanakh* and by Christians the Old Testament. As we have seen, it was first used to describe the kings of Israel who were marked out as chosen by God by being anointed with oil. In this way, for example, the prophet Samuel marked out David as being God's chosen ruler over the Jewish people.

When the Jewish Hebrew Bible was translated into Greek (c. 300–200 BC), the Hebrew word *mashiach* was translated by using the Greek word *christos*. This Greek-language version of the Jewish Bible is known as the *Septuagint*. As a result, the word "christ" was in the public domain, as it were, long before

Christians began using it to describe Jesus. This is important to remember because, by the time of Jesus, many Jews in the eastern Mediterranean were beginning to lose their Hebrew language and were increasingly speaking Greek. For these Greek-speaking Jews, the idea of "a christ" was a familiar one.

Back to the early kings and priests... It was thought that when a person was anointed they received from God the wisdom and ability to do the things expected of them. This became particularly associated with the power and responsibility of being a king. The first three kings of Israel – Saul, David, and Solomon – are all described as being anointed by a prophet. In this sense each one was a *mashiach* (a messiah) although this is not how we would think of them today. Even the non-Jewish Persian king, Cyrus, was described in this way when he was believed to be doing the will of God. Over time, though, the word began to take on even deeper meanings. It began to be used to describe a future messiah-king who would appear at the end of time, restore Israel, and bring in a new era of peace and justice. This future messiah-king would be the one chosen by God to bring all this about. He would be a descendant of the famous King David and would make Israel great once more. Through a time of suffering and judgment (often described as the "Day of the Lord") the Jewish people would finally be gathered together in a secure and peaceful ownership of their own land and there would be a golden age of peace. Foreign oppressors would be defeated and God's people would experience a moral awakening and transformation. At times the hope extended beyond Israel and encompassed the whole world in this longed-for future age, as all people would come to recognize and worship the God of Israel.

The ultimate "Christ"

When Jewish kings fell short of the ideal expected of them and when, eventually, the Jewish kingdom itself was destroyed by the Babylonians (in 586 BC), this future messiah-king became even more important and longed for. He became a "messiah" in the way that we now understand the meaning of the word. The promised future End Time messiah would be related to – but in a different league to – the earlier anointed kings of Israel. He would be in an even more intense way God's agent and representative. In this way the idea of the messiah-king both looked back to the "good old days" of great King David and also forward to a world that would be just and perfect. Sometimes one idea predominated; sometimes the other. In the Old Testament there are hints that this idea was developing. Ideas about the ideal king and the promised future age (sometimes without actually mentioning the messiah-king) can be found in the books of the Old Testament prophets such as Amos, Isaiah, Micah, Hosea, Ezekiel, and Jeremiah. But the idea really took off in the century or so before the birth of Jesus.

It seems clear that Jesus himself was very aware of the idea of the End Time coming of God's ultimate kingdom as it is found in the Old Testament prophet Isaiah. There are, in fact, so many echoes of this in so many places in the words of Jesus in the gospels that even someone making the most determined effort to interpret the gospels as the creations of the later church, rather than the authentic voice of Jesus, could probably be persuaded that this formed part, at least, of his original teaching. Overall, the evidence indicates that Jesus saw himself as playing a key part in the proclaiming of the promised and looked-for new world order, which was now imminent.

Given their loss of independence, as the Jewish people came under the foreign rule of Babylonians, Persians, Greeks, and

Romans, it is not surprising that the hope of a messiah-king grew in importance. In this there was a tension between those looking forward to a future *spiritual transformation* and those looking to a *political solution* to the problems and suffering faced by the Jewish people. The two were not necessarily in opposition but, when taken to extremes, could present very different views of what the age of the messiah-king might look like. But that he would be a king, with power and authority, was common to both strands of this belief.

Jewish ideas about "Christ" at the time of Jesus

Qumran and the Dead Sea Scrolls

We would like to know a lot more than we do about messiah-hopes at the time of Jesus. However there are clues. At Qumran, near the Dead Sea, a strictly hierarchical community was set up, probably by a Jewish group called the Essenes. The group seems to have been dedicated to separating themselves from society and living a life of religious purity, prayer, ritual washing, communal meals, and celibacy. It appears that the site was abandoned following an earthquake in about 31 BC but then reoccupied around the time of Jesus in the first century. Qumran was eventually destroyed and abandoned during the first Jewish uprising against Roman rule in AD 68.

What did this community believe? We cannot be entirely sure, but nearby the discovery in caves of the so-called Dead Sea Scrolls gives some insights into their beliefs. No scrolls were found at Qumran itself but the same type of pottery was found both at the site of Qumran and in the caves with the scrolls. This indicates that the two sites were connected since the pottery is unique to these two locations. Among the Dead Sea Scrolls survive what are probably the oldest extant copies of Old Testament books, along with sacred books not traditionally included in the Jewish Old Testament, as well as the rules of a religious community. The documents include some that are peculiar to the Qumran community. These reveal that they were greatly concerned with the End Times and studied the Jewish scriptures in the hope of finding prophetic references to contemporary and future events. They seem to have believed that only they would spot these as only they had "eyes to see". This is all very messianic and End Time-orientated and reveals that some Jews at the time of Jesus were certain that the coming of the messiah was imminent.

The "Teacher of Righteousness" mentioned in a number of the documents may have referred either to the original organizer of the community, to successive leaders of the group, or it may have had a future meaning. This last interpretation is possible since another name for a future revelation of this "Teacher" seems to have been "Expounder of the Law", who would make clear the rules by which righteous people should live. In one document this "Expounder of the Law" was specifically identified as representing the "star" mentioned in the Old Testament book of Numbers, which says: "a star shall come out of [the descendants of] Jacob" (Numbers 24:17).[1] Whether or not the future "Teacher" and the future "Expounder" were one and the same, what *is* clear is that belief in the "Expounder of the Law" was closely tied to messianic hopes, since it was thought that he would accompany one known as "the prince of all the congregation" and "the shoot of David", who was clearly the messiah and descended from King David. This combined great priest and great king would bring in the longed-for future age. This idea of priest-proclaimer and messiah-king finds an echo in the way in which the relationship of John the

Baptist and Jesus is referred to in the gospels. Clearly, there was a hope and a mindset common to both sets of documents and this suggests shared ideas about how the messiah would be revealed. This does not need to have involved any connection between the Qumran community and Jesus and his early followers, as it may simply have arisen out of a similar reading of the Old Testament. But clearly, a lot of conversations about the messiah were going on in the first half of the first century in Roman-occupied Palestine. The words "messiah" and "christ" were very much on the agendas of a significant number of people.

Resistance fighters against Roman occupation

Other clues about Jewish beliefs in the coming messiah-king may survive in some surprising places. The fact that one of Jesus' followers was named Simon the *Zealot* (a revolutionary anti-Roman Jewish group) and the possibility that the second name of Judas *Iscariot* may possibly mean something like "dagger-man" (derived from a group of anti-Roman assassins called the *Sicarii*), suggest that some, at least, of his followers had political and nationalist hopes regarding his impact on their contemporary society – at least at first. Similarly, at the start of the Acts of the Apostles the question is put to the resurrected Jesus: "Lord, is this the time when you will restore the kingdom to Israel?" (Acts 1:6). Many early followers of Jesus hoped that the future age was about to begin and with it a transformation of the fortunes of the Jewish people.

Other Jewish people, though, as we saw with regard to the community at Qumran, were putting their hopes elsewhere. When Simon ben Kosiba, known as *"Bar Kokhba"* (meaning "son of a star"), led a revolt against Rome between AD 132 and 135, his nickname suggests that he had messianic ideas about the nature of his revolt. This is because there was the tradition, mentioned earlier, that described the messiah as being like a star. It is uncertain whether he believed this, but he was descended from the royal family of King David (as indeed, to be fair, a great many Jews were by that time), which enhanced any messianic claims he may have made. There is evidence that at least one Jewish religious teacher – Rabbi Akiva ben Joseph (lived AD 50–135) – thought Bar Kokhba might be the messiah, although others rejected this. One is recorded to have said to him: "Akiva, grass will grow in your cheeks and still the son of David will not have come!" What is beyond doubt is that Bar Kokhba thought that he was restoring the kingdom to Israel and freeing the Jewish people from foreign oppression. He engaged in a hard-fought war against the Romans, defeated hardened Roman troops in open combat, and retook Jerusalem from Roman control. He resumed the traditional Jewish sacrifices at the site of the Jerusalem Temple (which had been destroyed by the Romans in AD 70, after a previous unsuccessful revolt) and was planning to rebuild the Temple. He set up a Jewish provisional government and began to issue coins in the name of this government. They carried inscriptions such as: "Year one of the redemption of Israel", "Year two of the freedom of Israel", and "For the freedom of Jerusalem". He described himself using the Hebrew word *nasi*, which could be translated by his time as "king", and which might have had messianic overtones. This is, though, uncertain as the leader of the Qumran community was described using the same word, and it could simply have meant "leader". Overall, though, the fighting warrior Bar Kokhba was what a lot of Jewish people were looking for in the longed-for messiah.

*Jewish ideas about "Christ"
after the failure of revolt*

After the destruction of Jerusalem by the Romans in AD 70 and the final crushing of the Bar Kokhba revolt in AD 135, the Jewish people continued to look for the eventual revealing of the messiah. In the following centuries there is abundant evidence concerning ways in which members of the Jewish community prepared themselves for the coming of the messiah, or hoped to make his coming more likely. These included reciting key sacred Bible verses; mystical meditation; punishing their bodies with self-inflicted pain; even the use of magic. These accompanied complex mathematical calculations (called "calculators of the ends") which were designed to try to identify when the messiah would come. Over the years various members of the Jewish community claimed either that they were the messiah or that their actions were about to usher in his appearance. These included David Reubeni and Solomon Molcho in sixteenth-century Portugal and Italy, and the Jewish mystic Sabbatai Zevi in seventeenth-century Greece and Turkey. These events deeply divided the Jewish community and it is not surprising that a number of Jewish religious leaders specifically tried to prohibit any actions designed to make the messiah come before the time chosen by God. For them the correct attitude was to leave the matter with God, while still believing that one day the messiah would come. The messiah-hope (whether regarded as a literal future event or a spiritual revelation) remains a part of Jewish belief. Among some religious Zionists there was and is the idea that the establishment of a Jewish state would, in a sense, be part of the fulfilment of the messiah-hope but on a natural level. Others disagree.

Overall, as centuries passed, there grew a tension between the hope and the reality of frustrated expectation. On one hand it was said, in a later Jewish tradition: "On the day that Jerusalem was destroyed the Redeemer was born." In other words, there is always hope of the messiah, even in the darkest hour. On the other hand, the delay in his coming could give rise to fables (even jokes) such as that of an eastern European Jewish community, said to have paid a small boy to stand at the edge of the village in order to greet the messiah when he arrived. When a passer-by commented that his wage was low, the boy quipped in reply: "But at least it's a permanent job!"

Did Jesus think he was "the Christ"?

This is an enormous question. We will return to this in chapter 3, but here we will just touch on it. The simple reality is that Jesus did not write any mission statement, nor was he in the right political position (as the Roman emperor was) to commission inscriptions about himself, his status, and his achievements. And even if he had been, there would, no doubt, still be tremendous debate about whether these statements actually represent *his own words*. As it is, we rely entirely on the records and assessments written by others. This is not unique. Few ancient people wrote their own biographies. Boudicca did not write her political manifesto to accompany her rebellion against Rome… Attila the Hun did not write a travelogue of his conquests… and we could go on. But this does mean that we need to explore the way that Jesus was presented *by others* in the gospels and letters and other first-century records. Virtually all biblical experts would agree that he called *himself* "the Son of Man" (note the emphatic definite article) and that his contemporaries called him "Jesus of Nazareth" and "Jesus son of Joseph". His consistent references to God as his father indicate that he had a particularly striking understanding of the intimacy of his relationship with God, although this *could* be argued to imply obedience rather than a unique nature. But did he claim to be "Christ" and was this title used to his face with his approval? Did he even go further and claim to be "the Son of God", in a way that took intimacy with God to new and controversial heights? This we will shortly return to.

How was the term messiah (Christ) understood by the early followers of Jesus?

Clearly the word "Christ", as it was used in the first century, had a long backstory and contained rich and varied meanings. However, what is clear is that the early Christians had developed a very different concept of the messiah/Christ than that of the all-conquering military leader and restorer of the kingdom of Israel. Their Christ was poor and persecuted. This would continue to be extremely controversial when Christianity expanded away from its Jewish roots and became a predominantly non-Jewish religion, but as long as it was a sect of Judaism, the contrast with the dominant image of the victorious messiah was profound. Even allowing for the possibility that some undercurrents in the first-century Jewish image of the messiah contained allusions to suffering servanthood, rather than triumphant kingship, something dramatic had happened in the mental history of what "the Christ" might be.

CHAPTER 2

Christ in Acts and the Early Letters

In the third decade of the first century a small but expanding sect within the Jewish community in Jerusalem and its surrounding area began to proclaim a very controversial and astonishing new set of beliefs. These were connected to a Galilean preacher, teacher, and miracle worker who had been condemned for blasphemy by the Jewish religious leadership in Jerusalem and executed by the Roman occupying power. Over the next sixty years this sect would expand out of its heartland in Jerusalem and within the Jewish community, as large numbers of Gentile Greek-speakers joined it and so totally changed its ethnic and cultural composition. Increasing conflict with the Jewish authorities led to the group's persecution. It was regarded as a blasphemous and heretical sect, and its Jewish members were expelled from synagogues. Suspicious Roman authorities also began sporadic and, at times, lethal persecution. Sometime around AD 90, the so-called "Benediction of the Heretics" was introduced into Jewish daily prayers. Pious Jews would thank God every morning that they were not a heretic, including a "*Nazarene*" (a Christian). By AD 100, therefore, Christianity had become a religion separate from its Jewish roots and most – some would argue all – of its central core writings had been written.

The evidence of early Christian beliefs about Christ

The question is: what was the nature of this new set of beliefs which led to this break with Judaism? What did these beliefs proclaim about the nature and significance of Jesus? In short: what was the Christology?

In order to explain this we will look at the Christology of Christianity's core writings, specifically those which are generally agreed to have been written during the so-called "Age of the Apostles" (the name given to the disciples who went on to become leaders in the early church). This is an area that still divides modern experts but, in order to make this manageable, we will focus on those generally agreed to have an early date. These include the following of Paul's letters: Romans, 1 Corinthians (2 Corinthians may be an amalgamation of a number of letters), Galatians, Colossians, 1 Thessalonians, Philemon, and Philippians. The traditional names of these letters are taken from each place receiving them: Rome, Corinth, Galatia (an area), Colossae, Thessalonica (an area), and Philippi. That of Philemon takes its name from the individual to whom the letter was addressed. These letters contain evidence of the beliefs developed by the Christian communities *before* Paul, as well as key points in Paul's own contribution to emerging Christian ideas about the nature and significance of Christ.

Who was Paul?

Paul (originally named Saul) was not one of the disciples of Jesus. He was a well-educated and well-connected member of the Jewish intellectual elite. He was changed from being a persecutor of early Christians into an enthusiastic and highly influential exponent of the new faith by a conversion experience while on the way to organize further acts of anti-Christian violence in Damascus. It was Paul (his name now changed from Saul) who was responsible for articulating many of the early faith-statements of Christian thought. He was and remains a controversial but highly important figure in early Christianity. He was very conscious both of his own former role as a persecutor of the Christian community and of being a late addition to the apostles. It took them some time to accept him too and tensions can be discerned in a number of places in Acts and in his own letters. Even today there are some Christians who are less comfortable with Paul's authority than with that of the compilers of the gospels. In traditional Christian teaching, though, his "apostolic authority" is accepted and his writings are considered on a par with the evidence in the gospels. To Paul, his authority came from his "road to Damascus" experience of the risen Christ; then an extended time of deep reflection under the influence of the Holy Spirit; ongoing spiritual revelation; and knowledge of "the Christ" that he gained from the teachings of the other apostles and their companions. It should be noted that he did not write his letters until quite some time after his conversion, and then on the basis of much reflection and teaching.

Christ as revealed in the book of Acts

In addition to Paul's letters, the book of Acts gives us evidence of how Christ was viewed soon after his resurrection. It may well have been written around AD 70, at about the same time as the gospels were being compiled (see chapter 3), and the evidence (internal stylistic features and early church tradition) suggests its writer was the same man who wrote the Gospel of Luke.

The importance of Acts lies in the fact that it contains a record of early preaching that is generally accepted as being representative of the earliest faith-statements of the church. Modern theologians call these by the Greek word *kerygma*, meaning "to proclaim". This was the early and core message of the Christian faith.

The earliest example is that of Peter, preaching to the crowds on the day of Pentecost. This is a key event in the New Testament. This occurred after the resurrection of Christ and his ascension into heaven and was the day on which his followers were empowered by the outpouring of the Holy Spirit.

Peter's speech contains key insights into what early Christians believed about Jesus and the nature of "the Christ". He describes him as: "Jesus of Nazareth, a man attested to you by God with deeds of power, wonders, and signs that God did through him" (Acts 2:23). This language could have described an idea of the messiah (Christ) that was familiar to many first-century Jews. It becomes more daring as Peter goes on to state: "God raised him up, having freed him from death" (Acts 2:24). While the Jewish tradition did not include that the messiah would experience resurrection, even this remains broadly within the boundaries of expectations, as it is explained that Jesus was a descendant of David (a traditional messianic characteristic). The exalted nature of the risen Jesus, although there are glimpses of this in Psalm 110,[1] then begins to stretch the boundaries of messiah-expectations. Not only has God raised him from the dead, but Jesus has been "exalted at the right hand of God" and, consequently, the Holy Spirit has been poured out on his followers (Acts 2:32–33). The conclusion is that: "God has made him both Lord and Messiah [Christ], this Jesus whom you crucified" (Acts 2:36).

In this understanding of the nature of Christ, we see a person whose legitimacy is expressed in terms borrowed from the Old Testament but whose exalted status would have caused disquiet in the Jewish community. But there is no mention of divine Sonship or of worship. The wording "God has made him…" (along with similar phrases occasionally used elsewhere in the New Testament) has sometimes been taken as evidence of "adoption" (see chapter 4), which would imply that at some point – Jesus' baptism or his exaltation to heaven after his resurrection – he was made Christ, Lord, or Son. This would mean he became something he had not been before. This was defined as a heresy in the later history of the church, as it strikes at the heart of the intrinsic nature of Christ. In fact, the context of the use of this term (especially when set alongside other statements of faith) does not imply "adoptionism". Instead, the term indicates appointment to a new office or a new role. This is the one through whom God will eventually judge the world and save those who have trusted in him. This was an End Time projection of Christ's significance, not a transformation of him from human to divine.

This image of a Christ whose exaltation may already be straining the boundaries of Judaism is seen elsewhere in Acts. Preaching in the vicinity of the Jerusalem Temple, Peter later declares: "The God of Abraham, the God of Isaac, and the God of Jacob, the God of our ancestors has glorified his servant [or child] Jesus" (Acts 3:13). Glory is the preserve of God but the more flexible listener may have interpreted this as: the Christ is exalted and brings glory *to* God. Similarly, the substitute reference to "child" in this context need not have implied more than faithful servant. In the same way, the next verse's reference to Christ as "the Holy and Righteous One" could be contained within contemporary expectations, but when described as "Author of life" (verse 15) who heals through "faith in his name" (verse 16) we see the way in which attributes of God are being ascribed to Jesus the Christ. A revolution in mindsets is occurring. It is therefore no surprise to learn that the Christ will be finally revealed at a future date, at "the time of universal restoration that God announced long ago through his holy prophets" (Acts 3:21).

Many of these early Christian definitions of "Christ" had this End Time theme and were linked to the events at the end of Jesus' life. In short, because he had died and been raised, he had then been exalted to a position from which he would return to judge the world. This way of expressing faith in Christ had less to say about the significance of Jesus' earthly life than some other statements that we will explore in due course.

The implications of the "Proclamations" in Acts

In these areas of Acts we see that Jesus is being freely accorded the Greek-language titles of *christos* (Christ) and *kyrios* (Lord). Both imply majesty, authority, and an exalted status. The second term had echoes of the way in which God is addressed in the Greek version of the Old Testament (the *Septuagint*), but is not conclusive proof that this was assumed with regard to Jesus, since the term could *also* be used to describe lesser lords and masters. However, the more elevated meaning rapidly became current among Christians, and in the emerging New Testament, the word "Lord" is reserved almost exclusively for God and the "Lord Jesus". The trajectory of thought is clear: God and Jesus are comparable. Eventual expulsion from the synagogues is not surprising, given the sound of this to many first-century Jews. What is remarkable is how quickly the followers of Jesus were expressing their beliefs in these terms. They were clearly becoming "Christians"; those whose exalted view of Jesus accorded him honours due only to the One God in Judaism. This is even more apparent in the writings of Paul, that once most rigid and determined defender of Jewish orthodoxy.

Christ in the early letters of Paul

A number of Paul's letters appear to quote from hymns and short statements of faith which were clearly drawn from existing expressions of belief. They reveal something of the Christian community's defining of Christ before Paul added his own contribution.

A clear example can be found in 1 Corinthians: "For I handed on to you as of first importance what I in turn had received: that Christ died for our sins in accordance with the scriptures, and that he was buried, and that he was raised on the third day in accordance with the scriptures, and that he appeared to Cephas [Peter], then to the twelve" (1 Corinthians 15:3–5). The wording explicitly states that Paul was himself given this information from earlier Christians and the style suggests a simple creed or faith-statement. The centrality of Christ's death and resurrection is clear, as is his fulfilment of (undisclosed) Old Testament prophecies; although his status and nature are not examined in this particular formulation.

Another example can be found in 1 Thessalonians where Paul speaks of the faith of a Christian community as: "you turned to God from idols, to serve a living and true God, and to wait for his Son from heaven, whom he raised from the dead – Jesus, who rescues us from the wrath that is coming" (1 Thessalonians 1:9–10). This has echoes of the same kind of ideas expressed in Peter's words in Acts.

A more explicit exploration of what this meant for an understanding of Christ's nature can be found in the Letter to the Romans. Here the wording has the clear structure of a creed. The "gospel" (good news) is expressed in God's Son: "who was descended from David according to the flesh and was declared to be Son of God with power according to the spirit of holiness by resurrection from the dead, Jesus Christ our Lord" (Romans 1:3–4). Here we see a rapid résumé of what was understood about Christ: messianic credentials through his descent from King David; being the Son of God (a leap onward from traditional Jewish beliefs about the messiah); all this status being confirmed when God raised him from the dead; encapsulated in the now familiar combination of personal name and titles: "Jesus Christ our Lord". The use of "Lord" here is typical of the newly enhanced definition of this term that was becoming established among Christians. In a construction which united *who* Jesus was with *what* Jesus did, Paul went on to use another phrase that may also echo earlier creeds. Paul stated that being made acceptable to God, "will be reckoned to us who believe in him who raised Jesus our Lord from the dead, who was handed over to death for our trespasses and was raised for our justification" (Romans 4:24–25). The last part certainly sounds like the kind of formula that served as a creed. What this meant for ordinary Christians in their progress to salvation is revealed in another statement that also clearly echoes a pre-existing creed: "if you confess with your lips that Jesus is Lord and believe in your heart that God raised him from the dead, you will be saved" (Romans 10:9). Again we see the combination of the exalted definition of "Lord" as applied to Jesus and belief in his resurrection as proof of that status.

Christ in Paul's words

When Paul expressed his own beliefs concerning the nature of Christ, the dramatic shift from classic Jewish understanding of the messiah becomes even starker than in the early Christian creeds regarding Christ. There had been evidence of this before, in these, but now it took on an even more explicit and dramatic nature.

In the first chapter of the Letter to the Colossians, Paul describes Christ as "the image of the invisible God" and "the firstborn of all creation" (Colossians 1:15). The first statement would later be expanded on hugely as church councils debated in what sense was Christ the way in which God revealed himself? How did Christ's nature act as an "image" of God? In precisely what way was God supremely seen in him as a true likeness? But the implication of divinity was clear. The reference to "the firstborn of all creation" would also run and run. Could this imply that Jesus was created? On strictly grammatical grounds in the Greek, the phrase "firstborn" *could* be construed to mean this. However, orthodox Christianity would reply "no". In context, it means that Jesus was not created. Instead, in a way that defies simplistic understanding, he was, as the Nicene Creed would later insist, "eternally begotten of the Father". We shall return to this phrase in due course because it is very important but, in its most simplistic definition, it means that Jesus always stood in relationship to God his Father as his Son, and not as a created being, however exalted. In this sense he was always in this intimate relationship with God. Clearly, Paul had something like this in mind as in verse 17 he declared of Christ that: "He himself is before all things."

In an echo of an understanding that would also inform the "Prologue" to the Gospel of John, Paul went on to say that it was "in him" (or "by him") that everything in heaven and earth was created. This includes every physical and spiritual aspect of creation. Such a view of "the Christ" accorded to him a power and authority reserved for the creator-God of Judaism. It was for such beliefs that Christians were expelled from the synagogues! As if this were not enough, the same passage goes on to assert that all of creation only holds together because of him, and "in him all the fullness of God was pleased to dwell" (verse 19) and, further, that it was through Christ's sacrifice on the cross that peace was made with God.

If we looked at nothing else in Paul's writings, this declaration of the nature of Christ would be sufficient to illustrate both the extraordinary way that the Jewish concept of messiah had changed as Christians reflected on Jesus, *and* the later reasons for the spilling of gallons of ink on parchment as later church leaders sought to clarify exactly what this meant.

Paul's words in Colossians focus on the nature of Christ that predated his earthly birth. In a similar way, a belief in Christ being sent by God to save the world combines the life of Jesus with the way in which that life ended, rather than focusing solely on the end of Jesus' life as occurs in some of the faith-statements we looked at earlier. One of the earliest examples of this idea of "sending" is found in Paul's Letter to the Galatians: "But when the fullness of time had come, God sent his Son, born of a woman, born under the law, in order to redeem those who were under the law, so that we might receive adoption as children" (Galatians 4:4–5). This reveals a number of the features of Christ's nature: fulfilling ancient expectations; God's Son, sent by God; truly human; subject to the Jewish religious Law but then freeing people from the (futile) obligation to live lives holy enough to gain salvation; making it possible for those believing in him to become children of God.

Among the Greek-speaking churches this idea of Christ's pre-existence in heaven (before his earthly birth) rapidly took hold. In this process, Christ became associated with the "Wisdom of God" that could be found in the Jewish Old Testament. In key Old Testament passages, Wisdom was associated with God's creative power, his revealing of himself, and his saving of people. By the first century, Greek-speaking Jews had come to think of this Wisdom or Word as being more than simply an attribute of God. Instead, *logos* had become thought of as a distinct personal entity within the nature and being of God. From this foundation, early Christians came to consider Jesus as more than simply the representative of Wisdom but, rather, the personification of that Wisdom and so of God. This presented him as representing this in his life and teaching and then in being exalted to heaven after his resurrection. This idea is found (even when not expressed explicitly) in early hymns quoted in Paul's letters and in the later Letter to the Hebrews, and in the Prologue to the Gospel of John (see chapter 3) where its author describes how "the Word became flesh" (John 1:14). This is called "Incarnation Christology". "Incarnation" (from the Latin for "in flesh") refers to the embodiment of God in the human life of Jesus. It is found mostly in this Gospel and in the letters associated with John. However it did, as we have seen, influence aspects of Paul's writing, and also that of the writer of the Hebrews. It was certainly not, as some have supposed, only something that occurred once the church became predominantly Gentile (that is, non-Jewish). It was, instead, a belief found among the earliest – and Jewish – Christians.

With such an elevated status, Christ in Paul's letters stands shoulder-to-shoulder with God the Father. Philemon is far from unique when it opens (verse 3) with greetings that encapsulate this: "Grace to you and peace from God our Father and the Lord Jesus Christ." The exact same wording appears in Romans, 1 Corinthians, and Galatians. It also appears in the Letter to the Philippians; and in this and similar forms (sometimes adding "mercy") in other letters about which there is more debate regarding Paul's authorship.

In Philippians we find another of those older Christian statements – in this case almost certainly a hymn (Philippians 2:6–11). This may have been written by Paul himself or have existed independent of him, to be quoted in this letter. It is worth quoting in full (as translated in the NRSV) but instead of how it is usually presented, it is here divided into what *might* have been verses of such a hymn. The way in which the nature of Christ was described and he was worshipped can be understood if one imagines a group of early Christians either reciting this or singing it together.

Though he was in the form of God,
[he] did not regard equality with God
as something to be exploited,

but emptied himself,
taking the form of a slave,
being born in human likeness.

And being found in human form,
he humbled himself
and became obedient to the point of death –
even death on a cross.

Therefore God also highly exalted him
and gave him the name
that is above every name,

so that at the name of Jesus
every knee should bend,
in heaven and on earth and under the earth,

and every tongue should confess
that Jesus Christ is Lord,
to the glory of God the Father.

As with other New Testament statements about Christ, there were ideas in this that would later be argued over, analysed, debated, and expanded into complex and legalistic formulae. But here the message is simple and unadorned: Christ possesses the nature of God; he did not cling to this status but freely humbled himself to become a human being; he accepted a humiliating death. As a consequence, God exalted him (either the resurrection or the ascension might be referred to here, or both); eventually all will have to recognize his Lordship; this brings glory to God.

Little in the contemporary Jewish ideas about the messiah would prepare anyone for such a hymn of worship to "the Christ". Nothing in Judaism, or later in Islam, could tolerate such worshipful veneration of a human being. Here are both the unique claims and the controversial nature of Christianity.

Summarizing what all of this reveals

The themes explored above also appear in later letters attributed to Paul (though the attribution is debated by modern experts). In addition, the anonymous writer of the Hebrews explored the way Christ fulfilled the Old Testament and was foreshadowed there. As we have seen, the letters associated with John take up and develop the incarnation theme. Those associated with Peter bring out themes of Christ's centrality to God's plan of salvation – despite him being rejected by people – and the certainty of his second coming. The book of Revelation, through its dramatic and challenging imagery, presents a glorious Christ who will return as part of God's reordering of the whole of creation.

The earliest Christian writings reveal a highly exalted verdict on the nature of Christ. Despite arguments to the contrary, *both* by those who insist that many of the key New Testament documents really represent later second-century beliefs, *and* by the wildest conspiracy theorists who see all orthodox Christian ideas about Christ as being foisted on the church by the creed writers in later centuries, early evidence points in a very different direction.

Worship and deity were soon central parts of the package of beliefs that the early Christians came to hold with regard to Christ and his nature. This occurred within the first generation of believers, including people who had known Jesus. It occurred long before much later Christians attempted to explain just how such a nature was possible. And it seems to have not created controversy within the early church. It was, it seems, accepted by them. We need to bear this in mind as we now go on to examine the evidence found in the gospels.

CHAPTER 3

Christ of the Gospels

The New Testament is made up of four gospels (named after Matthew, Mark, Luke, and John), Acts, a number of letters (mostly, but not exclusively, written by Paul), and the book of Revelation (attributed to John). Many of the letters, as we have seen in chapter 2, were written *before* the gospels, although the gospels are for most people foundational for their understanding of Jesus. In all printed copies of the New Testament they come first, and so are read first by most people who open a New Testament. In addition, they will be more familiar to the general reader, with their blending of events, parables, and observations. It is from these gospels, compiled by the early church, that we get our most striking view of Christ: his life, teachings, death, resurrection, and significance. It is important to state the obvious: none of the documents mentioned above were written by Jesus. Instead, they reveal the way that his importance was understood by early followers. They present his words and teaching in a way designed to communicate his significance. They are statements of faith.

The "Jesus of history" and the "Christ of faith"?

A number of those who have studied the New Testament make a distinction between the "Jesus of history" and the "Christ of faith". By this they mean the difference between what can be identified and understood about the Jewish man executed in about AD 30 by the Romans ("Jesus of history") and what is believed about him ("Christ of faith"). This sounds straightforward. Statements in the gospels that refer to Jesus preaching, or being tried by the Roman governor, are likely to be widely accepted as historical events regardless of a person's faith or non-faith, although it should be recognized that there are some who view anything written by any biblical author as being automatically suspect. On the other hand, some passages, such as the first chapter of the Gospel of John, that speak of a being called "the Word" (clearly referring to Christ before his earthly birth) existing before the creation of the world, are clearly of a different order. Although written in a very different style, even the more concise Gospel of Mark begins with a faith-statement: "The beginning of the good news of Jesus Christ, the Son of God" (Mark 1:1). The same would apply to points of reflection within the gospels, where the writer quotes from the Old Testament to make a point about Jesus ("As it is written in the prophet Isaiah...") or comments on the significance of an event ("After that no one dared to ask him any question"). However, the matter is actually more complex than it appears. For a start, the way material was selected and combined was done in order to make points and lead to conclusions. Our understanding of, and access to, the words of Jesus are always dependent on the gospel writer's decision as to what to include in the account. In addition, examples of people's reactions to Jesus and even the setting of an event may be carefully and skilfully crafted in order to underline a point of faith. To say this is not to catch the gospel writers out because that is *why* they wrote their gospels. As one puts it: "these are written so that you may come to believe that Jesus is the Messiah [the Christ], the Son of God, and that through believing you may have life in his name" (John 20:31). In this way the "Jesus of history" is always blending seamlessly into the "Christ of faith". And for believers, of course, there is often no conscious recognition of any difference between the two.

It is to that "Christ of faith" – what the compilers of the gospels believed about Jesus, his nature, and significance – that we will soon turn. Firstly though, we need to clarify some key points.

What is a gospel?

The word "gospel" is derived from an Old English (Anglo-Saxon) word meaning "good news". In turn it translates a Greek word – *euangelion* – which means the same. A gospel retells selected events and words of Jesus in order to communicate that in him God had acted uniquely to reveal himself to human beings and enable them to be forgiven and brought back into relationship with him. This is why they gained their title of "good news". Each of the four gospels in the New Testament, as we will shortly see, is associated in its name with a key character from the early history of Christianity. They have had these associations since at least the end of the second century and probably had gained them by the beginning of that century. However, there is no surviving evidence that they were called by these names in the first century.

When were the gospels written?

This is a controversial subject and takes us into a detective hunt that involves the analysis of ancient manuscripts. Entire bookshelves in university libraries are devoted to this, so this brief exploration will just scratch the surface of a very deep debate.

Many experts believe that the Gospel of Mark was the first gospel to be written, and that this occurred around AD 70. The same general agreement would extend to stating that the Gospel of Matthew and the Gospel of Luke were both composed sometime in the 80s. They seem to have been written independently of each other. However, despite this, they seem to have used a version of Mark but also both used material that was not in Mark. This may have been in the form of a collection of Jesus' sayings. This hypothetical collection of sayings is often referred to as "Q" (from the German word *quelle*, meaning "source"). "Q" may have been compiled very early; maybe as early as the 40s or 50s. This way of explaining the origins of these three gospels would answer the question: why are they so similar but not identical? In this scenario, the compilers of Matthew and Luke blended their own unique traditions with that supplied by Mark and by "Q". These three gospels are often referred to as the "synoptic gospels" from the Greek words *syn* (same) and *optic* (sight). In other words, these three gospels tend to see things in the same way. There is, however, still a very rich variety in these three gospels in the way they present Jesus as the Christ. Early church tradition – which divides modern experts – is that somewhere behind the Gospel of Matthew lay a much earlier work written in Aramaic, to which the later – Greek – gospel was in some way indebted.

Finally, we come to the Gospel of John. This gospel is very different to the other three and comes from a quite different literary tradition. There is much debate over its authorship. Some think it is the work of a single man described in this gospel as the "disciple that Jesus loved" who, it is claimed, wrote this gospel, three letters attributed to John, and Revelation. Others argue that there was a group of authors who wrote in a similar style, with numerous layers of careful editing. While this gospel is more developed, reflective, and symbolic, it concentrates on a narrower set of events and themes. It is, therefore, arguably more theological. But one should not overstate this, as the synoptic gospels are also clearly focused on making key points regarding belief.

The general consensus among experts is that the Gospel of John was compiled later than the other gospels but may still have drawn on much earlier oral traditions and even written sources now lost to us. It was once fashionable to give it a second-century date but, given that the earliest manuscript dates from about AD 120 and was probably copied several times before that and undoubtedly already had a backstory of circulating among churches in Asia Minor, it was almost certainly compiled much earlier than some have suggested. With its emphasis on Christians being thrown out of synagogues because of their faith (formal Jewish rejections of Christian belief date from about AD 90 but this was the culmination of such conflict), the gospel could have been compiled any time between about AD 70 and AD 100. This would put it on a par with some of the other gospels. So the matter is complex.

There are, though, occasional hints that things may have been more complex still. Claims have been made (and rejected by other scholars) that some fragments of Matthew may date from as early as the mid-60s. This is very controversial indeed, and has not been widely accepted, but reminds us that future discoveries (and new methods of dating evidence) *may* cause us to revise our dating system regarding the writing of the gospels and this could push their compilation even closer to the actual events described. Even at a more conservative estimate, the gospels were being compiled within around one generation of the events described and also drew on earlier traditions. Historians in many other areas of ancient history, it should be noted, would be very pleased to have evidence compiled so close to the events that they study. For example, the earliest surviving manuscript of the writings of Julius Caesar dates from 900 years later than the date at which the original was written.

According to the earliest church traditions, however, the gospels were written in the order they appear in the New Testament: Matthew, Mark, Luke, and John. There are other variations in the ordering of the gospels in early Christian literature (in all, there are eight early different order combinations). Modern scholarly opinion though – as outlined above – differs from this and places the more concise and fast-paced Mark as the first to be compiled.

Why were the gospels written?

In the first generation of the Christian church, there were no gospels. This is a surprising thought but was clearly the case. That is why chapter 2 of this book focused on the preaching that was later recorded in Acts and on some, at least, of the letters. It was this way for two main reasons. Firstly, early Christians were sure Christ would soon return so there was no need to get things on the record. Secondly, and as a direct consequence of this, the pressing job was getting on with spreading the "good news" as quickly as possible.

However, when Christ did not return, the first generation of witnesses began to die, and disputes arose over belief, there was an understandable need to produce a record of what was being claimed. These records were linked to particular early and authoritative Christians who – it was claimed – had either written these accounts or had an association with them in some way. That is why, in Greek, the title of a gospel is (for example): *Euangelion kata Matthaion*, the "Gospel *according to* Matthew", and so on. This may imply either a claim concerning who wrote them (authorship) or from whose tradition they arose (their ultimate human authority). Traditionally, the church has believed the former but it may also have included aspects of the latter. Early church accounts of their authorship, as recorded by mostly second-century church writers, claim that Matthew and John were written by, or represented the outlook of, the two men who were two of the "disciples" and "apostles" (followers called by Jesus and then leaders given authority by him). The same early church accounts state that Mark represents the traditions associated with the apostle Peter (but written by Mark) and Luke represents the traditions linked with a man connected to the group of churches associated with Paul and his associates. The word meaning "according to" may also have suggested that there was really just one gospel (one "good news") but that in the four individual cases, it was in the form associated with a particular person.

We know of something like fifty works that once were called "gospels". We cannot now say exactly how and why only four of these came to be accepted as authoritative and sacred. What we can say, though, is that this had happened by the late second century at the latest. The church leader Irenaeus (died c. 202) wrote: "It is not possible that the [four] Gospels be either more or fewer than they are." Early collections of the accepted books (*canons* – from a Greek word meaning "measuring stick") that date from the same period tell the same story: four acceptable and authoritative gospels. All of this suggests that this situation was well established and had probably existed since the early part of the second century. Church traditions claimed that these four gospels could be differentiated from the other "gospels" in existence because: they were written earlier; they were more reliable because they arose from or were linked to the first-generation Christian leaders; they were grounded in eyewitness testimony; and, though miraculous in content, they were without the magic found in some later "gospels" which often supported the viewpoints of breakaway sects. It is also likely that church leaders were prompted by the serious disputes in the early second-century church. A striking example of such a dispute was when a man named Marcion and his followers (see chapter 4) rejected the Jewish roots of the church, disputed key features of the message as passed down through, what were becoming accepted as, the "mainstream gospels", and proposed the acceptance only of an edited version of what later became Luke and ten of Paul's letters. Faced with this situation, there was an urgent need to establish what constituted reliable records of events.

How did the gospel writers present the origin of Christ?

On scraps of Matthew housed today at Magdalen College, Oxford, the name of Jesus is abbreviated to "IS". This may well have been a Christian variation of the Jewish practice of abbreviating the unutterable name of God in Greek versions of the Old Testament to "YHWH" (omitting the vowels). This may give us a hint as to how Jesus rapidly became venerated in the early Christian communities, so that he and God became the focus of a similar level of devotion. At the time this would have been extraordinarily controversial and for mainstream Jews (a little less for Greek ex-pagans) extremely shocking.

The accounts in Matthew and Luke, regarding the birth and upbringing of Jesus, were carefully retold in order to make powerful points about his significance. These contain the events that are traditionally associated with Christmas. In Matthew there is only the journey of the *magi* (the wise men) to the infant (not baby) Jesus. This signals a new world order that is reflected in the cosmic order (the star), has significance beyond Judaism (the non-Jewish *magi*), and is in conflict with this world's authorities (Herod's attempt to kill the child). In Luke alone do we find the now familiar account of the miraculous birth of John the Baptist, the visit of the angel Gabriel to Mary, the Roman census and the journey to Bethlehem, the baby in the manger, the angels, and the shepherds.

What both have in common, though, is a radical revision of the nature of the messiah (Christ). The Christ is not as expected, these accounts insist. It is easy to miss the radical and controversial nature of this message, given our familiarity with the Christian construction of what "the Christ" is like. But to a first-century audience, these claims regarding Jesus would have been offensive to many Jews and exotic – if not bizarre – to many Greeks. And this is before we consider the implications of a Christ who was executed by the Roman authorities and in a manner designed to humiliate its victim. Not surprisingly, the apostle Paul was to wrestle with the challenge of presenting this new view of "the Christ" when he described it as: "a stumbling-block to Jews and foolishness to Gentiles" (1 Corinthians 1:23). There is no kingly triumph but, instead, vulnerability and public execution.

Yet, despite this, Matthew and Luke are both explicit in their identification of Jesus as "the Christ" and his credentials as a descendant of King David. The Bethlehem connection reinforces this, since the town was closely associated with King David. Matthew starts his Gospel with: "An account of the genealogy of Jesus the Messiah [Christ], the son of David, the son of Abraham" (Matthew 1:1). Luke concurs, as he states Gabriel's message to Mary: "He will be great, and will be called the Son of the Most High, and the Lord God will give to him the throne of his ancestor David" (Luke 1:32). Luke adds his own version of the genealogy linking Jesus to David a little later in his Gospel. Mark, too, has Jesus identified as "Son of David"; but in Mark this occurs late in Jesus' life and is, significantly, just before his final dramatic entry into Jerusalem (Mark 10:47–48), with the crowds then emphasizing the same kingly theme as he enters the city. Being found in Mark, this suggests that the tradition of Davidic association was an early one.

Matthew and Luke both explicitly refer to Jesus' virgin birth through the Holy Spirit – a faith-statement which insists on his heavenly origin, while combining this with human birth through his mother, Mary. The complex debates about exactly what this implied regarding the nature of Christ and his relationship with God his Father – that would later split churches, occupy church councils, and lead to complex creeds – are absent here. All that was yet to come. In Matthew and Luke, the Christ is as he is: while Mary's son, he is in his ultimate origin the Son of God. Matthew is, to be fair, a little less explicit in this conclusion, calling Jesus "Emmanuel" ("God is with us"), but the implication (made explicit in Luke) seems clear. It has been argued that the references to conception by the Holy Spirit do not necessarily imply any more than that Jesus was marked out as chosen for a unique role from Mary's womb but this seems an unnecessary dilution of what, by any standards, is a profound claim about some kind of divine status. What has to be admitted though is that there is no evidence for belief in his pre-existence in the synoptic gospels that might parallel the incarnation (embodying deity in human form) found in John and in certain early hymns that are quoted in some of the letters. This does not mean that the compilers of the synoptic gospels were unaware of this belief, just that it did not form a major part of their presentation.

In contrast, Mark contains no account whatsoever of the birth of Jesus. Instead, Jesus bursts onto the scene in adulthood preaching the arrival of "the kingdom of God". However, Mark does contain the interesting piece of evidence whereby, at Jesus' baptism, God's voice declares: "You are my Son, the Beloved; with you I am well pleased" (Mark 1:11). In John there is, similarly, no account of the birth of Jesus. Instead, his Prologue reflects on the significance of the pre-existing "Word", through whom God created the world, who "became flesh and lived among us, and we have seen his glory, the glory as of a father's only son, full of grace and truth" (John 1:14). This is typical of John's more reflective style.

The nature of Christ, revealed in the life and teaching of Jesus

For the gospel writers this heavenly authority and origin is revealed in the power to heal, to drive out demons, and to forgive sins. The last is an attribute unique to God presented as causing consternation among many of his hearers: "It is blasphemy! Who can forgive sins but God alone?" (Mark 2:7). The way in which teachings, parables, healings, and exorcisms are presented is carefully crafted in order to build to the conclusion that this is the Christ and in him God's kingdom is breaking into the world.

While radically different to many contemporary assumptions, there are still clear echoes in this of the End Time expectations associated with Old Testament prophecy regarding the messiah. This is why Matthew, in particular, is keen to say again and again that events fulfil the Old Testament, particularly those prophecies found in the book of Isaiah. This is not unique to Matthew and the same rooting of events in Old Testament prophecy can also be found in Mark and in Luke. It is also found, though less frequently, woven into aspects of the very different style of John. This is fundamental to the gospel writers' presentation of the nature of Christ – what is described as their Christology. They were at pains to draw attention to these claims to fulfilment because these underscored the belief that Old Testament prophecy had been fulfilled in the life of Jesus and this pointed to the legitimacy of his credentials as "the Christ".

What becomes increasingly obvious the more closely one reads the gospel accounts is that, initially, Jesus could have been understood as a prophet of the End Times, declaring the dawning, in a new and dramatic way, of the rule of God on earth. He taught in the synagogues, drew together a group of disciples, and discussed beliefs with them and with onlookers. His style of preaching and teaching had parallels with the practices of contemporary Jewish rabbis. However, in other ways he was also strikingly different. There is a radical new direction in his demand for inner transformation and not mere outward conformity to the Jewish Law; in the emphasis on wholehearted love of God and of neighbour; most strikingly in his clear personal experience of God as father (not simply as a theological abstraction), one that could also be enjoyed by his followers. All of this was accompanied by an identification with outcasts and his self-styled title of "the Son of Man", which clearly implied identification with people and a self-effacing attitude – but may also have conveyed the idea of a new kind of humanity being presented for emulation, one that was possible through intimacy with God. It should also be noted that this title echoed a verse found in the Old Testament prophecy of Daniel: "I saw one like a human being [the Hebrew form of the Aramaic 'a son of man'] coming with the clouds of heaven" (Daniel 7:13). This title, therefore, had a clear messianic End Time meaning, which Jesus made even more emphatic by the use of the definite article: "*the* Son of Man".

In this we see the beginning of what is most radical in the gospels. The message of Jesus is presented as important – but the man himself is presented as being bigger than the message. Indeed, the man is the message. Time and again the compilers of the gospels record singular first-person pronouns such as: "Whoever welcomes you welcomes *me*, and whoever welcomes *me* welcomes the one who sent *me*" (Matthew 10:40); "Blessed is anyone who takes no offence at *me*" (Luke 7:23); "You have heard that it was said to those of ancient times… But *I* say to you…" (Matthew 5:21–22).

Overall (and this is a *very* broad-brush picture), the main contrasting characteristics of the way the four gospel writers present Jesus as "the Christ" can be summed up in this way. Matthew is determined to demonstrate Jesus' messiah-credentials as the fulfilment of Old Testament prophecies. He is Israel's messiah, the "Son of David", a title with kingly meaning as it links back to the great Old Testament king, David. Mark offers a gospel of action, End Time urgency, and a compressed version of events. The reality of "the Christ" is revealed in what he does. Mark, therefore, contains more miracles than the other gospels. Luke is rather more "intellectual", geared to a non-Jewish readership, and shows the perfection of God revealed in a perfect man. Christ goes to the outcast and breaks boundaries. Women are noticeably present and significant. Distinctions between the new religion and Judaism can be clearly seen. Finally, John records few parables and leaves out things as central as the establishing of the bread and wine of the "Lord's Supper" but, instead, has a Jesus who explains ideas concerning his nature and mission in depth and at length. And the gospel writer reflects on Jesus' pre-birth origins, the Christ-revealing nature of his miraculous signs, and the significance of his death.

These are the key features of "the Christ" as presented in the gospels: not merely the appearance of a new doctrine or set of principles but, instead, the radical demand of acceptance that this person is more than just a prophet. This is a crucial characteristic. There is clearly a significant difference between an insightful teacher... a prophet... the Christ... the Son of God. In the gospels we see a presentation which insists that Jesus is more than the first, beyond the second, and which recreates the concept of messiah so that it eventually becomes synonymous with the final and astonishing claim. And nothing would exemplify this more than the way in which the gospel writers presented his death and what, they insist, came after.

Death and resurrection: the ultimate demonstration of Christ's status

The gospel writers are unanimous in their belief that the Christ-status of Jesus is supremely revealed at the end of his life. Regarding his betrayal by Judas, Matthew states: "Then was fulfilled what had been spoken through the prophet Jeremiah..." (Matthew 27:9); and John says something similar about the soldiers casting lots for Jesus' clothes (John 19:24). Matthew goes on to describe darkness at noon (as does Mark and Luke) and an earthquake at Jesus' death. These three gospel writers insist that the cosmic order was shaken. Furthermore, the most unlikely people bear witness to the significance of the events. Mark has the Roman centurion exclaim: "Truly this man was God's Son!" (Mark 15:39), although Luke's words refer only to Jesus' innocence. Luke has one of the bandits crucified beside Jesus recognize the messiah-status of his fellow victim as he asks: "Jesus, remember me when you come into your kingdom" (Luke 23:42).

For all the complexity of the details in the different resurrection accounts, the one undisputable feature is that it forms the climax to all four gospels. The gospel writers clearly thought that it was crucial. It is after the resurrection that, in

John, the disciple Thomas declares to Jesus: "My Lord and my God!", which is literally in the Greek: "The Lord of me and the God of me" (John 20:28). For the reader of John, the journey from miracle-working prophet to a radically redefined understanding of "the Christ" is complete.

The views of Jesus and the conclusion of the church

There is a curious reluctance to declare his own status as "the Christ" on the part of Jesus. The sayings attributed to him, as we have seen, use the apparently preferred self-designation of "the Son of Man" (although this could be understood in a messianic way). Time and again those healed are told to keep the news to themselves. The parables reveal truths only to those "who have ears to hear". When exorcized demons refer to his status, they are commanded to silence. When Peter declares that Jesus is "the Messiah [Christ], the Son of the living God" (Matthew 16:16), Jesus declares this has been revealed to Peter by God *but* that the disciples are not to tell others. In Mark and Luke there is a similar wording, though without the reference to divine Sonship, but followed by the same command to secrecy. Within the gospels, therefore, we simultaneously find records of these statements by Jesus alongside the gospel writers' own declarations of the exalted status of Jesus as the redefined Christ.

This has sometimes been described as the "messianic secret" and has led to a lot of debate as to what it implies. To some it is evidence of the later church redefining Jesus as "the Christ" in a way different to how he defined himself but not doing it well enough to gloss over his reluctance to present himself as such. To others it suggests a concern on Jesus' part that mass interest in miraculous acts will get in the way of his fundamental message, or that the popular image of the messiah as a political leader will obscure the way that Jesus understood the status, nature, and role of "the Christ".

The debate will, no doubt, continue but suffice it to say that the dominant understanding in the gospels and the early church was that "the Christ" had indeed been radically redefined. It would be this understanding of Christ – with all its uncertainties, ambiguities, and complexities – that would fuel faith, argument, and images from that time onward. This was, in many ways, revealed most strikingly in John. In that gospel the idea of Christ's pre-incarnation existence in heaven, God's "Word" becoming a real human being (incarnation) and being revealed to people, before being exalted back to heaven, is most explicitly stated. But it is not confined solely to John's Gospel and the letters associated with him. John and those like him did not *cause* this trend; they were, instead, the *outcome* of a way of thinking that had been present since the very start of the Christian community. As we have seen in chapter 2, there is evidence of this in early hymns, in aspects of Paul's teaching, and in other letters too. In a very short period of time indeed the early church was, in effect, declaring both the full deity of Christ and his full humanity. Not that it was thought that Christ represented *all* that God is. Rather, that in his earthly life, Christ was and revealed that character (later creeds would say "person") within the divine being of God who creates, reveals, and saves. What we can describe as the "history of Christ" had started.

CHAPTER 4

Getting it "Right"…
Getting it "Wrong"…
Christ of the Creeds

As we have seen, something quite remarkable happened in the middle of what we now call the first century AD. A small – but growing – sect of Judaism centred on Jerusalem began to declare that a Jewish preacher and worker of miracles, named Jesus, who had been condemned by their own religious authorities and finally executed by the Roman occupying power, had risen from the dead. This, on its own, was controversial; but what was even more astonishing was that this group were according him honours that had previously been reserved for the one true God. Since this group was firmly rooted within the determinedly monotheistic religion of Judaism, such an attitude seemed to signal a dramatic break with their Jewish roots. And yet nothing was further from their intentions at this point. In this formative period these early followers of Jesus were confident that they were the true inheritors of Jewish traditions and their venerated risen leader was the culmination of Jewish messianic hopes. And, they had radically redefined their understanding of who the messiah was. In Jesus, they claimed, the one true God of Israel had revealed himself in human form and it was only possible to gain salvation by belief in this Christ who had died for our sins and been raised again to life. Given the spiritual earthquake that this seemed to threaten to the foundations of their Jewish traditions, and the ferocious debates about the nature of Christ that would soon dominate this community and its understanding, these early believers seem remarkably calm about the radical nature of their beliefs, even though they would appear blasphemous to most of their fellow Jews.

Questions, questions...

These beliefs soon attracted a significant following within Judaism but even more so among Greek-speaking communities in Asia Minor. Facing sporadic persecution from Jewish authorities, suspicious local pagans and, finally, the Roman imperial administration itself, it was for Christ that they suffered and began to die. The centrality of this key figure was clear within the early Christian community. Yet, as time went on, it became obvious that a number of questions could be raised about him. Some came from hostile critics; others from members of the Christian community itself as they began to explore the implications of their new beliefs. If God was revealed in Christ, then what precisely was the relationship between Jesus the Christ and the God of Israel as revealed in the Old Testament? Was the Old Testament God the same as the one Jesus called his Father in heaven?

Then what of the actual nature of Jesus the Christ? In what sense did he have the nature of God? Did this imply equality with or subservience to God? Did Jesus become "Christ" at a key moment in his life? Some Christian thinkers proposed his baptism as the occasion: but the very idea of such an "adoption" was strongly rejected by the mainstream. Did he have an existence prior to his earthly birth? If so, was this an existence from eternity, or one that saw him as the exalted "First" among all in creation? In short: did he have a beginning or not?

Then there were so many questions about how humanity and divinity were combined in Christ. Were these natures in some way distinct? Or were they inextricably mingled? Was humanity taken on by Christ, the Son of God, in such a way that he suffered pain? But how can God – who is beyond such earthly limitations – experience such things? Or did Christ only *appear* to suffer? And what about the mind of Christ? Did Jesus know everything, because he was God? Or were there limitations to his knowledge? Was he reliant on God for his understanding? And if so, in what sense was he God? For, surely, God's knowledge is unlimited.

Such questions were not easily answered. A dynamic and radical religious community was soon exploring uncharted territory. And these issues were not merely the preoccupations of theologians within the community (although they came to dominate these debates). They went to the very core of the central character of the new community. Christ was central; the church members were "Christians". It was vital to understand him accurately. And since it was firmly believed that it was through Christ that the world was saved, this understanding could have eternal implications. Those who did not believe correctly might not be saved. Eternal life in heaven might be reserved only for those who did. These arguments were therefore much more than matters of intellectual curiosity. One's Christology would have a direct impact on one's salvation. Since salvation was dependent on Christ, who he was, was a matter of eternal life and death. And it soon became a vital matter in this world as well.

Arguing from the Scriptures

As the first century gave way to the second century, it was increasingly common for those engaged in these debates to seek answers in what were becoming the established books and letters (now the New Testament). This, though, did not settle the matters. These books and letters were written by different sets of people, and there was diversity in the way in which Jesus' significance was expressed. The coalescing canon of the New Testament was not unified by a single editorial hand. In this it was and is very different from, for example, what Muslims believe about the Qur'an.

So, for those who were focused on a particular aspect of the Christ-debate, it was possible to identify a feature within a gospel and draw far-reaching conclusions from it, that probably went well beyond anything in the mind of the original author. For example, an emphasis might be laid on the pre-existing "Word" referred to at the beginning of John in order to demonstrate the pre-existence of Christ before his earthly birth. This was fair enough as John explicitly stated this. But the silence of the other gospels might be taken (it was argued) as evidence that they did not believe this and that the birth of Jesus was the start of his existence. Yet others, as we have seen, would point to the descent of the Holy Spirit on Jesus at his baptism as evidence that it was quite late in his life that Jesus became "Christ" and was, in some sense, adopted as God's Son. Others would argue for what we might call a more holistic approach and suggest that the reality of the nature of Christ could only be understood from the overall message of these different documents and that no one text could be used as the basis for an entire theological position.

The matter was made more complex by at least two factors. The first was that some approached the New Testament documents with their minds already made up and then quarried them for material which supported their position. The second was that the complexity of the debate soon led to the use of – and furious debate about – Greek technical terms that were themselves invented or adapted during these debates. Such terms might well have been justified as succinct expressions of otherwise opaque matters but these words were not found in Scripture. Yet everyone who used them was confident that their viewpoint (as expressed in these terms) represented the best understanding of Scripture. This is not to be dismissive of the creeds. It is a reminder that the creeds were works in progress. They were position statements as people sought to define things at a level of complexity that, at times, might seem unfamiliar to those who only read the Scriptures.

So, how did these debates reveal themselves over time? And what were the rival positions? How were they expressed and by whom? How were these matters resolved and what were the implications of this for the next 2,000 years? What decisions were made about the "right" and "wrong" understandings of who Christ was and is?

From these divisive debates would come such profound doctrines as the Trinity and the study of Christology. The very nature of God would be debated and defined as never before. The great ecumenical church councils convened to address these debates would include those at Nicaea (325), Constantinople (381), Ephesus (431), and Chalcedon (451) and their decisions were seen as binding on the whole Christian church. These great debates were to decide the nature of Christian understanding concerning the nature of Christ in a way that is difficult to exaggerate. Even in today's more fragmented and disparate church, the creeds produced at them still decide the shape of Christian debate. Across the Christian church such statements as the Nicene Creed, the Chalcedonian Definition, and the

Athanasian Creed still resonate with clarity and power. After 2,000 years, these statements possess a permanence that mask the ferocious debates, rivalries, and complex negotiations that gave rise to them.

Early controversies...

Among the earliest heretical sects (those whose beliefs were eventually rejected by the mainstream church) none have attracted so much attention as the so-called Gnostics. These were, in fact, a complex group of eastern Mediterranean sects who claimed access to secret "knowledge" which differentiated them from "unenlightened believers". Some of these beliefs related to the person of Christ. Saturninus of Antioch (early second century) held that Christ had no material existence; he only appeared to be human. Others also subscribed to this belief in *docetism* (Greek: "to seem") in various forms. Cerinthus, in late first-century Ephesus, taught that Jesus really was a man but that "Christ" descended and then left him before the crucifixion, since Christ could not suffer. This combined belief in the real physicality of Jesus with the concept that a pure spiritual being could not experience pain and death. Marcion of Sinope, though not a Gnostic, taught (c. 144) the dualistic belief that the God of the Old Testament was a tyrant or *demiurge* (creator of the material world), whereas Christ revealed a higher supreme God. He also taught that Christ was not born from Mary; instead he appeared as a grown man. Similarly, the suffering of Christ was apparent, not real.

There were also other sects seen as heretical outside the Gnostics. Jewish Christians, known as Ebionites, regarded Jesus as messiah but not divine. This meant rejection of his pre-existence, his divinity, the virgin birth (although some may have accepted this), his death to secure salvation, and his physical resurrection (although again some may have accepted this). Ebionites believed that, as the human son of Joseph and Mary, Jesus was chosen by God at his baptism when he was anointed with the Holy Spirit. This adoptionist understanding would appear in other schools of thought too. Sabellius (excommunicated in 220) taught a doctrine sometimes described as *modalist*, that God existed in different forms (modes) at different times, so: Father, Son, Holy Spirit.

Such views were in stark contrast to the early Christian insistence that Christ both was a real (and suffering) man and yet also revealed God the Father, previously known only through Old Testament scripture. Christ was the *Logos* referred to in John: the divine wisdom of God that went forth in creation, in revelation, and in the incarnation, where he was revealed as God's Son. But did this make the Son less than God the Father? And if God was Father, then when did the *Logos* become the Son? Tertullian (160–220) suggested this occurred prior to creation; Hippolytus (170–236) suggested at the historical moment of the birth of Jesus; Origen (182–254) argued, in contrast, that the terms "Father"/"Son" indicated an intimate relationship in the sense of the Son being eternally generated.

Tertullian coined terms (in Latin) that would be used in the church for centuries to come. God was one being (*substantia*) but three distinct persons (*personae*). God the Father was not divided when God the Son and God the Holy Spirit went forth; instead they proceeded from God the Father like sunrays. In the Greek-speaking church in the eastern Mediterranean, Origen used the Greek word *hypostaseis* in a similar way to Tertullian's use of *personae*. But this did not settle the question of whether the Son was subordinate to the Father. And the storm of that debate was soon to break on the church.

The Arian controversy

The ideas associated with Arius, who lived in what is today Egypt, first came to prominence in about 318. In that year he was in conflict with the bishop of Alexandria over his claim that only the Father was truly God. Arius argued that Christ, though highly exalted, did not possess of himself the nature of God. He was brought into being ("begotten") by the Father (before his earthly birth) and, before that, did not exist. In short: Christ was not eternal. Although, for Arius, Christ did not share in the being/nature of God, nevertheless God had created the world through Christ the Son. This left Christ with a position far exalted above the rest of creation but well below that of God the Father. Arius also believed that Christ was sinless and unchangeable, but that these were attributes made possible by God and not products of Christ's intrinsic nature. Similarly, Christ was endowed with sufficient knowledge to make God the Father known to human beings. But this was provided by God; it was not integral to Christ's nature and being.

In these ways Arius sought to remove some of the more difficult issues inherent in the belief in the "incarnation" (God becoming a human being). Arius had sidestepped all the complexities connected to the claim that, in Christ, God was revealed and lived an earthly life. All those debates about exactly how this could be possible were therefore unnecessary in his view since, to Arius, Christ was not God. Similarly, the complex question of how Jesus' humanity could be united with God was defused. Christ the Son (the *Logos* in John) was united with a human body at his birth in Bethlehem. He inhabited that body. There were no difficult questions about how the nature of God can be united with a human nature, since the *Logos* was not truly God and the relationship of the *Logos* with a human life was strictly differentiated. Arius' reduction of Christ's status looked to New Testament texts which referred to the unique nature of God and to other texts which described Christ as "God the only Son" (John 1:18), which can also be translated as "the Only Begotten", and "He [Christ] is the image of the invisible God, the firstborn of all creation" (Colossians 1:15). Others did not agree with Arius' interpretation of such texts.

Arius was excommunicated but the matter did not end. As the controversy drew in more church leaders and increased in intensity, the new emperor of a united East and West Roman empire, Constantine I (the Great), called a council at Nicaea. This condemned Arius' teaching and produced a statement known as the Creed of Nicaea (325). A later creed, with similar content, is known as the Nicene Creed and is generally accepted across Christian churches. The words of the Creed of Nicaea expressed belief:

> ... in one Lord, Jesus Christ, the Son of God, begotten from the Father, only-begotten, that is, from the substance of the Father, God from God, light from light, true God from true God, begotten not made, of one substance with the Father, through Whom all things came into being, things in heaven and things on earth, Who because of us men and because of our salvation came down and became incarnate, becoming man, suffered and rose again on the third day, ascended to the heavens, will come to judge the living and the dead.[1]

The fallout from the Arian controversy

The matter seemed settled and the understanding was expressed in some technical Greek terms. God the Son (that is, Christ) and God the Father were of the "same substance" (*homoousios*).

This word had earlier been used by Gnostics in a different sense when they used it to describe a common characteristic of all the heavenly powers. At Nicaea though it was used only to describe the Father and the Son. The implication was clear: Christ shared the divine nature of God the Father. Even after Nicaea, though, there were those who worried that the term might not be quite precise enough. The word was in everyday use to describe two *separate* objects made from the same substance. This was clearly *not* the way it was used at Nicaea but others might interpret it this way. And some did.

The Arian way of thinking did not go away. It became entangled with tensions between the Western Christian church (generally in favour of Nicaea) and the Eastern Christian church, where it was still far from universally accepted. Bishop Marcellus of Ancyra even revived an idea that God was one but then became three in the act of creation and redeeming the world and then became one again. This was strongly rejected by church leaders. But Arianism itself had a fairly wide following in the East. Other variants too, though not Arian, were at odds with the Creed of Nicaea. One such was expressed in the Second Creed of Antioch, which declared that Father, Son, and Holy Spirit were "three as persons" but one "in agreement". It was only their united will that made them one. At the Council of Sardica (343), Western representatives argued for such a unity of Father and Son that it left Eastern representatives concerned that this, in effect, denied the three recognizable "persons" of God: Father, Son, and Holy Spirit. In contrast, the Western representatives feared that the word preferred in Eastern terminology to describe the three persons of God (*hypostaseis*) might suggest that there were "three Gods".

A further boost to Arianism came when the barbarian Visigoths converted to an Arian form of Christianity, and took it with them as they invaded the Western Roman empire in 408.

More moderate forms of Arianism were also apparent. The priest, Basil of Ancyra (died in 362), argued that Christ was "of similar substance" (*homoiousios*) to God the Father but not "of the same substance" (*homoousios*). It looked as if the Christian church was becoming Arian, since the belief was becoming accepted by a large number of Christians at this point.

Reconciliation: the position of Christ and the nature of the Trinity

In 362 a major synod held in Alexandria finally decided broadly in favour of Nicaea. Describing God as being recognizably "three persons" did not constitute belief in three Gods. They did not have separate natures and were not separate beings. Instead, they possessed a single and uniting essence. Declaring the Son to be fully God was accompanied by the same understanding regarding the Holy Spirit. But when the Eastern Roman emperor Valens (ruled 364–78) declared in favour of the Arian outlook (as had his predecessor Emperor Constantius), the followers of Nicaea found themselves in conflict with the imperial authorities.

In time, though, the crisis was averted by the actions of Basil the Great, the bishop of Caesarea in Cappadocia (in modern Turkey). Under his influence it became accepted in the Eastern Roman empire that one could believe both in the united "substance" of God (*homoousios*) and that God existed in three recognizable but inseparable "persons" (*hypostaseis*). This view became widespread when supported by the new Eastern Roman emperor Theodosius (ruled 379–95). Under his rule the whole Roman empire was again briefly reunited. In 381 he summoned the Council of Constantinople and it was at this council (according to a fifth-century tradition) that the Creed of Nicaea was relaunched (in a modified form) as the Nicene Creed. The threat of Arianism was finally over. The position of Christ and the belief in the Trinity had been settled in a manner that would define the future outlook of the Christian church. There would, though, remain areas of contention. In the Western church it became accepted that the Holy Spirit proceeded *from* the Father *and* the Son. In the Eastern church the established view remained that the Holy Spirit proceeded *from* the Father, *through* the Son. This was a division affecting doctrines of the Trinity but the fundamental outlook on the nature of Christ and his relationship with God the Father was not disputed. There at least there was, finally, some unity.

Christ: fully God and fully man

After ferocious debate, the full divinity of Christ had become a mainstream belief. But what of his humanity? In what sense could someone who was fully and truly God become a real human being? Could God really have experienced a human life and, even more shocking, death by crucifixion?

In the 360s, Bishop Apollinarius of Laodicea (in modern Turkey) taught that Christ could not have possessed a human soul since that was corrupted in human nature. Consequently God, as it were, occupied the human body of Jesus but there was no unity in him of God and human, in terms of inner spiritual existence. This prompted more arguments since, it was counter-argued, if Christ had not also been fully human then it would not be possible for humans to be saved. There would always be something about a human being that had not been (and could not be) transformed by Christ's incarnation. This was, indeed, a matter of salvation: of life and death. It was no mere intellectual disagreement.

It also radically affected how one regarded Christ. If Christ was not fully human, as well as fully God, then his mental and emotional life, his ability to experience sorrow for example, would not be truly human. These things would not have been features of his nature or experience. He would always have been substantially distinct from humans, truly God – but not truly man. Christ's inner life would have been utterly unlike ours. The incarnation would lose its intimacy and its bridging of divine and human existence. Christ would simply have inhabited a human body.

Theologians, especially in the influential church at Antioch, argued strongly for the complete humanity of Christ which meant that he had a human body and soul as well as his divine nature. For them, Christ was divine and truly human too. This outlook, exemplified in the teachings of Nestorius (386–451), could easily become problematic if these two natures were envisaged as being in some way separate. This left Christ as being composed of two persons. They might merge but not be truly united. So Nestorius rejected calling Mary "God bearer" (*theotokos*) since he objected to the idea that God's nature could be born from a human woman. He was getting dangerously close to dividing off the divine nature of Christ from the suffering Jesus so clearly described in the gospels. In 431, Nestorius was condemned for heresy and deposed from his position as Archbishop of Constantinople.

Others, such as the monk Eutyches of Constantinople, argued for what almost amounted to a *monophysite* (single-nature) position, in which the humanity of Christ was absorbed into his divinity. It existed but was of little account, and his humanity could therefore not be compared with that of other human beings. Eutyches' ideas were condemned in 448 but political and inter-church rivalries meant that the matter was not fully settled until the Council of Chalcedon in 451. The Chalcedonian Definition asserted that Christ was:

> ... truly God and the same truly man... begotten from
> the Father before the ages in respect of the Godhead, and
> the same in the last days for us and for our salvation from
> the Virgin Mary the *Theotokos* in respect of the manhood,
> one and the same Christ, Son, Lord, Only-begotten,
> acknowledged in two natures without confusion, change,
> division, or separation (the difference of the natures being
> in no way destroyed by the union, but rather the distinctive
> character of each nature being preserved and coming
> together into one person and one hypostasis)... .[2]

However, the dissent continued. Although rejecting the description of being *monophysite*, the so-called "Oriental Orthodox churches" – those ancient churches that are now known as the Armenian Apostolic Church, Coptic Orthodox Church of Alexandria, Eritrean Orthodox Tewahedo Church, Ethiopian Orthodox Tewahedo Church, Malankara Syrian Orthodox Church, and the Syriac Orthodox Patriarchate of Antioch and All the East – were not reconciled on the subject with the Roman Catholic Church, the major Protestant churches, and the Eastern Orthodox Church, until the second half of the twentieth century.

In the seventh century though, these disputes in doctrine were to have social and political – as well as theological – ramifications. They added to the difficulties facing the Eastern Roman empire in mounting a united defence against Muslim invasion. Dissenting Christians, facing persecution from imperial authorities, were less inclined to defend the imperial system. Debates about the nature of Christ had unforeseen consequences.

CHAPTER 5

Now You See Him, Now You Don't… Portraying Christ

Most people today have a visual image of Christ. Even if not consciously formed, there is usually an assumption regarding his appearance. For those influenced by Western media this is usually informed by film and television. For older viewers this may mean Christ as portrayed by Swedish actor Max von Sydow in *The Greatest Story Ever Told* (1965), Robert Powell in *Jesus of Nazareth* (1977), or Brian Deacon in *The Jesus Film* (1979). More recently this might be Henry Ian Cusick in *The Gospel of John* (2003), Jim Caviezel in *The Passion of the Christ* (2004), or Diogo Morgado in *Son of God* (2014).

Long-haired and bearded, simply dressed in homespun cloth, portrayed with varying degrees of Middle Eastern appearance, often with an intense gaze, played by an attractive and characterful actor… these characteristics spring to mind.

These modern images, though, have a backstory that lies in 2,000 years of the portrayal of Jesus, working backwards through books, illustrated printed Bibles, devotional art, medieval illuminated manuscripts, Eastern Orthodox icons, imperial-sponsored Roman mosaics, and catacomb wall paintings. Consciously or unconsciously the most arresting modern visual images are simply the latest in a long line of portrayals that – though highly varied over the centuries – have settled on this, quite literally, iconic image. The Christian impulse to portray Jesus stands in dramatic contrast to Islamic prohibitions on portraying Muhammad but is not unique: similar easily recognizable iconography can be found in Hinduism and Buddhism where there is, similarly, no reluctance to portray central characters or divine beings. It may be helpful here to briefly explain that by "iconography" is meant: "the study of symbols used in a particular style of painting, etc., and their meaning".[1]

Faith and portrayal of Christ

For Christians, there is a theological impetus to portray Christ, because of their faith in the incarnation and that, in Christ's humanity "all the fullness of God was pleased to dwell" (Colossians 1:19). Therefore, to portray him in recognizable human form reinforces this faith, while challenging the viewer to accept the reality of the God-man and reflect on the implications of this reality for his followers.

The evidence of the New Testament

Given the modern, immediately recognizable, features of Christ it may be helpful for a moment to reflect on how the New Testament portrays him and how this compares with how we see him. But of course there is not one single description of Christ in the gospels or the letters. We may infer from John the Baptist's statement that he was not fit to untie Christ's sandal (John 1:27), that Jesus wore sandals. At the crucifixion we learn that his "tunic was seamless, woven in one piece from the top" (John 19:23). That is it. There is no other description and not a single reference to his appearance. We may make assumptions based on comparative cultural references and other evidence for the appearance of Jewish men in the first half of the first century AD but these are simply assumptions. Revelation contains descriptions of Christ but these are visionary descriptions of the resurrected and glorified Son of God. They are not intended to give any insight into his actual human appearance:

> ... in the midst of the lampstands I saw one like the Son of Man, clothed with a long robe and with a golden sash across his chest. His head and his hair were white as white wool, white as snow; his eyes were like a flame of fire, his feet were like burnished bronze, refined as in a furnace, and his voice was like the sound of many waters. In his right hand he held seven stars, and from his mouth came a sharp, two-edged sword, and his face was like the sun shining with full force. (Revelation 1:13–16)

This makes the question of where we get our strong visual image from all the more intriguing.

The earliest images of Christ

The Old Testament prohibition on making images means that we have no figural representations from Jewish communities in Judea from the first century AD whatsoever. By the third century this had changed among some Jews of the wider Jewish diaspora. The excavated synagogue at Dura Europos (in modern Syria) contains numerous colourful wall paintings of some fifty-eight scenes from the Old Testament. These include portrayals of Old

Testament characters such as Abraham and Isaac, Moses, the visions of Ezekiel, and the story of Esther. In line with traditional Jewish teaching, God is never portrayed but the "hand of God" is shown in order to illustrate divine intervention. Why did the Jewish community at Dura Europos overthrow generations of traditional opposition to the use of figural art? The answer is not certain. It may have been that Jewish figurative art was more widespread than the surviving evidence would suggest and so the absence of evidence may not constitute evidence of absence. On the other hand, the lack of comparative earlier Jewish artistic material of this type means this is conjectural. A more intriguing possibility is that the Jewish community at Dura Europos was reacting to a new and competing religious community in their town: Christians.

The excavated Christian church in the town appears to have been constructed (c. 230–40) a little before the phase of Jewish wall painting occurred. Since the church at Dura Europos contains many figurative paintings, it is possible that its visually striking interior may have contrasted with the (at the time) much plainer synagogue. What is beyond dispute is the range of pictures found in the church building. The baptistery contains a number of frescoes. These surviving pictures constitute probably the most ancient Christian paintings in the world. These include "the Good Shepherd" (borrowing from classical iconography to illustrate this self-description by Jesus), the "Healing of the paralysed man" referred to in the gospels, and a scene showing Christ and the apostle Peter miraculously walking on the water (again from a gospel account). Many experts in Christian art history consider these illustrations to constitute the earliest surviving depictions of Christ.

Other paintings depict three women (probably the three Marys visiting Christ's tomb), Adam and Eve, and David and

Goliath. The pictures do not have the artistic sophistication of the later ones from the nearby synagogue but, like them, they drew on a mixed artistic culture fusing Jewish and Greek ideas and images. What is striking is how un-iconic these representations of Christ are. That of the Good Shepherd is simply a man with no distinguishing features. His hair is short, as is his tunic. The same is true of the figure of Christ healing the paralysed man, although the tunic is longer. In the scene depicting the walking on the water, though, Christ appears to be bearded. The short hairstyle is consistent with the apostle Paul's comment: "Does not nature itself teach you that if a man wears long hair, it is degrading to him…?" (1 Corinthians 11:14).

What is clear is that there was no third-century Christian tradition of what Christ *should* look like. This is further illustrated by the example of another painting of the Good Shepherd, this time from the Catacomb of Callixtus, in Rome. Again dating from the third century, this portrait shows a clean-shaven man, with short hair, and wearing a thigh-length tunic. As with the figures of Christ from Dura Europos, the image simply represents contemporary fashions in terms of clothing and hairstyle. The man could be any man. It is the narrative element (sheep carried on shoulders) that reveals the man to be Christ; and this is only identifiable because it is reminiscent of the gospel account, not because the man himself is recognizable.

These third-century depictions of Christ, though, were beginning to break free from the Jewish prohibition on images that had earlier affected Christian attitudes towards portraying Christ. Church leaders had been reluctant to have such images in Christian places of worship. Irenaeus (died c. 202), Clement of Alexandria (died 215), Lactantius (c. 240–c. 320), and Eusebius of Caesarea (died c. 339) all disapproved of images of Jesus. This disapproval was revealed in other forms too. The Synod of Elvira in

Spain (306) maintained that: "It has been decreed that no pictures be had in the churches, and that which is worshipped or adored be not painted on the walls." Given the use of art and sculpture in pagan representations of gods and goddesses, this reluctance (combined with Jewish heritage) is readily understandable. On the other hand, by the third century this reluctance was weakening: most Christians were non-Jewish in their origins, were used to a visual culture of religious iconography, and were conscious of their separation from Judaism.

From the second century onwards, symbolic Christian art appears on tombs. These coded images included undoubted references to Christ. The fish (Greek *ichthus:* an acronym for the first letters, in Greek, of "Jesus Christ, Son of God, Saviour"), the anchor, the peacock (thought to have incorruptible flesh), the loaves and fishes all appear. Figurative representations developed more slowly. At first the characters depicted were allusions to aspects of Christ and his actions. These included: Moses striking the rock to produce water (a reference to Christ providing "living water" to refresh his followers); Jonah (his time in the stomach of the whale representing Christ in the tomb); Daniel in the lions' den (representing Christ's triumph over sin and death); and even the pagan mythological figure Orpheus charming animals (a reference to conquest of violence and disorder).

The last association, it must be admitted, is open to debate. Even the Good Shepherd theme was taken from classical usage and given a Christian meaning. In its classical, and pagan, form it was known as the *kriophoros* (ram-bearer) and represented a deity or a human carrying a sacrificial ram across their shoulders. In Christian art, this image changed to indicate not the carrying of a sacrificial ram but the rescuing of a lamb, and referred to Jesus' parable of the Good Shepherd, who leaves the ninety-nine sheep in order to find the one that was lost. It may also have had echoes of a second-century Christian literary work, known as *The Shepherd of Hermas.*

None of this, though, could be directly described as a portrait of Christ. Interestingly, none of these contain images that would later be intimately connected with Christianity: the Nativity, the crucifixion, the resurrection, or events from the life of Christ. It is possible that, because this art was fairly public, these images were withheld since they would only be understood by initiated believers. It may also have been because Christians knew how such sacred images could be misunderstood by non-believers. Criminal execution could be mocked and there is early evidence of this (see chapter 10); pagans accused Christians of cannibalism because they misunderstood the use of the bread and wine at communion, and the words involved, of body and blood. It may well have been to protect such sacred concepts that they were not depicted, and this would also apply to the figure of Christ himself. This reluctance continued for most Christians through much of the third century.

Although the third-century wall paintings at Dura Europos contain some images of Christ, the majority of early portrayals are from the fourth century. These depict Christ as a baby receiving the three gifts of the *magi*. The earliest are from paintings in catacombs and sarcophagus reliefs. The depiction draws on secular images of barbarians submitting to the authority of a Roman emperor. Scenes from Christ's adult life also appear. In the Catacombs of Domitilla, Christ is seen among his disciples. He is depicted curly-haired and dressed in classical costume (the toga) and holds a scroll in his left hand. His right hand is outstretched in the so-called *ad locutio* gesture ("the gesture of the orator"). These features – dress, scroll, gesture – all emphasize the authority of Christ. The picture presents him as a philosopher surrounded by his students. The style of the painting suggests a fourth-century origin. It is often described as being a painting of the Last Supper but may not necessarily represent this event.

A fourth-century glass plate recently found by archaeologists excavating within the ruins of what was probably a church in Castulo, in Andalusia, contains another illustration of Christ. In this example, Christ is – characteristically for this period of history – shown clean-shaven; he has short curly hair and is wearing the same philosopher's toga as seen in the Catacombs of Domitilla. Christ has a halo, something that appears from the fourth century onwards to symbolize holiness, and he stands between two other haloed figures (apostles?). All three are flanked by palm trees.

From the Catacombs of Commodilla (also dating from the fourth century) comes the first known representation of Christ that would be familiar to a twenty-first-century viewer. His hair and beard are long and he is robed (though, since the portrait depicts from the chest upwards, we cannot comment further on his dress but it appears to be a toga). His head is encased within a halo. To either side of his head are the first and last letters of the Greek alphabet: alpha and omega; Christ is the beginning and the end. Truly, this portrait is recognizably "Christ". In the so-called "cubiculum of the coronation" in the Catacombs of Praetextatus we find a rare depiction of Christ wearing the crown of thorns. Other fourth-century catacomb paintings also show Christ long-haired and bearded. One has him haloed with a cross behind his head. The painter was no longer reluctant to depict this symbol of Roman execution, with the church now ascendant within Roman society and an emperor – Constantine I, the Great – having legalized Christianity. According to tradition, he had seen a vision of the cross before the battle that secured him the imperial throne, and it was inscribed with the words: "By this conquer!"

While the image of the bearded Christ would be highly influential, the clean-shaven image would continue to appear in Christian art. A fourth-century mosaic from Hinton St Mary (Dorset, England) depicts a beardless and short-haired Christ, with the Chi-Rho symbol behind his head (the first two letters of Christ's title in Greek) and flanked by pomegranates (symbols of eternal life). A sixth-century mosaic from Ravenna (Italy) combines a clean-shaven Christ with a jewelled cross behind his head, all within a halo. Another Ravenna mosaic (this time fifth-century) of Christ's baptism combines a beardless appearance with long hair. A recent find of a sixth-century wall painting from the ruins of Oxyrhynchus (Egypt) revealed the familiar form of a young man with curly hair; he is dressed in a short tunic and has his hand raised, as if giving a blessing. Armenian manuscripts from the tenth century feature beardless figures. In Western Christian art, a beardless Christ continued to be depicted as late as the twelfth century, but among Eastern Christians the bearded Christ had become the norm from the sixth century onwards. This included those shown on wall paintings, on icon boards, and on coins of the Byzantine empire (the Eastern Roman empire which survived until 1453).

The significance of the features of Christ

Early Christian thinkers did not consider it necessary to portray a handsome Christ. Indeed Tertullian (died 220) quoted the Old Testament passage that many Christians believed referred to Christ to support this view: "… he had no form or majesty that we should look at him, nothing in his appearance that we should desire him" (Isaiah 53:2). This led some pagans to ridicule Christians for having an unattractive God. As a reaction against this attitude, and in an attempt to reflect spiritual perfection in human beauty, later Christian writers such as Jerome (died 420) and Augustine of Hippo (died 430) argued that portrayals of

Christ should show him exemplifying perfection in every way. A handsome Christ therefore became mandatory.

The shift to a bearded Christ by the sixth century is noteworthy. It was once thought that this was a decision within Eastern Christianity but it is now clear that the trend was also occurring in the West. This shift is quite dramatic as it greatly altered the appearance of Christ and has influenced Christian visualization ever since. Why did this occur? It is likely that the long hair and the beard were finally chosen because they were culturally associated with philosophers, along with the centre parting of the hair. There may even have been visual echoes of how the healing god Asclepius (a pagan Greek deity borrowed by Roman culture) and Jupiter, the chief god of pagan Rome, were portrayed: long-haired and bearded. This in no way compromises the Christ-icon; it is simply that things such as hair have cultural resonance and associations. In this sense the long hair and beard were culturally associated with wisdom, learning, divinity, and healing. When transferred to Christ they had been shorn of their pagan connotations. Interestingly, other bearded Christian figures – such as the apostle Paul – are always shown (if bearded) with a neatly trimmed beard and hair. It is clear that the association of long hair and beard with Christ was not accidental; instead it communicated meaning. In the crossover period from clean-shaven to bearded there may have been a tendency to depict Christ in his priestly majestic role bearded, but in scenes from his life as clean-shaven. Once again this would point towards the significance of the beard.

What is certain is that the image struck a chord. The fifteenth-century forgery, the so-called *Letter of Lentulus*, purported to have been written to the Roman Senate in the first century during the reign of Emperor Tiberius, by a certain Publius Lentulus, governor of Judea before Pontius Pilate. It contained a fictional description of Jesus:

He has hair the color of an unripe hazelnut, smooth almost to the ears, but below his ears curling... hanging over his shoulders, and having a parting in the middle of his head.... His brow is smooth and quite serene; his face is without wrinkle or blemish, and a slight ruddiness makes it handsome. No fault can be found with his nose and mouth; he has a full beard of the color of his hair, not long but divided in two at the chin. His facial expression is guileless and mature; his eyes are greyish and clear.[2]

Apparently, it was just too frustrating that, when everyone "knew" (!) what Christ looked like, there was no first-century description of him. "Publius Lentulus, governor of Judea" filled the vacuum. It may be noted that there was no governor of Judea of this name.

Portraying Christ: now you see him... The role of icons

As we shall see (in chapter 6), the imperial conversion to Christianity had dramatic effects on how Christ was understood and presented. There was now an imperial Christ where there had once been a humble Galilean.

In theological terms this was reflected in the way in which Christ was portrayed in both Eastern and Western Roman art and in the art of the barbarians who converted to Christianity (see chapter 7). But at this point we will pause to ask another question: If a picture is a visual representation of Christ, does that make it holy?

In the Eastern half of the Roman empire, from the fourth century onwards, an exalted view of the role of icons developed. It was alleged that Luke had painted an icon of the Virgin Mary, and that a miraculous depiction of Jesus (formed from a towel pressed against his face) had been sent to the king of Edessa in the first century. Adopting a high-status approach to Christian pictures (that is, icons) almost certainly had some of its cultural roots in the Roman imperial practice of burning candles and offering incense to the emperor's image. With the official conversion to Christianity during the fourth century it is possible to trace this being transferred to Christ, who alone was seen as truly worthy of worship.

As icons developed, they took on distinct characteristics in order to convey particular spiritual truths. This tended to mean that a deep conservatism prevailed in their production as new painters copied the style and content of previous icons. Developments did occur but distinct types can still be identified. Icons only appear to have "width" and "height". The sense of three-dimensional "depth", which today is such a feature of art, is missing. Partly it is because this third dimension (the "depth") is considered to only exist spiritually, in the mind of the viewer. Eastern Orthodoxy teaches that in the *image* of the invisible is the *presence* of the invisible. While icons often contain pictures of the Virgin Mary and saints, many focus on Christ. Such icons emphasize certain aspects of his character and role; and this was the very recognizable bearded and long-haired Christ that we have earlier described. These include: "Christ the Teacher", "Christ the Redeemer", "Christ *Pantocrator*" ("ruler of all"). The latter title – traditionally used to describe God the Father – is a direct result of the shift in theological thinking that occurred in the fourth century in terms of the relationship between Christ and God the Father (see chapter 4).

There was, though, a thin line between using an image as a visual aid and considering that it was itself holy because of whom it represented. Within Eastern Orthodoxy (the official church within the surviving Eastern Roman empire) there was great popular devotion towards icons.

Portraying Christ: now you don't...
The reaction against icons

The use of icons was seriously challenged by the Eastern Roman (Byzantine) imperial authorities in the eighth century. There had been disquiet in some quarters for some time and a fear that veneration of an icon of Christ could become worship of that icon. Islamic opposition to images may also have heightened government anxieties as imperial authorities prepared both military and spiritual defences against the Islamic threat. The imperial government decided it was time for radical action.

The so-called Iconoclastic Period began when images were banned by Emperor Leo III, the Isaurian (ruled 716–41). In 726 he published an edict declaring images to be idols. He claimed they came under the category of "idols" forbidden by Exodus 20:4–5. Leo commanded that all such images in churches be destroyed throughout the empire. When the picture of Christ, called "Christ *Antiphonetes*" ("the Guarantor"), that hung over the gate of the palace at Constantinople was removed, a serious riot occurred in the city. The patriarch of Constantinople protested, and he was deposed. When conservative monks led the opposition to Leo, he began a systematic campaign against monasteries. Pope Gregory II (pope 713–31) responded to an appeal by the deposed patriarch with a long defence of images and argued that they were not the same as idols. In 731, a new pope, Gregory III, held a synod at St Peter's, Rome. It declared that all persons who broke and defiled images of Christ, his mother, the apostles, or other saints were excommunicated. In retaliation, Leo then sent a fleet to Italy to punish the pope but it was wrecked in a storm.

When Leo died in 741 the cause was continued by his son, Constantine V, Copronymus (ruled 741–75). In 754 a council he convened declared that all such images of Christ were either *monophysite* or Nestorian (see chapter 8). This, it argued, was because as it is impossible to represent Christ's divinity, such icons either denied or split Christ's two natures.

Constantine V died in 775 and was succeeded by his son Leo IV (ruled 775–80). He was more moderate, allowed the exiled monks to return, and tried to reconcile the conflicting groups. When he died in 780, he was succeeded by the Empress Irene. She was regent for her son Constantine VI (ruled 780–97), who was aged nine in 780. She was in favour of icons and immediately set about undoing the work of the Iconoclasts. Pictures were restored to the churches and the monasteries were reopened.

The matter though was not over. The ban was reinforced by Emperor Leo V in 815. Finally, though, the veneration (but not worship) of icons was permanently restored by Empress Regent Theodora in 842. Icons would remain a major feature of Eastern Orthodox worship. In the West they would also be venerated until the sixteenth-century Reformation, when those who took the Protestant line abandoned them to the Roman Catholic Church, but they would never have as central a place in the life of the Christian community as in the East.

The familiar images of Christ were once more back on display for public veneration. All in all, the history of portraying Christ had come a long way, by a rough road, since the first wall paintings at Dura Europos.

The legacy of these images for the portrayal of Christ beyond the year 1000

The developments that we have explored in this chapter have influenced the way many Christians have visualized Christ ever since. Such images were not uniform and, as we shall see, in Africa, Asia, and South America, indigenous developments would reflect the vibrant Christian cultures of these communities. But much of the pictorial outlook had been decided by 600, even if it took time for this to fully settle as the norm.

When Michelangelo painted a clean-shaven Christ in his Last Judgment fresco in the Sistine Chapel (1534–41) he found himself in trouble. The figure, as depicted there, was rather Apollo-like and not as expected. That it was reverting to a pre-fifth-century manner of depicting Christ was clearly lost on the sixteenth-century detractors of the artist. They knew what Christ looked like. And they wanted no messing with how he should appear.

CHAPTER 6

Imperial Christ

Today, in the Louvre, it is possible to see a carving that was once one of the Christian treasures of Constantinople. This city, originally known as Byzantium, became the new capital of the Roman empire under Emperor Constantine the Great, after whom it was renamed, in 330. It was solemnly dedicated in this new role that same year. The city was initially capital of the whole Roman empire and then, with the collapse of the empire in the West in the fifth century, that of the surviving Eastern Roman – or Byzantine – empire until 1453. There was also a short-lived, so-called, Latin empire (1204–61) when Western Catholic Christian knights sacked the city and set up their base there. Following this, it returned to Byzantine control. It was the capital of the Islamic Ottoman Empire from 1453 until 1922. It was renamed Istanbul in 1923, as capital of the new country of Turkey, which emerged after the defeat of the Ottoman Turks in the First World War and the break-up of the Ottoman empire.

But back to the exquisite carving that was produced in Christian Constantinople. Carved from ivory in the middle of the tenth century, it is today known as the Harbaville Triptych. A triptych is a three-part construction consisting of a central scene flanked by two hinged panels or leaves (also decorated). These flanking leaves can be shut like doors or opened to present a three-part set of scenes.

It is what is known in Byzantine art, and then in later Eastern Orthodox art, as a *Deesis* or *Deisis*. The term is derived from a Greek word meaning "prayer" or "supplication". These show a figure described as "Christ in Majesty" or "Christ *Pantocrator*". Christ is depicted enthroned and carrying a book. He is flanked by the Virgin Mary and by John the Baptist. Sometimes other saints and/or angels are shown. Mary and John (along with any other human figures present) face Christ with their hands raised in supplication. They plead with Christ on behalf of humanity.

The craft skills employed in the production of the Harbaville Triptych are magnificent and the workshop which produced it was almost certainly closely associated with the imperial court of the Eastern Roman emperor. On the Harbaville Triptych the central panel has the *Deesis* scene of Christ, Mary, and John the Baptist at the top. The bearded Christ is seated on a magnificently carved throne with his feet on a footrest. His head is surrounded by a halo combined with a cross. His right hand is raised in blessing and his piercing look is directed straight ahead at the viewer. His face carries a look of concentrated reflection. Below is a separate scene depicting the apostles James, John, Peter, Paul, and Andrew. On each of the flanking panels, two military saints stand guard. Below each pair of soldier-saints are four other saints. The whole scene is reminiscent of an imperial ruler sat in judgment, amid his closest trusted advisors, his court, and his military bodyguard. This is an "Imperial Christ".

The triptych can be contrasted with another example of political and religious art from the Eastern Roman empire. Also produced in the middle of the tenth century, this carved ivory depicts Christ crowning Emperor Romanos (ruled 948–63) and Empress Eudokia. It is now in the Bibliothèque Nationale de France. Christ stands between them and is elevated on a three-tiered pedestal. He is cross-haloed as on the Harbaville Triptych and his hands rest on the heads of the emperor and the empress. These two are sumptuously robed and, like Mary and John the Baptist on a *Deesis*, they have their hands raised in supplication. This time, though, the implication is a little different: they are receiving Christ's power and authority while also, perhaps, representing in their persons the empire before Christ. Both supplication and empowerment are depicted. The Imperial Christ has made the emperor and empress his divinely sanctioned representatives on earth. They are thus "God-Crowned". Christ and emperor stand together in imperial majesty and unity. We will return to this in due course but, at this point, it might be helpful to briefly explain how this had come about.

Christ triumphant

Christ was executed, in the first century, by the governor of a Roman province, acting in concert with the Jerusalem elite of Judaism. By the beginning of the fourth century the influence of this once-derided faith and its God-man central figure was dramatically increasing.

As we have seen, the Christian historian Eusebius of Caesarea records that in 312, during a civil war over rule of the Roman empire, one of the contenders – Constantine – saw a noontime vision of a cross placed over the sun and the words "By this conquer!" The cross was, of course, the dramatic and controversial symbol of Christ's crucifixion. Then, in a night-time vision, Christ appeared to Constantine and commanded that he use a sign in battle to ensure victory. Another Roman historian – Lactantius – claimed that this Chi-Rho symbol (the first two letters of "Christ" in Greek) was then painted on the shields of Constantine's soldiers. Constantine defeated Maxentius, his enemy, and became emperor. Whatever the truth of this tradition, the figure of

Christ had dramatically been superimposed on Roman imperial politics. The tradition clearly caught people's imagination. On the sarcophagus of Junius Bassus – from the Catacomb of Domitilla, Rome, and dating from 359 – the central carving of Christ's cross merges into Constantine's Chi-Rho standard.

Under Constantine, Christianity became the favoured religion within the Roman empire. It was, though, not the only religion. It would be some time before Christianity achieved this position. But the change was dramatic. In this period of transition there is evidence to show that the way Christ was interpreted and presented bridged the old and new phases of religious dominance. Constantine, along with previous emperors since the 270s and soldiers generally, had earlier favoured the worship of the "Unconquered Sun" (Latin *Sol Invictus*) and the sun/cross vision may show he considered there was some connection between this deity and Christ. He may simply have considered that his favourite god commanded him to henceforth worship Christ, or perhaps that Christ was now revealed as the deity who had previously been worshipped as the "Unconquered Sun". We cannot now be sure exactly how Constantine saw the situation. The Christian title used for Christ (and used by himself in the gospels) of "the Light of the World" may have assisted this process. Christian writers regarded Christ as the messianic fulfilment of the Old Testament prophecy: "But for you who revere my name the sun of righteousness shall rise, with healing in its wings. You shall go out leaping like calves from the stall" (Malachi 4:2). This refers to the sun as a metaphor and not as a deity of any kind.

That there was a pagan reverence for the sun as a deity meant that Christians might use some pagan sun-god imagery to express ideas about Christ who was regarded as the Son of the only true God. Under St Peter's in the Vatican, Rome, the grave known as "Mausoleum M" (and dating from the third century) is decorated with a mosaic that depicts Christ in the traditional image of Sol, driving a chariot across the sky. Clearly, a well-known pagan image could be used to convey the new truth of the message of Christ. The choice of 25 December as the celebration of Christ's birth (the gospels give no date) may have been influenced by it already being the pagan festival of *Natalis Invicti* (named from *Sol Invictus*) and dedicated to the birthday of the sun. The general location around this date of the winter solstice may also have prompted this selection of date but, either way, the relationship to the sun was comparable as a factor. Emperor Constantine's coinage continued to carry images of Sol until 325. A gold medallion from his reign combines the emperor's bust with that of *Sol Invictus*. On it the words *INVICTUS CONSTANTINUS* combine the title of Sol with the name of Constantine: "Unconquered Constantine". In 321, when Constantine decreed that the Christian sabbath would be the Roman day of rest, he selected *dies Solis*, the day of the sun (modern Sunday). Emerging imperial Christology was clearly going to be complex in its imagery and the way in which it related the new beliefs about Christ to previous pagan ones.

The same process would affect the way Christ has been communicated in South America, Africa, and India for example. And for some Roman worshippers of Christ there was undeniably some confusion. In the middle of the fifth century, Pope Leo I criticized some who bowed to the sun before entering the Christian church of St Peter's in Rome. There are more than hints of this in some South American and African Christian practices today and, similarly, there have been debates about the appropriateness of the use of some Hindu imagery and concepts to describe Christ among modern Indian Christians. Old complexities have not vanished.

Although Constantine's Christianity may have been rather complex and questionable he nevertheless greatly elevated the person of Christ within his religious policies. It was under Constantine that the Holy Sepulchre (the place of Christ's burial and resurrection) was "found" in Jerusalem in 325, after pagan temples there were demolished. Constantine's mother, Helena, it was claimed, also discovered the True Cross, on which Christ died, at the same time. In 335 the newly constructed Church of the Holy Sepulchre was inaugurated. It should be noted that Jerusalem had ceased to be a Jewish city after the crushing of the Bar Kokhba revolt against Roman rule in 135. In 335 it became a Christian city. The figure of Christ was central in this reinvention of Jerusalem.

Imperial politics and the debates about the nature of Christ

We have seen how the leaders of the church debated the exact nature of Christ. In this there were various factions grouped about different major churches which were powerhouses of study and learning in their regions. These included key "players" such as the church communities at Antioch, Alexandria, Rome, and Constantinople. But there was another set of players who wielded great power and influence over this period of debate, controversy, and division: those at the top of imperial Roman government and society, the emperors.

Constantine inherited a role in which emperors were high priests of the pagan cults of the Roman empire. Consequently, it would not have seemed odd to him to intervene in disputes within the church. Indeed, certain factions within the church openly appealed to him to support them in the controversies that divided the church in the fourth century. To the role of these emperors in the emerging understanding about Christ we will shortly turn.

By way of explanation, though, some of the emperors mentioned below ruled the whole empire, while some ruled only in the West or East. It could get very complicated because a ruler might start off ruling one half of the empire and end up controlling it all. The situation with regard to co-emperors and junior-emperors was more complicated still, but that lies beyond the focus of this examination of Christian faith.

Imperial interference in the debates about the nature of Christ revealed itself in a number of dramatic ways. And, for such is the nature of politics, this did not follow one clear trajectory. The figure of Christ was now grasped by factions and political expediencies.

By 324 Constantine was firmly in control of both the West and East of the Roman empire. He found that in the East he had arrived right in the middle of the Arian crisis and he was determined to settle it. As a successful soldier and politician it took him some time to appreciate just how much heat there was in these disagreements. At first he described it as "very trifling". To those involved it was anything but. It was due to his intervention that the first ever ecumenical council, that at Nicaea, was called. It was actually Constantine who suggested the word *homoousios* (Greek: "same substance") to describe Christ and God the Father. Constantine's decisive technical intervention was probably on the instigation of one of his advisers but the impact of his imperial excursion into Christology would be long-lasting. Also important was the precedent which he had set: that the emperor had an active role to play in church affairs. In the West, this would disintegrate with the collapse of that half of the Roman empire. But in the East (witness the ivory of the crowning of Emperor Romanos and Empress Eudokia) the emperor would remain Christ's empowered representative on earth. And that included authority over the church.

Just how influential emperors could be was made clear after Constantine's death in 337. His son, Constantius II (emperor 337–61), favoured Arianism and so this once again was resurgent. When challenged by some church leaders who appealed to canons (church rulings on faith matters), he allegedly retorted: "Whatever I will shall be regarded as a canon." Some church leaders, such as Athanasius and Ossius of Cordoba, begin to rethink the wisdom and validity of imperial interference in matters of faith. They may, though, have been more favourable when Constantius closed pagan temples and banned pagan sacrifices in 356.

Just how influential an emperor could be in a negative sense (from a Christian perspective) was revealed during the reign of Julian "the Apostate" (emperor of the whole empire 361–63) who attempted a pagan revival, although he based his reorganized paganism on the more successful aspects of church structure and conduct. The pendulum swung back the other way when Julian was succeeded by Jovian (emperor of the whole empire 363–64) and Valentinian I (emperor of the West 364–75) who were both Christians. Valentinian I was not Arian but pursued a policy of toleration regarding them and other heretics. Valens (emperor in the East 364–78) was pro-Arian and so things reverted to a situation reminiscent of the reign of Constantius II. Imperial faith-preferences and Christology were getting tightly entwined. After Valens' death in battle, in 378, all later emperors (East and West) were Nicaean-believing Catholics and this ensured the eventual defeat of Arianism and the victory of Trinitarian beliefs.

In 391, Theodosius I (emperor 379–92 in the East and 392–95 over the whole empire) finally banned all pagan sacrifices and shut all pagan temples. In 392 he made private pagan worship illegal as well. He also acted energetically against those in the church who were accused of heresy. Under the Western rebel-emperor

Magnus Maximus (ruled 383–88) the first death penalties were enacted for heresy. This was not widespread, though, and a number of church leaders condemned its use but it showed how much had changed in the church (and in church–state relations) on the question of getting faith in Christ "right" or "wrong".

Christ and the elites in the late Roman empire

Once Christianity became acceptable, it also became fashionable. On one hand this meant that those who had once kept their Christian allegiances secret or who practised the faith discreetly could now do so openly. On the other hand, as the power and influence of the Christian faith and church increased during the fourth century, it actually became politically expedient to attach oneself to the new faith. Christianity and Christ had come a long way from Galilee and Judea, as a socially marginalized and, at times, persecuted faith. Now, association with Christ was a political and social necessity. This revealed itself in a number of ways.

Educated late Roman villa owners, whose grandparents had declared their classical education through scenes from Virgil depicted in their floor mosaics, might now include Christ in the artwork. At times their blend of pagan and Christian imagery might seem to indicate syncretism at odds with the singular focus of Christians on Christ. For example, at Hinton St Mary (Dorset, England), the head of Christ in the central roundel (backed by a Chi-Rho and flanked by pomegranates) is surrounded by four unidentified figures in each corner; a tree is depicted beneath the central figure and flanking scenes (with a third above the head of Christ) show a dog chasing a stag. On a nearby section of paving the pagan myth is illustrated of Bellerophon riding Pegasus and slaying the Chimera. It looks as if Christ has simply been added to the repertoire of a mosaic maker's pattern book.

However, this may be too simplistic. The Christ-mosaic may tell us far more about how Christ was understood in one of the western provinces of the Roman empire in the last century of its existence. The four figures *may* represent the four gospel writers; the tree *may* represent the Tree of Life; the hunting scenes *may* represent the pursuit of eternal life; Bellerophon and Chimera *may* represent the defeat of death and evil. In short, this mosaic, far from revealing a shallow attachment to Christ, may instead instruct us in how an educated late Roman family used its grasp of wide-ranging literary and artistic devices to communicate what Christ meant to them. Given the passing similarity of the central roundel to a coin of the Western rebel-emperor Magnentius (ruled 350–53), it is possible that the images found on the obverse (a distinctive head of Magnentius) and reverse (Chi-Rho between an Alpha and Omega) of that coin have been combined and adapted to make this Christian statement. To portray Christ in a way reminiscent of an emperor may have seemed to make perfect sense to the mosaic designers. It was, as we shall shortly see, certainly an idea developed in the Eastern Roman empire and beyond in the centuries to come. The fact that in the same period similar images were produced at Lullingstone Roman villa (Kent), and at Frampton Roman villa (Devon), which also combine the Chi-Rho symbol and Bellerophon, suggests we are looking at a set of religious images about Christ that would have been recognized by other Christians.

In the same way, educated Christians expressed Christ in the language of classical education when they portrayed him in the guise of Orpheus, as appears in fourth-century contexts in the Catacombs of Peter and Marcellus and also in the Catacombs of Domitilla, all in Rome. Orpheus' mythical ability to tame wild animals with his song, his heroic journey to the underworld, and his meeting a violent death would have reminded fourth-century educated Christians of Christ who was executed, in the tomb for three days, and triumphed over the forces of sin and evil. Indeed, the priest and theologian Clement of Alexandria (150–215) was clearly well aware of this since he wrote that Christ, unlike Orpheus, tames even the wildest of beasts: humans. Clearly, Christ could become part of intellectual cultural debate. We would like to know more about what less educated citizens thought of Christ in this period of imperial acceptance but, as usual, the poor are voiceless.

Christ and imperial power

At the heart of imperial politics the official nature of Christianity meant that the position of Christ and the role of the emperor were now closely aligned. This followed a curious trajectory which first saw Christ displace the emperor, and then the sacred power of the central imperial political figure being enhanced by his association with Christ. Three objects illustrate this very well.

The first object is the so-called Missorium of Theodosius (I), preserved in the Real Academia de la Historia, in Madrid. It is a large ceremonial silver dish, made in 388 to mark the tenth anniversary of the emperor's accession. It is full of the imperial images of grandeur that were associated with Roman emperors. Centre stage sits the emperor within an arcade. He hands down a scroll to a smaller (but still senior) official. The scroll was probably a letter of appointment. Theodosius is flanked by two co-emperors. All three emperors have haloes, clearly indicating their exalted status. Beyond are armed bodyguards. There is nothing of Christ in this object.

But fast-forward 550 years to the production of the Harbaville

Triptych (the second object) and a transformation has occurred. Now the central figure is Christ enthroned; the flanking figures are Mary and John the Baptist; the bodyguards beyond are soldier-saints. As we have seen, Christ is the emperor now. Not that we have to wait five and a half centuries to see this. We can see Christ depicted as "Christ *Pantocrator*" ("ruler of all") in the Byzantine world from the sixth century onwards. This half-length image of Christ sets him alone in imperial splendour. By the seventh century the figure of Christ *Pantocrator* – recognizable with him holding a book (the gospels) and raising his right hand in blessing – had become established in the form that it still retains in Eastern Orthodoxy. It is a small step from this to the accompanied *Deesis* figures that effectively took over the imperial power-art of objects such as the Missorium of Theodosius. In the Western tradition a slightly different version emerged known as "Christ in Majesty" or "Christ in Glory" (Latin: *Majestas Domini*). In these depictions, Christ appears seated on a throne as ruler of the world. He is always seen frontally in the centre of the object; often he is flanked by other sacred figures. A variant on this theme of an exalted Christ is the form known as "Christ Triumphant", where he is usually shown standing and often with both hands raised high. Christ has displaced the emperor.

This displacement of the emperor by Christ, though, was accompanied by other developments. This brings us to the third object. As early as the sixth century, the decoration of the Church of San Vitale in Ravenna (Italy) portrays an emperor, Justinian, combining the elevated image of a haloed and purple-robed emperor, with the humility of Justinian's gesture as he carries the bread of the Eucharist in an act of homage to Christ (who appears in the nearby apse mosaic). There Christ, dressed in purple and seated on an orb, displays his universal power. In the mosaic below he offers the crown to Justinian. The message is clear: Christ is ruler of all but the emperor is his agent on earth. It is reminiscent of the mid-tenth-century crowning of Emperor Romanos and Empress Eudokia that we considered earlier. The emperor's role has actually been enhanced by his close association with Christ who has displaced him as the ultimate figure in sacred iconography.

This revealed itself strikingly on Byzantine coinage. An example (and there are many) is the gold coin – known as a *histamenon nomisma* (full-weight gold *solidus*) – of Emperor Nicephorus II (ruled 963–69). On one side the bearded Christ, haloed and holding a gospel book, raises his hand in blessing. His title, which includes Latin abbreviations, reads: *IHS XPS REX REGNANTINM* ("Jesus Christ King of Kings"). On the reverse the emperor stands beside the Virgin Mary and between them they are holding a processional cross. Mary has a halo, the emperor is ornately crowned. The emperor's power is sacred because it is blessed by Christ and by the support of Mary his mother.

The same concept was also taken up by the "barbarian" Germanic inheritors of the Roman empire in the West. As they reinvented themselves as the "new Romans" they proclaimed the same outlook concerning their sacred royal authority as was to be found in the surviving Eastern Roman empire. Almost identical to the crowning of Emperor Romanos and Empress Eudokia is the carved ivory of Christ crowning the German emperor Otto II as Holy Roman Emperor in the West (ruled 973–83) and Empress Theophanou. Otto II married the daughter of a Byzantine emperor and was heavily influenced by the political and religious art and ideology of the Byzantine empire, as can be seen in the way that he had his crowning represented.

The process is clear in all of this. Christ has now been publicly elevated to cosmic imperial power; but even as he takes to himself the representations of authority once reserved solely for emperors, he also transforms the imperial role to that of the holy representative of Christ *Pantocrator* on earth. Both images have been transformed in the process. Now we have Imperial Christ and God-crowned emperor in close relationship. We have come a long way from a Roman execution on the outskirts of Jerusalem.

Christ: the continuation of old certainties and the appearance of new possibilities

In the eastern Mediterranean the Eastern Roman empire survived until 1453, when it finally fell to the Islamic armies of the Ottoman Turks. In those intervening centuries, despite ups and increasingly dramatic downs, an attempt was made to keep "Roman-ness" alive. In this the "God-crowned" relationship of the emperor with the church (outlined above) continued. Eastern Orthodox Christianity, with its striking emphasis on icons and the imperial family, the grandeur of liturgy, and the particularly Orthodox views of the Trinity (the Holy Spirit proceeding from the Father and not from the Son), survived. This was despite the divisions and tensions over Christological beliefs and other matters of theology that had not gone away, even with the resolution of the creedal debates. It survived in the face of the rise of Islam and the loss of vast tracts of land in the Middle East and North Africa to Muslim invaders. Despite all this, a continuous (if at times tenuous) thread links the intervening Emperor Constantine the Great in the fourth century and the succeeding emperors of the diminishing Eastern Roman empire that finally vanished in the fifteenth century.

In the West, though, there was a rupture with the past that occurred far earlier. The last Western Roman emperor – Romulus Augustus or Augustulus – was deposed in 476. He was overthrown by Odoacer, the Germanic commander of the (mostly Germanic) army who now made up the majority of the Roman military forces in Italy. So-called "barbarians" (whose cultural roots lay beyond the boundaries of the empire) were now in the ascendant.[1] The Roman empire in the West, already in turmoil, had finally collapsed. Odoacer ruled as king of Italy until 493, when he was murdered by another Germanic chieftain, the Ostrogoth known as Theodoric the Great. Theodoric himself was put up to this by Zeno the Eastern Roman emperor. He had been happy to see one troublesome barbarian set about another troublesome barbarian.

Odoacer was an Arian Christian ruling in an Italy that was now dominated by the Trinitarian, Nicaean-believing, Roman Catholic Church. It has to be admitted that this had little influence on how he interacted with the church in Italy. Across the West a mixed bag of barbarian tribes were the inheritors of Roman power, from the Danube to the upper Thames, and from North Africa to the Rhine. Some were already Arian Christians, others were pagans who eventually converted to Catholic Christianity. In this cocktail of chaotic new ethnic identities and shifting politics, the figure of Christ would once again play a central role as new allegiances were forged and identities constructed. Defenders of the rapidly diminishing empire would see allegiance to Christ as one of the key features of their "civilized" identity that differentiated them from the barbarians. In contrast, barbarian arrivistes would rapidly see devotion to Christ as the hallmark of the legitimacy and acceptability that they desired in order to cloak their seizure of power by the sword.

Between 400 and 1000 the Christian faith would also spread far beyond the now defunct boundaries of the old empire. There would be competing religious identities and debates over the place of Christ within these emerging barbarian kingdoms. From Ireland (where Christianity was dominant by the year 550) to Scandinavia (where the process of conversion was still underway in the year 1000), new ways of understanding Christ and communicating these ideas would be dramatically explored. "Christ of the barbarians" would be the successor to "Imperial Christ" in the West.

In the south and south-east of the old empire, the rise of Islam in the seventh century led to the emergence of a very different set of understandings about Christ and a different challenge to the Orthodox Christian Church as it faced a new set of rulers with a new religious ideology.

It is to the emergence of these new views of Christ that we now turn.

CHAPTER 7

Christ of the Barbarians... Beyond the Mediterranean Heartlands

The original heartland of Christianity was in the eastern Mediterranean. From there it spread across the Roman empire. The key players in the debates about the way Christ should be understood and communicated until the year 500 remained centred on the Mediterranean, in places such as Antioch, Alexandria, Constantinople, and Rome.

It was not to stay this way. Christianity spread not only across the empire but beyond it. Although the Western empire had collapsed in the fifth century, the Christian faith continued to extend its geographical reach. In the south it spread down the Nile valley into Ethiopia. In the east it extended across the Jordan valley into modern-day Jordan and Syria. In the north-east, its extension into Armenia had occurred during the fourth century. In the north, the barbarian tribes of the Goths and Burgundians converted to an Arian form of Christianity (they were later reconverted to Catholic beliefs) which meant that –

temporarily – a heretical form of Christianity dominated the societies that these migrating tribes ruled between the Adriatic and the Danube, on the upper Rhine, in central and southern France, and in much of the Iberian peninsula. In North Africa, the aggressively Arian kingdom of the Vandals survived until 534, when they were defeated by the Byzantine empire. Along the Rhine and in northern France, the pagan Franks converted to Catholic Christianity and were followed in the seventh century by the pagan kingdoms of Anglo-Saxon England. In the far west and north-west of the British Isles, that is, the areas now known as Wales, southern Scotland, and Cornwall, Christianity survived unbroken from the Roman empire. Missionaries from Britain took the faith to Ireland in the fifth century.

By the year 1000, Christianity could also be found throughout the Germanic kingdoms beyond the Rhine, although Scandinavia took some time to see the conversion become secure and it was not until the year 1000 that Scandinavia's far-flung colony of settlers in Iceland decided to adopt Christianity. When Þorgeir Þorkelsson, law speaker of Iceland, threw his pagan idols into the thundering waterfall of Goðafoss, on the River Skjálfandafljót in north-eastern Iceland, he completed the Christian conversion of the northern Germanic peoples.

In each of these areas the understanding of Christ combined ideas and images that we have already come across, with aspects of the tribal and warrior cultures of these people who had never known Roman rule. From the abbreviated facial features of the two-dimensional Christ found in Ethiopian gospel books, through Christ portrayed as a Frankish warrior or framed by Celtic interlace patterns, to the crucified Christ entangled in branches reminiscent of legends of Odin... we see Christ beyond the early heartlands. He was also Christ of the "barbarians".

Christ of the Germanic Arians

In a strange twist of theological history many of the barbarian Germanic tribes that invaded the Roman empire and became its immediate successors held a view of Christ that was on its way to defeat within the mainstream of Christianity.

Ulfilas (died 383) was an Arian Christian missionary and also a member of the Germanic tribe of the Goths. Sixth-century traditions would later claim that the Goths' original homeland was in Scandinavia and that from there they migrated to the shores of the Black Sea, via Pomerania. What is clear is that, in the third century, this tribal group (an amalgamation by this time of a number of allied tribes) invaded the Balkans and Greece. For a brief period they ruled over a confederation that stretched from the River Danube as far east as the River Volga. Under pressure from the westward-moving Huns, a large group of Goths entered the Roman empire. Relations with the Roman government deteriorated and, in 378, they defeated the Roman emperor, Valens, at the Battle of Adrianople (modern Edirne in Turkey, close to the border with Greece and Bulgaria). By this time, though, many of them had converted to Christianity. Which brings us back to Ulfilas. With mixed Goth/Greek parentage he was a missionary who was successful in converting many Goths to the Arian form of Christianity (see chapter 4). By the time that these Goths finally established successor-kingdoms in the western parts of the Roman empire, many had been Arian Christians for over a century.

One group of Goths – the Ostrogoths – eventually settled in and dominated Italy, in the second half of the fifth century. Another group – the Visigoths – sacked Rome itself in 410 and went on to establish kingdoms in Aquitaine (modern south-western France) and modern Spain, after they were driven out of France by another Germanic group, the Franks.

The migrations of these Arian Christians created a strange situation in which different social groups in the new kingdoms adhered to quite different understandings of the nature of Christ. In fact, there coexisted separate Arian and Nicene Churches. They had parallel hierarchies, serving different communities of believers. It was the unintended and unforeseen consequence of the great creed debates that had rocked the fourth- and fifth-century church. In these kingdoms the new Germanic elites were Arians, and the majority population was made up of Nicene-believing Catholics. This may have been reinforced as a mixed theological and political strategy by the newcomers, designed to set them apart from their new subjects. However, the new Arian rulers did not attempt to force their beliefs on their subjects, with the exception of the Vandals in North Africa. There the Vandals banished the clergy and shut the monasteries of the opposing, Catholic, tradition.

How this situation would eventually have developed is hard to guess. Which outlook on Christ would have triumphed, if the groups had continued to coexist? As it was, the Arian view of Christ failed to thrive. By 700 these Arian kingdoms had either been defeated by Nicene-believing Catholic rivals from neighbouring areas (in the case of the Ostrogoths, Vandals, and Burgundians) or the pull of mainstream Christianity had led to the conversion of the Arian elites to Nicene Catholic beliefs (in the case of the Visigoths and the Lombards). Garibald (briefly king of the Lombards in 671) was the last Arian king in Europe.

Christ of the Germanic Catholics

In contrast to the Arian Germanic barbarians who entered the empire as Arian Christians and eventually accepted the mainstream Catholic understanding of Christ, the Franks (who invaded Roman Gaul, roughly modern France and Belgium) and the Anglo-Saxons (who invaded Roman Britain) did so as pagans, but converted to Nicene-believing Catholic Christianity.

In 496, the Frankish king, Clovis (founder of the Frankish Merovingian dynasty), converted to Christianity. This would have a huge impact on the lands of the expanding Frankish empire in what is today France and Germany. When the Frankish tribes of the Rhineland and northern France converted to Christianity they were adopting, in Christ, a motif of Roman power and culture. Accepting Christ made these conquerors of Roman power the heirs to its authority (albeit in a much reduced form). Given that the authority of Christian bishops was all that had survived the collapse of Roman rule in many areas, it is not surprising that Christ was seen as a link to the mighty empire that had once ruled the lands now occupied by barbarian tribes. This combination of the Christian faith with echoes of imperial power and with the warrior culture of Frankish kings meant that a very military Christ could sometimes be celebrated.

At Grésin, Puy-de-Dôme (France), a seventh-century terracotta funerary plaque helps illustrate how Christ appealed to such warriors and how they then identified with him. This Christ is depicted helmeted, spear in one hand and sword at his side. A snake lies trampled beneath his feet. This is the victorious warrior-Christ who triumphs over evil. The warrior figure is even depicted with a long phallus. To anyone who thinks they know about how Christ is depicted in Christian art this is a shock. But here the anatomical detail borrows from pagan images of virile power, just as the bearded and long-haired Christ of the late Roman empire borrowed the culturally identifiable hairstyles associated with Jupiter and Asclepius.

The idea of this warrior-Christ, as found at Grésin, is not unique. Another example is the artefact known as the Landelinus plate-buckle, from Ladoix-Serrigny (France), which was buried with a Burgundian man armed with a *scramasax* (a one-edged sword) who was clearly a warrior. The horseman on the buckle clearly represents Christ as he features in Revelation. To his right are the cross and the Alpha and Omega. To his left, the beast represents anti-Christ and evil. The halo on Christ is inspired by late Roman art; extended ears represent Christ's ability to discern all; his mouth is fanged to represent the words of Revelation: "From his mouth comes a sharp sword with which to strike down the nations, and he will rule them with a rod of iron" (Revelation 19:15). This Christ is at war. In his right hand he holds a *francisca* (a war-axe from which the Franks derived their name) and in his left an *angon* (a kind of lance associated with Frankish warriors). The prominent word *numen* (the spirit or divine power presiding over a thing or place) on the buckle was meant to remind viewers of Christ's power to save. It may even have suggested that the object itself had protective power because it was imbued with references to Christ as conqueror. In addition, there may also have once been a cloth relic secreted between the buckle and the belt.[1] The prominent erection depicted on the horse was, again, intended to communicate strength and dominance in a way readily understood by those experienced in the art motifs of the Germanic barbarian tribes, rather than to those used to decoding Christian art.

In Anglo-Saxon England, Æthelbert (the ruler of Kent c. 560–616) converted to Christianity in 597 and then used his influence to encourage the conversion of other south-eastern Anglo-Saxon kingdoms in Essex and East Anglia. The unique nature of Christ was not always fully understood by this first generation of convert-kings. The later Anglo-Saxon Christian historian, Bede (writing c. 731), recorded how Rædwald, king of East Anglia, tried to serve both Christ and the ancient gods, and he had in the same temple an altar for the holy Sacrifice of Christ side by side with an altar on which victims were offered to devils [the pagan Germanic gods].[2]

To other Anglo-Saxon converts – of a more conventional and committed type – the conversion to Christianity did not lead to any new developments in Christology as such. They were fully orthodox believers. However, the way that Christ was understood and communicated reflected something of the values of their world. It was not that they were compromising their Christ-beliefs; rather that they expressed these beliefs in ways that resonated with their culture. On the early eighth-century whalebone Franks Casket a scene showing the Adoration of Christ by the *magi* is accompanied by scenes from Roman and Germanic legend. The Germanic mythical character, Weland the Smith, makes a cup from the skull of his enemy's son preparatory to drugging and raping the man's sister; the Germanic hero, Egil the Archer, defends his home from attack; the Roman general, Titus, besieges Jerusalem; the wolf suckles Romulus and Remus. Though random at first glance, this mixture of scenes is nothing of the sort. Decoding its scenes tells us about the nature of kingship, good and bad rule, and the universal history of all peoples that find their culmination in the incarnation of Christ. It is Christology in whalebone. Christ is known through indigenous culture.

In a similar way – as among the Franks – Christ was regarded as a warrior-saviour. Although some of the descriptions used of him may be unfamiliar to modern ears, they are simply Anglo-Saxon ways of expressing kingship, sovereignty, and victory over evil. In the poem known as "The Dream of the Rood", the cross (the *rood*) speaks of the suffering and victory of the young warrior-Christ on the cross:

> Then I saw, marching toward me [the Cross], mankind's
> brave King [Christ]… Almighty God ungirded Him, eager to
> mount the gallows, unafraid in the sight of many: He would
> set free mankind.[3]

The military nature of this Christ is clear. He is "marching", he is "unafraid", he is "eager" for battle. In another section of the poem he is described as: "the great King, liege lord of the heavens…" This is nobility as any Anglo-Saxon king or warrior would recognize it. And this way of representing Christ clearly caught the Anglo-Saxon imagination. The poem survives in whole or part on three items: in the Northumbrian Old English dialect and carved in runes on the eighth-century Ruthwell Cross (Dumfriesshire, Scotland); written in an expanded form in a late tenth-century anthology of Anglo-Saxon prose and verse that is now known as the *Vercelli Book*; and as a quotation on the early eleventh-century silver reliquary that was made to hold a fragment of the "True Cross" and is now known as the Brussels Cross. On the last named (now held in the treasury of the St Michael and St Gudula Cathedral, Brussels), the Old English quotation is dramatic in its stark simplicity: "*Rod is min nama; geo ic ricne Cyning bær byfigynde, blod bestemed*" ("Rood is my name. Trembling once, I bore a powerful king, made wet with blood").[4]

As in the Byzantine empire, as among the Franks, the Anglo-Saxon kings not only expressed Christ in their own terms but also linked their own royal authority to him and enhanced it by association with him. Anglo-Saxon kings frequently emphasized their distinct nature by the genealogies composed at their courts which linked them back to the Germanic pagan god Woden (Seaxnet in the kingdom of Essex) and other figures from Germanic mythology. After the Christian conversion these continued to be composed but with these pagan figures now transformed into heroic ancestors who had become worshipped in pagan times. But in the *Anglo-Saxon Chronicle* entry for 855, the annalist extended the genealogy of Æthelwulf, Alfred the Great's father, back beyond this to Noah and even further back in time to: "Adam the first man and our father, i.e. Christ. Amen."[5] The message was clear: warrior kings were ultimately descended from warrior-Christ. This holy authority by association reveals itself in many ways. When King Edgar was crowned at Bath, in 973, the event occurred when he was about thirty years of age. In this there were clear parallels with the age at which Jesus Christ began his ministry and when he was baptized in the River Jordan, by John the Baptist. It is likely that a work of Anglo-Saxon church liturgy – *Æthelwold's Benedictional*, which has an emphasis on Christ's kingship and baptism and draws a link between baptismal anointing with oil (*chrism*) and a king's coronation – was actually produced for Edgar's coronation. The Christological pointers can easily be read: King Edgar was God's anointed ruler and modelled on Christ himself. Furthermore, the coronation took place at Pentecost, when the gift of God's Holy Spirit was poured on the church, as recorded in the book of Acts in the New Testament. As all Catholic Christians (in contrast to the Eastern Orthodox) knew well, the Holy Spirit proceeds from the Father and the Son. The date further emphasized the sanctity of Edgar.

This association was perhaps even more important to those whose claim to the throne was questionable. In 1016, Cnut of Denmark took the throne by military might. In 1031, he and his wife, Queen Emma, presented a gold cross to the royal church at Winchester. The scene is depicted in a manuscript known as the New Minster *Liber Vitae*. Cnut stands by the altar; his left hand is on his sword hilt (his warrior status); his right hand clutches the golden cross on the altar (his Christian commitment); he is crowned by an angel who points above, to where Christ is seated in majesty. Christ holds a book and raises one hand in blessing. He is reminiscent of Christ *Pantocrator* and Cnut is both reminded of Christ's majesty and enhanced by association with Christ. To such a majestic figure the faithful could cry for help. He was and is Christ the Saviour.

The Coppergate Helmet dates from the second half of the eighth century and was found in York in 1982. On the crest of the helmet is an inscription, in Latin. In translation it reads: "In the name of our Lord Jesus Christ, the Holy Spirit and God; and to all we say amen Oshere [a man's name]." Clearly, the Northumbrian nobleman Oshere (whoever he was) invoked the name of Christ as his protection in battle. Similarly, in scenes from late Anglo-Saxon manuscripts that depict the "Harrowing of Hell", Christ is depicted entering hell in triumph (a huge figure who stands tall above the demons and human figures) and rescues people from hell. Such a rescue could be sought from political and military crises too. When Æthelred II, the Unready (ruled 978–1016), and his people were suffering from Viking raids, he issued a new set of coins – probably in 1009 – featuring the *Agnus Dei* (Latin for "Lamb of God"). Only twenty-one have been discovered. And all but four of them were found in Scandinavia or the Baltic. One of the latest to come to light, though, was found near Epping (Essex), in 2008. The overall distribution of these coins reminds us of how much wealth was bleeding out to the Viking homelands. On these coins there is no image of the human king. Instead, Christ – in the appearance of the sacrificed and victorious Lamb of God – is shown. On the reverse the Holy Spirit descends. These beautiful coins remind us of how Anglo-Saxons looked to Christ for rescue from worldly as well as spiritual dangers. The warrior-Christ was also the peace-bringing Lamb of God.

Christ beyond the ocean

As with the Anglo-Saxons, Irish Christians were orthodox Catholic Nicaeans in their understanding of Christ but they nevertheless enriched the way in which this was expressed with insights and understandings derived from their own particular culture. This, though, should not be overstated since – despite much that is claimed today – the church in Ireland was no more focused on women's rights or the environment than any other Christian community. These assumptions owe more to the nineteenth-century Romantic Movement and to modern priorities than to historical reality. Nevertheless, there were recognizable characteristics of early Irish Christology that stand out. One was a sense of personal self-denial in imitation of Christ. This was by no means unique to Ireland since Middle Eastern Christian ascetics had blazed this trail before. They had fasted severely, and lived in mountain caves. One, allegedly, never turned his face to the west for twenty-five years. Another, allegedly, spent ten years in a tub which was suspended in mid-air from poles. Most famously, in 423, Simeon Stylites the Elder took up residence on top of a pillar for thirty-seven years. He had a number of imitators, mostly in Syria and Palestine. But it was the Irish who coined the phrase "*peregrinatio pro Christo*", meaning "exile for Christ", to express a particular form of self-denial. This Irish imitation of Christ (who had no fixed home and was rejected by the world) involved permanently leaving home and being totally dependent on God. When this involved leaving Ireland for ever, it was known as "White Martyrdom". In related forms this urge to imitate Christ led to embracing forms of monasticism which emphasized personal isolation (inspired by the monastics of faraway Egypt) or living as a hermit in an extremely isolated situation, such as on Skellig Michael, an island in the Atlantic, seven miles west of the Iveragh Peninsula, County Kerry. In such situations of physical isolation and in communion with God and creation, such "exiles for Christ" clearly felt that their lifestyle choice was a direct outworking of their understanding of how Christ had lived his life.

Irish insights were also felt abroad. John Scotus Eriugena was an Irish theologian living at the Frankish court of the Holy Roman Emperor, Charles the Bald (king of West Francia 843–877, king of Italy 875–877, and Holy Roman Emperor 875–877), the grandson of the famous Frankish ruler, Charlemagne. The name "Scotus" indicated his Irish origins, since the "Scots" had originally been an Irish people. However, John Scotus Eriugena's ideas drew on both Latin and Greek traditions. He got into trouble due to his thinking on predestination and Holy Communion (which he saw as a purely spiritual experience and not in any way a physical partaking of Christ's body and blood) and also on the relationship of God to creation, which was later condemned as being *pantheistic* (God is one with nature). Where he explored the nature of Christ, he uneasily combined Neoplatonism, empiricism (the idea that knowledge comes primarily from sensory experience, as taught by Aristotle), and Christian ideas about creation, with what might be regarded as a mystical approach that may have owed something to his Irish origins. According to him, when Christ returned to heaven he took with him not only his human soul but also his senses and his body. In this way the whole of creation (physical and spiritual) began a process of returning to God.

African Christ

Christianity was widespread in Egypt before the Islamic conquests of the seventh century and from here it spread southward along the Nile Valley and along the Red Sea coast into Ethiopia. Here the church also claimed a tradition that the faith was even older still, dating from the conversion of the Ethiopian official by Philip, as described in chapter 8 of Acts. Even after the Arab Islamic conquest of Egypt, the church in Ethiopia continued to have a close relationship with the Coptic Orthodox Church of Egypt. Whatever its ultimate roots, Ethiopian Orthodox Christianity became the established church of the Axumite kingdom (centred on Eritrea and northern Ethiopia) in the fourth century. It was not until the seventeenth century that the connection with Egypt was severed when the Axumite kingdom briefly became officially Catholic; however in 1632 the Ethiopian Orthodox Church again became the official church.

The Christian community in Ethiopia, in line with the Coptic Church in Egypt, rejected the concept of Christ set out in the Chalcedonian Definition. They are often described as being *monophysites,* who believe that the humanity of Christ was absorbed into his divinity, ensuring he only had one nature. However, modern Ethiopians have preferred the term *miaphysite* ("united nature"). This belief is expressed in the Geʿez or Ethiopic word *tewahedo* meaning "unified".

The tensions within this view of the nature of Christ surfaced in the post-medieval Ethiopian church, suggesting that the matter had not been laid to rest. One strand, later condemned as heretical, believed that the full union of the divine and human natures of Christ only occurred at his baptism. This sounded very like the old heresy of adoptionism. A version of this suggested that Christ became the Son of God by the grace of the Holy Spirit. In contrast, the official Ethiopian position insisted on the eternal nature of all the persons of the Trinity in formulae such as: "The Son Himself is the one who anoints, the Son Himself is the one who is anointed, and the Son Himself is the anointment."[6]

Perhaps the most striking legacy of Ethiopian views of Christ, though, is the Africanization of the icons that the church inherited from its Coptic Orthodox roots and adapted in local artistic style. A brown-skinned Christ, with wide, staring, almond-shaped eyes, contrasts with vibrantly coloured robes. Red is the colour of Christ. These images contrast with the style of icons found in other Eastern Orthodox churches, while still demonstrating their debt to them. In this they reveal how cultures see and represent Christ in a way that also holds up a mirror to their own humanity and artistic styles.

Viking Christ

Few cultures offer us a more striking combination of indigenous culture and artistic imagery with established Christian understanding of Christ, than the last of the Germanic peoples to convert to Christianity: the Vikings. In the early Christian art of tenth-century Viking England and then, a little later, in the Scandinavian homelands themselves, we see a fusion even more striking than we have seen in the warrior-Christ figures of the Frankish sixth century. But this too was embedded in the idea that familiar pagan imagery could be adapted and revised in order to convey the new iconography of Christian understanding.

The very first representation of the crucified Christ to be found in Scandinavia dates from the early tenth century. In Grave 660, from the cemetery at Birka, in the Swedish province of Uppland, a wealthy woman declared her Christian faith but in a way very recognizably Scandinavian. On a crucifix pendant, Christ is dressed in trousers, like a contemporary male, and is *bound* to the cross. Clearly, the concept of nailed crucifixion had not been fully understood or was not considered a vital part of the depiction. It is, though, clearly based on contemporary art from further south and does not necessarily use pagan imagery, unless the bound Christ was a reworking of the Norse myth of the binding of Odin in order to gain power over runes. This apart (and it may not carry an Odin association), the indigenous character in this case is largely a matter of male fashion and artistic style.

Similarly, the vine-entwined crucifixion scene from the royal memorial stone at Jelling in Denmark (dating from the third quarter of the tenth century and marking the conversion of the Danes), was inspired by a style of representation found across western Europe; although on closer inspection it can be seen that Christ stands with arms wide but there is actually no cross. It does though, as at Birka, represent a *bound* Christ rather than one *nailed* to the cross. It is not until about the year 1100 that we start to see Scandinavian representations of Christ on the cross that indicate the experience of suffering. So far, so relatively conventional, with the exception of the trousers at Birka and the nail-less binding by vines.

More striking by far was when pagan motifs and ideology were reinvented in order to convey the message of Christ. This can be seen most obviously in tenth-century examples from the British Isles. On the strikingly tall Gosforth Cross, from Cumbria, the figure of the crucified Christ is accompanied by a Valkyrie-like female figure. A warrior-Christ is reminiscent of the representation in Anglo-Saxon literature in "The Dream of the Rood".

Other scenes on the Gosforth Cross relate to the Norse myth of Ragnarok (the destruction of the gods): the watchman-god Heimdall confronts two open-jawed serpents; the wife of the god Loki attempts to prevent serpent-venom from dripping on him. Similarly, at Kirk Andreas, on the Isle of Man, an elaborately carved cross depicts to one side of the cross a scene straight from Norse pagan myth: Odin, identified by his raven on his shoulder, is being devoured by the wolf Fenrir. These dramatic meldings of Christian and pagan iconography can simply be dismissed as *syncretism*: Christ has been awkwardly bolted onto the pantheon of pagan Norse gods. In a similar way, silver pennies minted for Sihtric (Viking king of York 921–27), recently found as part of a hoard at Thurcaston, near Leicester, carry a picture of a hammer of the Norse god Thor and a sword on one side, and a Christian cross on the other. There are even little crosses next to the sword. A related phenomenon (but not from a Christian perspective) can be seen today in the way that images of Christ can be found added to those of Hindu gods and goddesses in some Hindu *mandirs* (temples).

We do not, though, have to view these Viking examples as the naïve art of first-generation converts who had not really understood the Christian understanding about Christ – a Viking version of the Anglo-Saxon King Rædwald of the East Angles. It is just as possible that something far more profound was going on in this aspect of the history of Christ. It is more likely that the Ragnarok scenes were simply evoking thoughts of the Christian concept of Judgment Day, but communicated in a traditional style. Indeed, the fact that Ragnarok told the tale of the destruction of the Norse gods may have had particular resonance as it proclaimed the victory of Christ over them. In this case, these images of a Viking-Christ are actually carefully communicated and profoundly Christian. They are not naïve misunderstandings or ideological compromises. They are, instead, important stages in the communication of Christ to the people of the north. It is even possible that the traditional pagan Norse stories themselves had already been altered by being filtered through the outlook of Christian writers, even before they were adapted further in order to express ideas about Christ in a Scandinavian form. If so, there is little of Norse paganism that can now be discerned that has not been influenced by ideas about Christ.

CHAPTER 8

Christ of the Crusaders

One of the most striking features of inter-faith conflict in the Middle Ages is that of the crusades. The crusades were wars called by popes against both internal and external enemies of that great medieval community of Christians known as Christendom. Those who went on crusade often took a sacred vow to do so. The church frequently promised indulgences which meant that their sins would be forgiven in return for them taking up this dangerous sacred duty. In this way the crusades were seen as combining holy warfare and holy pilgrimage. Those who went on them considered themselves "soldiers of Christ", defending his cause and the lives and property of other Christians. Not surprisingly this became intertwined with personal desires for adventure, loot, and political advantage. Nevertheless, the religious devotion – whatever we now feel about these events – was very real and apparent at the time.

Where were the crusades fought?

The most famous crusades were those fought in order to capture Jerusalem from Islamic rulers and restore it to its previous status as a Christian city (as it was under the Late Roman and Byzantine empires). However, there were a number of other examples in which military adventures were promoted as crusades and in the pursuit of which knights took crusader-vows and were promised spiritual benefits. Such crusades were fought in Spain and Sicily (again against Islamic armies); in the Baltic (against pagans in Estonia, Latvia, Lithuania, and Prussia); in Italy (a political crusade against the pope's enemies); and in southern France (the Albigensian Crusade against those regarded as Christian heretics).

The launch of the First Crusade

The first of the great crusades was launched against Islamic rule and its threat to the Byzantine empire, establishing the predominant image of a crusade as being war against Islamic forces. This, in turn, was entwined with the importance of Jerusalem to Christians. As early as the year 638, Jerusalem had been captured by an Islamic army. Given the central place of Jerusalem within the life of Christ, this Jewish holy city had inevitably become a Christian holy place. Furthermore, Christians believed Christ would return in glory to Jerusalem at his second coming. Consequently, Jerusalem is closely associated with the history of Christ. The city was also regarded as holy by Muslims, since they believed that Muhammad had miraculously been transported from Mecca (Makkah) to Jerusalem during what is known as the "Night Flight" and, while in Jerusalem, had briefly ascended into heaven.

The capture of Jerusalem by Muslims did not lead to the launching of the crusades. Indeed for over 400 years, it remained under Islamic rule with Christian pilgrims visiting it. Islamic rule in the area had been facilitated by the fact that – as a consequence of the great creed-debates – there were numerous Christians in Syria and Palestine who had not accepted the conclusions drawn at Nicaea and Chalcedon and who were regarded as heretics by the Orthodox Greek Church of the Byzantine empire. Condemned by the Byzantine rulers as being *"monophysites"* (see chapter 4), those persecuted for their refusal to accept these decisions are sometimes described as "Jacobites" after Jacob Baradai, a monk from a monastery near Edessa (present-day Urfa in south-eastern Turkey). Another tradition claimed they were named after the Old Testament figure, Jacob, and were descended from Jewish converts. Yet another tradition claimed that the name was linked to that of James the brother of Jesus, a first-century leader of the Jewish Christian church in Jerusalem. Whatever the origins of their name, they became based in Antioch and were very influential in Syria, Palestine, and what is now Iraq. They had a church structure and hierarchy that stood in opposition to the official Byzantine church.

In Syria and Palestine, therefore, many Christians did not feel a sense of loyalty to the Byzantine empire and enjoyed more freedom under Islamic rule, even given the imposition of a special tax (*jizya*) that was paid by non-Muslims. Consequently, it is not going too far to say that the religious and political advantage, from the unwillingness of such communities to defend the Byzantine empire, which this gave to the new Islamic rulers was a direct result of the debates that had gripped the Christian church over the nature of Christ. These had not been uniformly resolved or accepted, despite the official positions adopted by both the Latin Catholic Church and the Greek Orthodox Church. The same was true in Egypt, which was also home to large numbers of Christians who had not accepted the decisions concerning the nature of Christ. In Palestine, it was only *after* the Islamic conquests that Nestorian monasteries appeared; previous to this they had been driven into neighbouring Persian territory by Byzantine persecution.

Others who were becoming increasingly persecuted by the Byzantines (who were, of course, Christian) and to whom the Islamic conquests appeared as liberation were Jews and Samaritans. The latter were a breakaway group from Judaism. As a result of Byzantine intolerance there had been a number of Samaritan revolts in the sixth century. Early seventh-century Jews had assisted Muslim Persian invaders since they had seemed to offer relief from Byzantine persecution.[1] Clearly, Byzantine religious intolerance had helped undermine their own system of rule in significant areas of the Middle East and had aided the Islamic conquests.

Over time, though, life for Christians, Jews, and Samaritans under Islamic rule became increasingly difficult and burdened with an expanding range of restrictions, alongside their general status as second-class citizens. Despite this, it was not until the eleventh century that the crusading movement was born. It arose out of a combination of factors. Conflicts within Islamic-controlled areas made pilgrimage to Jerusalem for Christians increasingly difficult, and the pope's power and influence had increased. The growth of an aggressive and militaristic knightly culture in western Europe encouraged the idea of a holy adventure in the East, raids by Muslim Turks were increasingly threatening remaining Byzantine territory, and an attempt to reverse this had led to a major Byzantine defeat at the Battle of Manzikert, in 1071. In Asia Minor, the Christian communities suffered greatly at the hands of conquering Turks, while a new Byzantine ruler, Alexius Comnenus, was beginning to recapture some lost land in other parts of Asia Minor. Finally, infighting among Muslims weakened their resistance to incursions from the West. It was in this context that Alexius wrote an appeal to Western Christians for help to resist the Muslims. The appeal was sent to Pope Urban II (pope 1088–99) and the result was an enthusiastic response that was greater than Alexius could ever have imagined. It had struck a chord among thousands of Western Christians that would have an impact on the eastern Mediterranean and far beyond for centuries to come. The crusades had started and with them a new chapter in the history of Christ.

A succession of crusades

The First Crusade was launched in 1095, with the aim of recapturing Jerusalem for Christendom. It succeeded in so doing and it established the Kingdom of Jerusalem and the principalities of Edessa, Antioch, and Tripoli. The reconquest of Edessa by Islamic forces, in 1144, led to the Second Crusade, which ended in a military disaster. The capture of Jerusalem by Sultan Saladin (Salah al-Din Yusuf ibn Ayubb), in 1187, triggered the Third Crusade. This was famously led by the Holy Roman Emperor Frederick Barbarossa, King Philip II of France, and King Richard I "the Lionheart" of England. It failed to recapture Jerusalem but, by 1191, Richard had conquered the city of Acre after a lengthy siege and had secured a narrow strip of land along the coast. Jerusalem remained under Islamic rule. The Fourth Crusade, of 1203–04, only succeeded in severely damaging the Christian Byzantine empire when Western – Latin – forces sacked Constantinople and set up their own short-lived Latin Kingdom of Constantinople, accompanied by other states in Greece. Jerusalem was regained by Christians in 1229 and finally lost in 1244. In 1291 the last Crusader State in the Middle East ended when the city of Acre was finally taken by Islamic forces. The Christian Crusader states of *Outremer* (literally: "overseas") were no more.

This did not see the end of the crusading movement however. Later crusades tended to focus on non-Islamic enemies, as we have seen. There had already been crusades in the Baltic. As late as the fourteenth century there were several crusades fought against pagan Lithuanians and against Mongols in Hungary and in Poland. The king of Sweden also led a crusade against pagans in Finland.

The militarization of Christ

We have seen how, among the warrior elites of the barbarian successor-states to Rome, Christ was frequently reinterpreted as a warrior like themselves. His violent death resonated with those who faced violent ends in battle. His victory over sin and evil could be communicated using the language of contemporary battle, while his return in glory, bringing triumph for his followers and eternal judgment, was viewed as if he was a conqueror in an earthly battle. His reigning in heaven was depicted in a way reminiscent of an earthly king or lord ruling over his court.

These trends accelerated during the Middle Ages and aspects of them were particularly sharpened during the crusades. This is not surprising as every generation borrows from its contemporary vocabulary to describe what is important in its religious beliefs. What is surprising is just how far this developed during the era of the crusades. In short, Christ was becoming militarized and feudalized.

According to the chronicler, Fulcher of Chartres, this was apparent from the first in Pope Urban II's speech at Clermont in France in 1095:

Arm for the rescue of Jerusalem under your captain Christ. Wear His cross as your badge. If you die your sins will be pardoned and you will go straight to Heaven.[2]

The event clearly made an impression on Fulcher. He was there that day at Clermont and went on the First Crusade. He wrote his account in 1105, not long afterwards.

The leadership of Christ was presented in military terms as a fighting response to a perceived military threat. It was the way any noble lord might view transgressions against his honour or territory. And what was proposed was a full-scale military response; one led by Christ himself. This was the church both *militant* and *military*.

A fourteenth-century manuscript, known as the *Queen Mary Apocalypse*, which is held in the British Library, illustrates scenes from the Apocalypse (Revelation). Inspired by words that foretell End Time battles, the defeat of worldly and evil forces, and the establishment of God's eternal kingdom, the artist (in about 1320) drew on his own history and values to illustrate these vast spiritual themes. But in his work they became very concrete indeed. In one scene (on folio 37) it is crusade that provides the inspiration. Mounted on a knight's robed charger, Christ leads crusaders forward into battle. His left hand holds the reins, while his right hand lifts up a gospel book. He grips a sword in his teeth; the artist was clearly inspired by the same passage from Revelation that prompted the maker of the Burgundian Landelinus plate-buckle to depict Christ as being fanged (Revelation 19:15). But in the fourteenth-century picture Christ leads crusaders. Behind him ride a group of knights, all protected by mail, and the lead knight has his face concealed behind a great helmet. A red crusader-cross adorns both their shields and the pennants on their angled lances. This is captain-Christ leading forward his feudal army. The illustrator clearly saw no incongruity in this, and neither had crusaders in the 300 years leading up to the production of this striking image.

Founded in 1118, the knightly crusading order of the Knights Templar was blessed by Bernard of Clairvaux, who was a champion of the Cistercian monastic order. The words with which he sought to sum up their fighting militancy are quite explicit:

The knight of Christ [is] glorified in slaying the infidel [meaning Muslims]... because thereby Christ is glorified.[3]

The associations of Christ with the knight and the knight with Christ and the act of killing "the infidel" as a holy occupation were clear in the mind of Bernard and, no doubt, in the minds of many who heard and read his words.

On the fifteenth-century *Hyghalmen Roll*, which is now held at the College of Arms, in London, Christ himself is actually represented as a knight. His face is hidden within a great helm and the helm itself supports symbols which mirror the heraldic devices carried on knights' helmets. The symbols are a high wooden cross with nails driven into it, a three-tailed whip with metal pieces tied into the leather, and a six-branched wooden scourge. These represent Christ's passion, his suffering, and his death. In his right hand he holds a lance, with a pennant depicting the Lamb of God holding a cross-standard and standing beside the chalice of the Eucharist. In his left hand he raises his shield. On a blue background is pictured the head of Christ: the medieval relic called the "Veil of Veronica" or "Veronica's Handkerchief". This was thought to bear the miraculous imprint of Christ's face, produced when, according to church tradition, Veronica gave him the cloth to wipe his face on the way to his crucifixion.

The crusades and the second coming of Christ

It is, as we have seen, a core belief in Christianity that Christ will return at the end of the age. Given the belief that this event – though universal – would be centred on Jerusalem, it is not surprising that the idea of restoring Jerusalem to Christian rule soon became closely associated in the minds of some Christians with the events leading to the second coming (eschatology).

Some wandering preachers, who were encouraging people to embark on crusade in the late eleventh century, spoke as if the recapture of the earthly Jerusalem would lead to the appearance of the "New Jerusalem". This referred to an event mentioned in Revelation, when God would establish his kingdom on earth. The hope of hastening the second coming of Christ was therefore part of the crusading motivation for many Christian believers. They were part of a *millenarian* strand of Christianity, a significant part of Christian faith. We will return to this in much more detail later (see chapter 12) but suffice it to say here that this belief in Christ's literal second coming and the transformation of the whole cosmic order has been part of Christianity since its beginning in the first century. The late eleventh century was one of the times when it was particularly prominent within the Christian community.

This millenarian zeal helped stimulate some of the less organized crusading treks to the Middle East. Sometimes referred to as the Peasants' Crusade, but actually comprised of a number of lower-class movements, the impractical nature of these poorly armed and poorly disciplined movements was not at the forefront of the minds of those engaged on them because they believed that they were part of an End Time mission. Movements such as those led by Walter the Penniless and by Peter the Hermit (1096) and the so-called "Children's Crusades" (1212) were undoubtedly influenced by such beliefs. Those on the Children's Crusades believed that the Mediterranean Sea would part and allow them access to the Holy Land. These crusades ended in disaster.

It would be wrong to assume that the great military crusades were motivated in the same way but there is no doubt that this aspect of faith in Christ played a significant part in the history of the crusading movement.

The emphasis on the cross

The focus on Jerusalem and on being soldiers of Christ sharpened up attention to what was known as the "True Cross". Ever since Helena, the mother of Emperor Constantine the Great, had claimed to have discovered relics of the cross in the fourth century, pieces of it had appeared in a number of locations in Christendom as holy relics. We have already come across a reference to the largest surviving piece that is now preserved in Brussels in a silver reliquary which has engraved on it lines from the Old English poem "The Dream of the Rood".

At Sétif (modern-day Algeria) an inscription, dating from about 359, referred to the *ligno crucis* (wood of the cross). And one a little earlier in date, at Rasgunia (again in Algeria), referred to the *sancto ligno* (holy wood).

In 614, the Persian ruler Khosrau II seized part of the cross when he captured Jerusalem and took it as a trophy. However, in 628, the Byzantine emperor, Heraclius, defeated him and recaptured the relic. From there it went to Constantinople and then back to Jerusalem. Pieces of the True Cross were highly prized since Christians believed they could touch the very object on which Christ had achieved salvation. Some people began to treat these objects in a way that could drift dangerously close to idolatry. In 869, the Eighth Ecumenical Council at Constantinople defined exactly what attitudes should be adopted towards such objects. It was right and proper to "salute" and "venerate" such a sacred relic but not to accord it "true adoration". Such should only be accorded to God.

In the early eleventh century, the holy relic in Jerusalem was hidden to protect it and it was not revealed again until crusader knights retook the city in 1099. It became the most treasured relic of the crusader kingdom of Jerusalem and was kept in the Church of the Holy Sepulchre. It was captured by the Islamic ruler Saladin during the Battle of Hattin, in 1187, in which he crushed the army of the Kingdom of Jerusalem. After this it was paraded upside-down on a lance through the streets of Damascus. From there, it vanishes from history.

The drama of this loss is arrestingly illustrated in the account of the defeat at Hattin by the St Albans chronicler, Matthew Paris (1200–59), in his *Chronica Majora* (*Major Chronicles*) on folio 279. This depicts the height of the battle, in which two crusaders – King Guy of Jerusalem and Count Raymond – grapple with Saladin for possession of the True Cross. Saladin seizes the two arms of the cross which are also being gripped by King Guy who is being pulled backward from his horse; Count Raymond leans forward in his saddle to grab the foot of the cross in a vain attempt to stop its loss. Other warriors are also engaged in the fight, and beneath the hooves of their horses can be seen the severed heads and limbs of the slain. The manuscript can now be found in the library of Corpus Christi College, Cambridge University. The contrast between its peaceful academic resting place and the bloody clash of cultures that is depicted on the vellum page is profound.

This militarization of Christ and emphasis on the True Cross was the foundation for Pope Urban's exhortation to his listeners to "take the cross" when he preached to the First Crusade at

Clermont. Cloth crosses were distributed and worn by those vowing to go to Jerusalem. In time the main knightly crusading orders took the sign of the cross as their emblem: the red cross of the Templars; the white cross on black of the Hospitallers (Knights of St John); the black cross on white of the Teutonic Knights; the red cross and sword of the Brethren of the Sword.

Today there are a number of places which house fragments claimed as pieces of the True Cross. These fragments derive from a relic that was kept at Constantinople and seized when Western crusaders looted the city in 1204. In contrast to these Constantinople-derived pieces, the Ethiopian Orthodox Tewahedo Church claims to have the right arm of the True Cross. It is buried in the monastery of Gishen Mariam, Ethiopia. In Ethiopia there is an annual religious holiday which commemorates the discovery of the True Cross by Helena in the fourth century.

Christianity and Islam...
the pivotal figure of Christ

We will return to the way that Jesus is depicted in Islamic traditions right up to the twenty-first century in greater detail later (see chapter 18) but as this exploration of the crusades draws to its close it is only right that it should do so by focusing on the person of Christ. There were many areas in which Christianity and Islam both conflicted and cooperated during the crusading years of Islamic conquest and the attempted Christian reconquest. Economics, politics, medicine, and culture were all, at various times, spheres in which the different groups involved interacted. Sometimes this occurred through mutual understandings and collaborations; at other times incomprehension and hostility characterized their relationship. This was very much the case with regard to the person of Christ.

Simply put, Christians believe that God revealed himself to humanity through his relationship with the Jewish people, culminating in his final revelation through the supreme person of the Father's only Son, Jesus. All other comparable revelations can only be understood inasmuch as they relate to, compare with, or reflect aspects of this revealed truth as seen in the history of Judaism and finally in the life, death, and resurrection of Christ. Given the monotheistic character of Islam, its references to Abraham, Moses, and Jesus, and the fact that it appeared over 600 years after the life of Jesus (and following a period of turmoil within Christianity over the nature of orthodox belief), it is hardly surprising that, to start with, some Christians considered the faith preached by Muhammad to be the latest in a series of developments of, and deviations from, orthodox Christianity. At first, therefore, some Christians considered Islam to be a Christian heresy. John of Damascus (c. 675–750) thought that Islamic teachings were a combination of Old and New Testament traditions, influenced by Arianism. Others, such as the *monophysite* Armenian bishop, Sebĕos, writing in 661, thought them a fulfilment of Judaism. This misunderstanding was not to last, as it soon became apparent that Islam represented something quite different.

For Muslims a core belief is that Islam is not a new religion derived from aspects of Judaism and Christianity and then finally completed through the teachings of Muhammad. They believe that it represents the oldest of all monotheistic religions, and is derived from the original faith of Abraham (claimed to be a Muslim himself who had submitted to God), from which Judaism and Christianity developed. Accordingly, Muhammad's mission had been to recall people to this original religion and he was the means by which God gave his last and final revelation to humanity.

As Islam spread into Syria, Egypt, Iraq, and beyond, from the seventh century onwards, the differences between the two beliefs became increasingly pronounced. Developing Islamic rites, lifestyle, and even architecture began to increasingly differentiate the conquerors from the Christian- and Jewish-majority populations that they had conquered. What differentiated them most however was the belief in who represented the *final* revelation of God to humanity: was this Jesus who was proclaimed to be "the Christ" or Muhammad who was believed to be the final Prophet? To Muslims, Jesus was a venerated human prophetic messenger from God, whose mission had preceded the finalizing mission of Muhammad. To Christians – after centuries of debate concerning the nature of Jesus and his relationship with God – this was not acceptable as a characterization of Jesus, his role, and his nature. For them, Christ was and is God. The divinity of Christ was and is a non-negotiable and central (indeed defining) feature of Christianity.

This then was the first of three huge ways in which Christianity and Islam disagreed over Christ. The second – and this flowed from the first – was the Islamic rejection of the Trinity. In the tenth century, the Christian philosopher Yahyā ibn Adī wrote a defence of the Trinity called *Unity and Trinity of God* because Muslims joked that Christians were not numerate since "with them, one is three and three is one". To Muslims the doctrine of the Trinity was incompatible with the Islamic belief in the oneness of Allah. The third difference was the Islamic claim that Christ had not died on the cross. This went further and led to Islamic accusations that Christian veneration of the cross was idolatrous. In the *Pact of Umar*, traditionally attributed to the second caliph Umar ibn Khattab (579–644), which defined relations between Muslims and the Christians of Syria, Christians were forbidden to display the cross in public. This attitude towards the cross and Christian devotion to it led to the disrespect shown to the True Cross as it was paraded through Damascus, following the battle at Hattin.

Despite these deep differences, there were still examples of doctrinal dialogue. The Nestorian patriarch, Timothy (728–823), in *The Parable of the Pearl* compared Muhammad to Moses for his opposition to idolatry. Nicetas of Byzantium, in the late ninth century, was aware of other Christians who held that, despite differences, Muslims still worshipped the one true God. Nicolas Mystikos, Patriarch of Constantinople (901–907 and again 912–25), wrote in a conciliatory manner to the Muslim caliph that both the gospels and the Qur'an were derived "from the same Source". As late as 1076, Pope Gregory VII could write that Christians and Muslims both "believe in and confess one God, admittedly in a different way".[4] In reality, that "different way" was enormously significant, indeed defining. The difference centred on Christ. It was a difference that could not be bridged or ignored, regardless of other areas of cultural, political, and economic interaction and dialogue. When it came to faith, decisions over the person of Christ would, in Jesus' own words, not "bring peace, but a sword" (Matthew 10:34). We often interpret this metaphorically. But during the crusades and, indeed, at other points in history, the "sword" proved very literal indeed.

CHAPTER 9

The Many-sided Christ
of the Middle Ages

When were the Middle Ages? In England this has traditionally been dated to the period of time between the Battle of Hastings that ended Anglo-Saxon England, in 1066, and the victory of Henry Tudor at the Battle of Bosworth Field, in 1485. These are, though, very artificial date bookends. In other countries of the British Isles, let alone western Europe, the dates 1066 and 1485 have either little or no meaning. And in English historical circles the period is now much more fluid in its date-range. Its beginning has been stretched back to the successor-states that filled the vacuum caused by the collapsed Roman empire and that were emerging from the sixth century onwards. In this scheme Anglo-Saxon England lies in the early Middle Ages. At its other end the political change brought by the arrival of the Tudors was not accompanied by significant cultural or economic change and so a loose date somewhere around Edward VI's determined efforts to break from Catholic traditions that had survived his father, Henry VIII, seems more fitting. So, in this scheme, the Middle Ages can be considered to have lingered until around 1553 (Edward died that year). This is what we might call the "long Middle Ages".

Having looked at Anglo-Saxon England and the successor-states to Rome in our exploration of "Christ of the barbarians" (chapter 7), we will take a fairly traditional start date of the eleventh century in this chapter. This works reasonably well in other areas too, as Viking attacks were finally over by this date in western Europe, and in the Middle East the crusades were about to commence. Then, the turmoil of the early Reformation (both on the continent and in England) gives us a date in the first half of the sixteenth century when we will draw it to a close. No date-range is perfect but this longish Middle Ages will do as a reasonable focus.

Medieval Christology – for all the complexities of the church in this time period – was fairly consistent with all that had been established by the end of the Roman empire. Indeed, at first glance it might seem that little fundamentally changed with regard to ideas about the nature of Christ, until some of the more radical (and heretical) strands of the Reformation come to our attention. But this is too simple. The Christian community in the Middle Ages contained a great many different ideas about Christ and how to communicate him to others. These ranged from scholars at the emerging universities seeking to reconcile Christianity with Greek philosophy and also with an increasingly critical view of the world, through female writers using feminine language to describe Christ, to those seeking an intimate and highly personal relationship with God. Meditations on Christ's death and humanity became increasingly realistic and arresting. Personal piety and a daily walk with Christ were real features of later fifteenth-century developments. The Middle Ages were not just marking time in the history of Christ, as they waited for the Reformation to happen.

The *"Filioque*-Clause" and the "Great Schism" of 1054

Tensions between the Western (Latin) church and the Eastern (Orthodox) church had been growing for some time. In fact, as far back as Nicaea and Chalcedon it could be noted that West and East (though not easily pigeonholed into two camps) did not always see eye to eye. This revealed itself in a number of important areas and one of these went to the heart of the relationship between the persons of the Trinity and the way in which the Trinity is seen as reaching out to creation and to humanity.

By the ninth century a gap was clearly opening up between West and East over the so-called "*Filioque*-Clause", from the Latin *filioque*, meaning "and from (the) Son". This maintained that the Holy Spirit proceeds from both the Father *and* the Son. In 883, the Orthodox Patriarch of Constantinople had claimed that some in the West were introducing the idea and earlier, during the time of Pope Leo III (died in 816), it is apparent that some in the East regarded this belief as a Western Latin heresy. The idea, though, was older than this since the formula was found in the Athanasian Creed of the sixth century, the first creed to explicitly state the equality of the three persons of the Trinity. It in turn drew on the ideas of Augustine of Hippo (354–430). He had famously written:

> For the Holy Spirit is God, even as the Son of God is God, and the Father God. I have said "God" thrice, but not three Gods; for indeed it is God *thrice* rather than three Gods; because the Father, and the Son, and the Holy Ghost are one God.[1]

In the East there was opposition to what they considered an addition to the Nicene Creed (see chapter 4) being imposed on the universal church. The issue – from the perspective of the East – was that only an *ecumenical* council of the whole universal church could make such an addition to a creed that had been agreed by just such a universal council. Any deviation from this was therefore, they argued, a break from the idea of one universal ("catholic" in its most exact definition) church.

It was disagreement over the *Filioque*-Clause that played a major part in the so-called "Great Schism" of 1054, when Pope Leo IX and Patriarch Michael I excommunicated each other. The matter had been brewing for some time. The pope claimed authority over the four Eastern patriarchs (Alexandria, Antioch, Constantinople, and Jerusalem). In contrast, the four Eastern patriarchs claimed that the authority of Rome was only honorary. In other words: the pope only had authority over Western Christians. In addition, they also disagreed over matters of liturgy. But the major difference over theology, rather than over church organization and jurisdiction, was centred on the *Filioque*-Clause and the right of the Latin Church to encourage its use (even though popes had shown hesitation over making it a matter of dogma). In the history of Christ, it is significant that a particular debate over Christology – the roots of which went back to the fifth century – lay behind a major division in the church which continues to the twenty-first century. Even today, though moderated by better relations, both claim that they are in fact the "One Holy Catholic and Apostolic Church" and that it was the other that, in effect, walked out of the True Church in 1054.

What did Christ do?

Alongside the great discussions over Christology, the Christian community had always debated just how Christ brought salvation to believers. But in the Middle Ages this debate became increasingly intense. How had Christ reconciled us to God? How had he satisfied his Father's righteous anger at sin? And how could this be securely grasped by believers? These were questions of *eternal* life and *eternal* death.

Christians had long believed that Christ had paid a debt on the cross that human beings could not pay, meaning they had been slaves to sin and death. Christ had bought salvation with his blood, paying a huge ransom and freeing those who could not pay it themselves. But who was being paid? This was the problem in the so-called "Ransom Theory". Early church thinkers such as Origen (182–254) had explained that Christ "bought back" humanity who had earlier been "bought" by the devil, since in sinning humans had, in effect, entered into his employment and belonged to him; Jerome (347–420) had written of the devil having "rights" over humanity. Gregory of Nyssa (335–94) believed that the price had been paid to the devil. John of Damascus rejected this as totally unacceptable and argued, instead, that the price had been paid to God. It was against God that humanity had sinned. Alternative theories suggested that Christ's sinless death had trapped the devil and forced him to release humanity. Something like this was advanced by Augustine of Hippo.

The matter was clearly complex and we can barely touch on its depth. However, what is relevant to how Christ is understood is a contribution made by a later thinker, Anselm (1033–1109), archbishop of Canterbury from 1093 to 1109. He recognized the problem that no one but God can make satisfaction to God. On the other hand – since God has no faults – only a human being can provide satisfaction since it is only humans who are required to do so. It was a conundrum solved by the incarnation; a complex knot that was cut by the Christian belief that the Word had become flesh. As Anselm summed it up:

If no one but God can make that satisfaction and no one but man is obliged to make it, then it is necessary that a God-Man make it.[2]

Such a God-man must be both truly divine and truly human. The laying down of the life of such a unique being would be sufficient to satisfy the honour of God. This was a very medieval combination of faith in the incarnation, with a world of feudal obligations and satisfaction of noble honour. The Son died but was in no need of any reward; therefore the reward was enjoyed by those for whom Christ had died. God's justice and mercy are therefore both completely satisfied. For Anselm, the divinity of Christ was not only a matter of understanding the complexity of his nature; it was the only way that salvation could be achieved and understood. Christ as God and Christ as Saviour were inextricably linked.

While Anselm's emphasis rather reduced attention to the significance of Christ's life spent ministering on earth, he did produce a powerful analysis of how the very nature of Christ was fundamental to the workings of salvation. Nevertheless, it could have a rather "cold" legacy. Christ, in Anselm's construction, was engaged in a highly legal transaction with God the Father, who was deeply concerned with his own honour. This made humanity's relationship with God a very legalistic one. Later writers (at the time of the Reformation particularly) would argue that the New Testament was more varied than this and that something gracious and intimate had been rather sidelined by Anselm's elegant logic of Christ and his relationship with his Father, and the transactional relationship between God and humanity. And, furthermore, Christ's teachings could rather drift out of focus.

Peter Abelard (c. 1079–1142) certainly thought so. For him it was clear that Christ suffered and bought humanity with his blood but he came to do more. Christ came to show what true love is and, by teaching us through example, he awoke in us the desire to live similar Christlike lives of love. Christ's suffering and death were an awe-inspiring and life-changing revelation of divine love. At the time, Abelard (although immensely popular with many students) met a lot of opposition from a church whose world view was formed by experiences of satisfaction and honour. Love and compassion, it might be argued, were rather higher on his agenda than on the agendas of his fiercest critics.

These included the great monastic reformer, Bernard of Clairvaux (1090–1153). Abelard, though he could be difficult to get on with at times, was no stranger to both human love and earthly trials. He is well known for his doomed love affair with Héloïse which ended in their physical separation and Abelard being castrated by a gang set to the task by Fulbert, Héloïse's uncle and guardian. When he died, Abelard was originally buried at the priory of St Marcel, near Chalon-sur-Saône (France). Later, his remains were taken to the Oratory of the Paraclete, near Nogent-sur-Seine in Champagne. Here they were cared for by Héloïse. When she died, in 1163, she was buried with him. There seems a lot more warmth in Abelard than in some of his steely opponents and his semi-tragic life seems strangely connected with his theological outlook which, among other things, focused on the compassion inherent in the life of Christ.

Devotion to Christ as "friend", "brother", "mother"…

Bernard of Clairvaux, though highly critical of aspects of Abelard's thinking, nevertheless had a highly spiritual and mystical understanding of the believer's relationship with Christ. Others who came after him developed this concept of a devotion to Christ as revealed in the human experience of Jesus' life. This was particularly apparent in the life and teachings of Francis of Assisi (1181–1226). He stressed the humility of Christ who was born in poverty and laid in a manger. It was Francis and his followers (the Franciscan friars) who first popularized Nativity scenes, with their memorable depiction of the baby in the stable. It would inspire later art and the dramas of the medieval mystery plays and continues to inform the way Christians understand the incarnation and celebrate Christmas. Francis and his followers sought to emulate the poverty and rejection of worldly things that they saw in the life of Christ. It was a Christology that challenged the power and wealth of both church and state and communicated a radical view of Christ. Christ was "friend" and "brother" to the poor. Even Francis' legendary preaching to the birds and to a man-eating wolf reflected an outlook which taught that whoever sought to follow Christ should live in harmony with creation, reach out to the outcast, and not despise small things. One take on his preaching to the birds suggests that he actually preached to the kites and crows who were feeding on bodies hanging from gallows. Another tradition claims that Francis asked to be buried outside Assisi in the area assigned to executed criminals. In 1219, as a result of this universal interpretation of Christ's love and mission, Francis even preached before the Islamic sultan.

Hildegard of Bingen (1098–1179) and Julian of Norwich (c. 1342–c. 1413) went even further in the language that they used to refer to Christ. Their writings emphasized how the concept of "motherhood" could be used to express the compassionate and caring nature of Christ and the Trinity. Like a mother, Christ loves, feeds, and teaches the individual believer. Hildegard used the Latin feminine form, "*sapientia Dei*" ("wisdom of God"), whenever she referred to Christ. This was similar to how Julian of Norwich used the term: "God our Mother". The vividness of this can be seen in her writings: *The Shewings of Julian of Norwich*. The striking simplicity of this expression of Christ in maternal and feminine terms is apparent when she wrote:

> [Jesus is] our very Moder in kynde, of our first makyng; and He is our very Moder in grace, be takyng of our kynde made. All the fair werkyng and all the swete kindly office of dereworthy moderhede is impropried to the Second Person.[3]

This, in modern English, would read something like:

> [Jesus is] our true mother in nature through our first creation, and he is our true mother in grace, by taking on our human nature. All the fair working and all the sweet, kind office of dear motherhood is found in the Second Person [of the Trinity].

In other words, because Christ is the one through whom God the Father made the world, Christ can be described as "Our Mother". Not only this, but this motherly love is also seen in the incarnation, since it was compassion and care – feminine attributes to Julian – that exemplified this event to save and restore humanity to relationship with God. To those who might object to this approach, Julian would argue that since Christ shared in our *entire* humanity, such feminine description is both fully appropriate and highly meaningful. This could be very explicit: Julian identified a parallel between women shedding blood and water in childbirth and Christ shedding blood and water on the cross out of love for humanity. It was his "dereworthy blode and pretious water which He lete poure al oute for love" ("dear blood and precious water which he let pour all out for love"). The femininity of Christ's incarnate humanity provided the way and manner through which salvation would be achieved. But Julian was insistent that this pointed to the all-encompassing nature of God, *not* that God was female. While she used the term "God our Mother" to describe Christ, she always referred to Christ as "He". Nevertheless, such use of feminine language was very striking and would not again be explored so explicitly until the feminist-inspired theologies of the twentieth and the twenty-first centuries.

This medieval feminization of Christological language was encouraged by how Christ had famously referred to himself on one occasion:

> Jerusalem, Jerusalem, the city that kills the prophets and stones those who are sent to it! How often have I desired to gather your children together as a hen gathers her brood under her wings, and you were not willing! (Matthew 23:37)

In addition, the passionate language of the Old Testament book, the Song of Songs, further encouraged the idea of both feminine and, indeed, romantic language to describe the relationship between the Christian and Christ. During the twelfth century a number of influential commentaries were written on this book.

Christ of the universities

Thomas Aquinas (1225–74) was one of the great intellectuals of the Middle Ages. For Aquinas the incarnation would not have occurred without the presence of human sin, since it was to deal with this that the *Logos* had become human in Christ. However, Aquinas was aware that the incarnation was also part of – indeed the supreme example of – God's revealing of himself to men and women. The life of Christ was therefore the supreme example of God's self-communication. It was not only the method by which salvation was achieved. Although Aquinas did not fully develop this, it was a very important step towards an idea that would become more highly developed in twentieth-century theology. Christ exemplifies par excellence that God is relational and that he wishes to have relationship with humanity. The Christ so revealed takes people to the Father-heart of God. God is, after all, not only God but also Father; and this Father is as loving as he is holy. This very twenty-first-century view of Christ and the Father is running ahead of what Aquinas wrote but there are, at least, ingredients of it in his thinking.

Aquinas also identified how the incarnation revealed the perfection of humanity, achievable through divine love and grace, and shown in a human life lived in complete obedience to God. This too has echoes in some aspects of modern theology. Even the different outlook of Pierre Teilhard de Chardin (1881–1955), who controversially argued that humanity was evolving over time towards a maximum level of complexity and consciousness that he called the "Omega Point", owed something to the ideas of Aquinas in this area.

To Aquinas, writing in his work the *Summa Theologica* (*Complete Theology*), humanity had achieved the highest possible state by being "assumed" by God's Son. As a consequence, believers (who were members of his mystical "body", the church) could, by the unmerited grace of God, share in this state of holy union with God. So the perfection of the nature of humanity in the life of Christ meant that from the very moment of Christ's conception his mind had full and intimate communion with God. Consequently, Christ always knew all things. His experiential knowledge, as part of living a human life, was therefore always "infused" with divine insight. The problem with such a view is that it raises questions about just how "human" is such a "humanity" as defined by Aquinas?

Aquinas, unlike Anselm, paid much greater attention to the details of Christ's life. These details were those that were particularly identified in the synoptic gospels (see chapter 3): his baptism, his temptation in the wilderness, his miracles, his teaching, his transfiguration. This was what we might call a historical Christology, which meditated on the key aspects of Christ's life in order to fully understand both his nature and the nature of his mission and message. In this Christology, Christ did not only come to die. The whole of his life was rich in meaning. Only by reflecting on this, alongside his death and resurrection, could a Christian fully understand the completeness of the redemption that Christ brought. This reflection on the "mysteries of Christ's life" continued as a strand in more holistic explorations of the impact of Christ until the seventeenth century. Thereafter it rather lapsed until the twentieth century. To be fair to Anselm, he too took very seriously the humanity of Christ, and argued that God assumed "the littleness and weakness of human nature for the sake of its renewal".[4] He emphasized what could be learned from all aspects of this life of the Word lived as flesh.

For Aquinas, Christ combined both a contemplative and an active life. This seemed a justification for the kind of monastic life that Aquinas lived and one can see in this the familiar fact that each generation seeks to understand and express Christ in the language of its own outlook. In this way, certain constant features are continually being combined with those that seem particular to the time at which they are expressed; be that the thirteenth or the twenty-first century.

In Aquinas' writings, he explicitly states that God always loved us and that this was a constant feature both before and after Christ's sacrifice had reconciled humanity to God. However, despite this, his use of the term "placating" left rather a different impression. It meant that Christ's death could be seen as a "penal sacrifice" which placated an angry and vengeful God. It left an impression and a legacy which was much harder than that found in Anselm. It was, perhaps, not wholly surprising, given the complex balance of punishment and justice with love and mercy that Christians see combined in the reason for the death of Christ. Nevertheless, and despite this, in Aquinas we are again reminded that, however we understand this complex balance, Christ went freely and lovingly to the cross and in this action both divine initiative and perfected humanity played their part. He was both messiah (God-man) and supreme priest, king and prophet. His humanity was not to be ignored when contemplating his divinity. When raised to life, his glorified humanity could achieve a transformation of awesome power and extent.

Thomas Aquinas and similar medieval scholars drew on a combination of Scripture, the great ecumenical councils which had produced the creeds, the writings of Augustine of Hippo, and the rediscovery of classical Greek philosophy as exemplified in the writings of Aristotle. They also drew on an intellectual tradition from the late Roman empire – later called Neoplatonism – with its emphasis on "emanation and return". This meant all things proceed from the same divine origin and ultimately return to that source. As Christians, they found support for exploring the implications of this in the emphasis in the Gospel of John on Christ's coming from the Father and his return to the Father. In this fusion of intellectual traditions, the divine revelation and human reason combined to produce an intellectually challenging and closely argued understanding of Christ that would influence Christian thinking for centuries. Others who also formed part of this medieval intellectual tradition included Giovanni di Fidanza, known as Bonaventure (1221–74), Alexander of Hales (1185–1245), and Philip the Chancellor (1160–1236), among others.

However, intellectual debate was not the only medieval legacy. Medieval Christianity also contained an intensely intimate strand of relationship with Christ. This found its culmination in the writings of the sixteenth-century Spanish mystic, Teresa of Avila.

Christ as lover

Just as the Song of Songs justified the use of feminine language to express divine truth, so the New Testament image of the church as "bride" (and so by implication Christ as "bridegroom") meant that the language of sexual union could be employed to describe the intimacy of believers' relationship with Christ. These metaphors are found in Revelation where Christ is described as "the Lamb" and his people are described as "his bride":

> Let us rejoice and exult
> and give him the glory,
> for the marriage of the Lamb has come,
> and his bride has made herself ready. (Revelation 19:7)

It was inspired by this concept that the Spanish mystic, Teresa of Avila (1515–1582) – whose life witnessed the fragmentation of Catholic Christendom with the arrival of the Reformation – could describe her experiences in terms of religious intimacy and ecstasy. This came from extended periods of intense contemplation. Through these she came to an experience of union with God. In 1559, she became convinced that Christ had revealed himself to her in bodily form, though he was invisible. These experiences continued for over two years and were expressed in a way that was almost physical. In one she described how an angel appeared to her:

> I saw in his hand a long spear of gold, and at the iron's point
> there seemed to be a little fire. He appeared to me to be
> thrusting it at times into my heart, and to pierce my very
> entrails; when he drew it out, he seemed to draw them out
> also, and to leave me all on fire with a great love of God.[5]

The sexual undertones of this description are difficult to ignore and have often been commented on. Modern readers may be more aware of these than sixteenth-century ones but it seems clear that, for Teresa, there was a physicality in her spirituality that seems to have drawn on her sexuality and which was focused on Christ as divine lover. This is not to impute anything sordid to Teresa. It merely admits the range of ways in which Christ was approached and described in medieval writings. Alongside Christ as "brother" and "mother" there certainly could be the image of Christ as "lover". While this may have been particularly appealing as an image and metaphor to a celibate nun denied any other form of sexual expression or fulfilment, it could be justified as a spiritual form of the bodily union enjoyed by husband and wife. No doubt, those celibates who described the spiritual union in these terms would have said that the physical sexual union was itself a pale reflection of the ultimate union between the soul and God. This, indeed, was why Christ was described as a bridegroom in Revelation. The lover image was also found in the Old Testament book Song of Songs.

The experience recounted by Teresa is vividly depicted in the sculpture known as "The Ecstasy of Saint Teresa" by Bernini. It is today in the Basilica of Santa Maria della Vittoria, in Rome. Its physicality is undeniable and it expresses what Teresa herself described (in her description of the four-stage ascent of the soul) as "devotion of union" (the third stage) and finally the "devotion of ecstasy or rapture" (the fourth stage). This was, for

Teresa, the climax of the mystical experience and the ultimate union with Christ. It was an unexpected outcome of belief in the incarnation of Christ. While still remaining God, he had crossed the divide between Creator and created. For some it may seem that Teresa's Christ is described in terms that are *too* intimate and *too* much like a human lover. Nevertheless, though extreme in its terminology, her descriptions are rooted in Trinitarian faith and in the concept that the Word became flesh. God pours his love into creation through his Son, in order to draw humanity into loving relationship with him. This is undoubtedly how Teresa saw the matter, even if she expressed it in terms that may appear overtly sexualized to twenty-first-century readers.

This, all too brief, exploration of Christ of the Middle Ages should dispel ideas that medieval Christians had a dry and impersonal relationship with Christ, dominated by ecclesiastical authorities and waiting for the Reformation to make it personal and dynamic. The reality was that many medieval Christians had an intimate understanding of their connection with Christ and they reflected deeply on his nature. Fifteenth-century Books of Hours encouraged personal prayer as part of the believer's contemplation of Christ, especially during the Mass as they reflected on his death, sacrifice, and union with believers in the sacrament. When this old world of Catholic values was being threatened in Tudor England the rallying point of the Catholic rebellion known as the Pilgrimage of Grace, in 1536–37, was, fittingly, the banner of the "Five Wounds of Christ". Devotion to the sacrifice of Christ revealed itself in the popularity of the image of Mary cradling the body of Christ and known as Our Lady of Pity. Clearly, medieval devotion, particularly to Christ and his suffering, was intense and it is to the depiction of his sacrificial death – his Passion – that we now turn.

CHAPTER 10

Reigning from the Cross or Suffering on the Cross?

The cross has always been a striking feature of Christian understanding concerning the nature of Christ and his mission on earth. Representing his death, it has always been recognized as having a central role within Christian explanations of how Christ saves humankind. This in turn directly relates to what is believed about his nature and status. This is seen in the gospel accounts, the letters of Paul, and in the writings and art of the church for 2,000 years. Its most vivid representation is in the form of the *crucifix*. This term is from the Latin words *cruci* and *fixus* and means: "fixed to a cross". In contrast to the plain cross, the crucifix carries the body of Christ nailed to it. As such, it offers many opportunities for Christian artists and craftspeople to communicate what they believe about this event and the nature of Christ.

There was a dramatic change in the depiction of Christ's crucifixion from the period of the early church to the late Middle Ages. The factors influencing the portrayal of the moment of Christ's death included beliefs about his role as saviour, his nature as both God and man, and the identification of Christ the man with human suffering.

Roman attitudes towards the cross

In the first century, crucifixion was a normal mode of Roman execution for violent criminals and more importantly it was a humiliating form of execution. Set against an Old Testament background, it had the added element of suggesting divine disapproval as in Deuteronomy 21:23 it was declared that "anyone hung on a tree is under God's curse". Emperor Julian "the Apostate" (ruled 361–63) spoke of Christians "worshipping the vile wood of a criminal's cross". The earliest known crucifix illustration is not a Christian image of adoration but a derogatory piece of anti-Christian graffiti. It shows a crucified man with an ass's head accompanied by the inscription: "Alexamenos worships his god", and was discovered in 1857, carved in plaster on a wall near the Palatine Hill in Rome. It is a mockery of Christian faith. This raises the question of how did this symbol of degradation and scandal become a symbol of Christianity? When did the crucifix lose its shameful connotations and take on redemptive associations? And exactly how should the dying Christ be depicted?

The cross as the means of salvation

Within the very first generation of Christianity, the cross came to represent eternal salvation won by Christ's death and resurrection. The early church wished to promote the acceptability of the cross but visually there was more emphasis on the resurrection. With the legalization of Christianity under Emperor Constantine I, "the Great" (ruled 306–37), the cross became a powerful symbol of sacrifice which led to the triumph of the believer. In addition, the supposed discovery of the True Cross by Helena, in 326, also added to fascination with the event of Christ's death. It was not until after the reign of Constantine the Great that *crucifixion* images appeared; before this (when crosses were depicted) it was simply the cross rather than Jesus dying on the cross which was displayed. However, from the fifth century the focus shifted from the instrument of death to both the instrument and the dying person. It was then that the crucifix image really emerged.

One of the earliest surviving Christian crucifix images is an ivory relief dating from 420; Jesus is calm and alive, illustrated by his open eyes, and he is reigning from the cross. This reflects a view found in John, where Jesus is not passive in his death but instead chooses to die, saying: "I am the good shepherd... And I lay down my life for the sheep... I lay it down of my own accord" (John 10:14–18). For Christ, this was not a moment of human weakness but divine victory. And he went to it willingly. For later Christians, it contested both pagan and Jewish opposition to Christ's divinity and omnipotence. The hymn *Vexilla Regis*, attributed to Fortunatus in the sixth century, and written for a relic of the True Cross, likewise celebrates Christ as a successful king, hailing him as: "God ruling the nations from a Tree." Overall, it was not the mode of death but rather the event of the death itself and the salvation implications which came into focus. The serene Christ on the fifth-century crucifix did not bring to mind the agonizing brutality of this form of execution. It was clear in this that theological understanding was triumphing over historical realism. This was to encourage a whole new way of approaching the depiction of Christ on the cross.

From cross of triumph to jewelled cross

In the early medieval period, the crucifix was transformed into the "*crux gemmata*" (jewelled cross), such as the Cross of Otto and Mathilda, made in the late tenth century. This cross is named after the two persons appearing on the enamel plaque below the figure of Christ: Otto I, Duke of Swabia and Bavaria and his sister, Mathilda, who was abbess of the abbey at Essen. The cross is encrusted with jewels and precious metals demonstrating Christ's regal nature. This change reflected the continued understanding of the cross as a symbol of honour, while also presenting Christ's death as an idealized event that heralded glory for believers. The figure of Christ, glorious in his death, had now become the dramatic focal point.

This inherently symbolic portrayal of the crucified Christ was prevalent across this early period and, similarly, Christian icons of Mary and Christ also displayed their majesty. Theological influences on this artistic style are clear, and particularly so with regard to the development of the crucifix. These crucifixes challenge one to find majestic beauty and celebration in the death of Jesus. As Augustine stated: Christ was "beautiful in his flagellation, beautiful giving up his Spirit... beautiful on the cross".[1] The act of crucifixion is undeniably ugly, but the death of Jesus in Christian understanding is glorious and good, as an instrument of salvation. The first Christian crucifix images then consistently display Jesus in his humanity and divinity: in his human death he is the Son of God who overcame death for the redemption of humanity. This image both portrayed Christ the human who died on the cross and signalled his divine origins.

The importance of the two features of Christ's nature for the church was demonstrated in the seventh century by the condemnation of the *monothelite* heresy by the sixth ecumenical council of Constantinople, in 681. The council objected to an understanding which was inclined to accentuate Christ's divine nature, while marginalizing his human nature and suffering. It stated: "we shall remember his mortal life, his passion and his death".[2] The *monophysite* heresy, which similarly was condemned, also stressed the single divine nature of Christ. The orthodox doctrine, which wished to express the equal status of both divine and human natures within Christ, shaped the interpretation of such sacred images and consequently the teaching of the church and the beliefs of the faithful. As Pope Gregory the Great (pope 590–604) recounted: "for what the Scripture teaches those who read, this same the image shows to those who cannot read but see".[3] Therefore such images allow all to access the message of salvation. The evolution of this doctrine governed and is reflected in the evolution of the crucifix images from the fifth to the tenth century. These images made no attempt to stimulate the believer to empathize with Christ's suffering. This was not to last.

The beginning of realism...

During the Iconoclastic controversy in the Byzantine empire, between 726 and 843 (see chapter 5), references to the physical death of Christ were deployed as providing justification for, and confirmation of, the significance of images of Christ. Such images were to bring the believer closer to the reality of Christ, by uniting reflection on his human existence with faith in his heavenly glory. Theological teaching on the role of imagery in Christian doctrine and aesthetics came together to create a new representation of Christ on the cross. A new realistic and reflective mood influenced such depictions.

Gradually then, and certainly by the high Middle Ages, the crucifixion was beginning to be displayed in a more realistic fashion. The figure of Jesus appears dead on the cross with eyes closed, bowed head, and sagging body. "*Christus patiens*" (Christ suffering) had now succeeded "*Christus triumphans*" (Christ triumphant) of the earlier period. The humanity and divinity of Christ's nature had become established in Christian doctrine. But how did the transformation to this later medieval image of suffering take place? Was it the result of an emphasis on the virtue of pain in the life of the believer; a shift in other areas of doctrine; or a development in devotion or identification in Christian imagination? To this we shall now turn.

Some have argued that this heightened, reflective focus upon a suffering Christ was the result of a triumph of masochism in the minds of medieval Christians. In this argument, the evolution of the image from this period onwards – and which dominated the remainder of the Middle Ages – demonstrates a focus upon a helpless Christ who submits voluntarily to his executioners. This, it is argued, justified self-inflicted pain on the part of the viewer. Furthermore, the crucifix icon of the high Middle Ages appeared to reinforce the belief that the omnipotent Father chose death for the Son. The church's teaching and liturgy – such as the Liturgy of Good Friday – began to explain the event through the death and *passivity* of Christ, to reach his eventual triumph. The church's approach to the crucifix image moved away from the need to show a glorified Christ or a warrior Christ, towards the depiction of his suffering, and on to the redemption through which humanity is able to identify with Christ.

However, the negative take on these more brutal images, and the accusation of masochism, are unjustified. It can as easily be argued that they aimed to provoke a response to the death of Christ in the heart of the believer. The emphasis on Christ's humanity greatly influenced devotional practices and this changed the purpose of such crucifixion images. The observer was intended to take ownership of such images and the Christian focus moved away from establishing doctrine to establishing how the individual should respond to such core beliefs. The period 1100–1300 revealed an increasing need for a human response to God's invitation to believe in what was achieved on the cross. In the thirteenth century, the production of devotional images by communities of monks and friars led to widespread dissemination of crucifixes with graphic images. Francis of Assisi had a marked and deeply personal devotion to the crucified Christ. He was influential in this movement and thus in the transformation of the appearance of the crucified Christ to show him dead on the cross. This focus upon private devotional images of Christ's Passion had the intention of enhancing the piety of believers. So passionate was Francis' devotion to the suffering Christ that it was believed that he received the five *stigmata* wounds on his own body, a visual sign of his identification with the crucified Christ. In this way, meditational devotion in the thirteenth century became more emotional to coincide with realistic depictions of Christ's anguish and individual empathy with him. This progression took place as part of an individual's desire for an intimate relationship with the suffering Christ; the Franciscans led such sense-experiences. The Franciscan teacher, Bonaventure (1221–74), insisted upon: "martyrdom as essential to evangelical perfection".[4] This reflected the words of Jesus in Matthew 16:24: "If any want to become my followers, let them deny themselves and take up their cross and follow me."

This increasing portrayal of the suffering of Jesus on the cross was stimulated by increased emphasis on the humanity of Christ, revealed in the incarnation of Jesus; God truly became man. Graphic wounds displayed humanity and weakness explicitly and physically. These images declared that in Christ's human-ness, he draws people to himself. This emphasis (though always present in Christian theology) focused particularly on how it was through Christ's suffering that salvation was won. As Anselm had earlier stated: the "sacrifice of Christ is an offering of his perfect humanity on behalf of sinful man".[5]

Consequently, as the church began to emphasize the importance of the humanity of Christ doctrinally, so artists began to expose the human emotions and bodily weakness of Christ visually. Portrayals that placed emphasis on Christ as a human being also incorporated images of the Virgin and Child: by the fourteenth century Mary was similarly displayed in a more realistic, human manner. The attempts at physical accuracy in such paintings as the Italian artist Cimabue's distemper on wood painting, *Crucifix* (c. 1265), aided the spiritual understanding of the event. In this painting, Christ is portrayed in a more naturalistic and physically accurate way than in most earlier portrayals. It is a graphic depiction of suffering and death.

Alongside thirteenth-century Franciscan devotion, the Catholic definition of the Eucharist resulted in the theological expression of divinity revealed in humanity with its emphasis on Christ's physical body and blood. Christ, in his sacrificial human suffering, was the victor; the sacrificial nature of the cross as an earthly event is the focus of these realistic depictions, clearly portraying Christ as the means of saving humanity. Thomas Aquinas, as he laid down his teaching on the Eucharist, emphasized how the crucified Christ is present across time in that sacrament. In the *Tantum ergo Sacramentum* (*Hence so Great a Sacrament*), a medieval Latin hymn, Aquinas wrote: "Down in adoration falling, Lo! the sacred Host we hail; Lo! o'er ancient forms departing, Newer rites of grace prevail."[6] The story of redemption unfolds in this medieval Christian imagery: the more realistic crucifixion represented a visual reminder of the Eucharist in which Christ continues to live in believers. There was a remarkable convergence of these strands of Christology.

Christ on the cross: reflection of a world of suffering

Even as the movement, emphasizing empathetic engagement with Christ as a man crucified for humanity, gained strength in the fourteenth century, traumatic social events also influenced this religious mentality. With the catastrophic effects of the Black Death across Europe, and the resulting intensified exposure to the frailty of human life, there was both a growing emphasis on human mortality in art generally and an accelerated emphasis on the particular subject of portraying the human Christ at the point of death. Death, life, and salvation were looked upon in a different way as death became more present; believers' own sufferings were reflected in the image of Christ's death on the cross.

At this time a strand of Christian thought, which called for personal crucifixion of one's sinful human nature in order to replicate Christ's suffering and subsequently win salvation, became more prominent. Morbid fascination with death and personal mortification of the flesh reflected the horrifying experiences of the fourteenth century and the perceived imminence of God's judgment. It was an era of penitential enthusiasm. The "Brethren of the Common Life" or "Flagellants" (a lay community founded in Flanders in the fourteenth century) would contemplate bloodletting fantasies and a Christ who was "so wounded, so bloodied, so mutilated".[7] Practitioners of mortification would whip their own bodies as a demonstration of piety and penance in an attempt to satisfy God's wrath and alleviate his supposed divine judgment as seen in the Black Death. As well as an act of personal atonement, flagellation arguably gave an insight into what God in Christ experienced and might also explain why this experience was being expressed in this way in contemporary art. By meditating on the cross one became united with Christ and was oneself crucified; this could, the Flagellants argued, also be shown externally. Devotion to the crucified Christ appears to have moved from an internal, spiritual experience to a public, physical experience. Attention to the five wounds of crucifixion marked on Christ's body became one of the principal devotions of the late Middle Ages.

However, it is clear that while the triumph of seemingly masochistic Flagellant practices may have been a contributory factor to the increasing intensity of graphic late fourteenth-century depictions, it was not the trigger-factor which instigated this stage in the development of crucifixion images. Such bloody images were already in existence before the rise of the Flagellants and may themselves have encouraged this self-flagellating trend.

It is clear that the change in appearance of the crucifix image illustrates a widening awakening of emotional identification, rather than simply physical imitation. Devotion to the crucified Christ had come to involve personal reactions to the imagery, engaging the imagination to stimulate emotional identification with the suffering Christ. As the writer, known as "Pseudo-Bede", stated in 1300: the believer "must feel grief as if the Lord were suffering before their very eyes".[8] From such graphic images extended an urgent call to respond to the display of divine love. Such art wished to exemplify Christ's sorrow as opposed to just his physical pain.

"Man of Sorrows"

As well as crucifix images, "Man of Sorrows" images emerged in the fifteenth century, such as Geertgen van Haarlem's 1436 Flemish depiction. These showed how throughout his life Christ suffered rejection and sorrow. The tears, bloody body, and direct, despondent gaze found in such pictures all served to emphasize his suffering humanity. Through such images believers sought consolation from and expressed identification with Christ, a fellow human being.

The intention of such images is clear. The sympathy denied to Christ at the time of his death is thus compensated for by the present sympathy of the believer. The observer is moved to reflect upon their own shameful sin which caused such pain to the innocent, and by extension they begin a process of identification with all who suffer. An appeal to compassion in the believer attempted to erase the barrier between man and God. Christ, who shared in universal human suffering, invites humanity to share in his work of redemption.

The overall pattern

It appears that both images of victory and suffering existed alongside each other for some centuries, demonstrating that there was not a simple, rapid change from early majestic images to suffering images. While, for the most part, medieval art is dominated by crucifixes showing graphic images of suffering, yet even here there are some exceptions. Some twelfth-century Spanish images display a calm and peaceful smiling Christ, the extensive gilding and jewels of such crucifixes exhibiting his regal nature and triumph. Yet, for the most part, a new intensity of affliction, physical and emotional, is found in late medieval art as applied to the figure of Christ on the cross. There was clearly a gradual process of development from an emphasis on the omnipotent Son of God, to intensely personal meditation on his broken human body which was allowed to be injured in order to achieve salvation. This latter image of Christ, well-established by the fourteenth century, was to prevail and remain through to the twenty-first century.

The first crucifixes are characterized by the early church's gradual establishment and clarification of doctrine. As doctrine became established, individual reflection and devotion became the focus in Christian imagination. The evolution of the crucifix mirrors such devotional changes. Initially, a reworking of theology drove the progression, but at its climax, individual meditation inspired the development.

The Christian image of Christ on the cross evolved from the royal victor to the one who truly suffers with humanity. Within this evolution, bloody crucifix images surface, yet the late medieval practices of self-denial and flagellation should not dominate one's view when analysing the cause of such a change. These ascetic practices, with seemingly masochistic elements, were not the driving force behind the evolving graphic crucifixion images, they merely accentuated the trend. Graphic crucifixion images did not derive from these self-flagellating tendencies but, instead, from the empathetic identification with Christ and from the devotion felt by the believer. In these ways, the developing medieval image of Christ on the cross offers a very revealing insight into changing attitudes during this period in the history of Christ.

CHAPTER 11

"Reformed" Church... "Reformed" Ideas About Christ?

During the sixteenth century a revolution occurred in the Western Christian church. Looking back from the twenty-first century it is easy to point out the spiritual and organizational problems of the late medieval church. There was corruption and vice; there were entanglements in politics in which the leaders of the church seemed no different to other unscrupulous rulers. Money was raised by the sale of "indulgences" which claimed to offer forgiveness of sins or reductions in eternal punishments in return for cash, while the trade in relics often included fraud and even theft. However, we should not overemphasize these aspects of the late medieval church, as the vast majority of its members believed in its central doctrines, respected its leaders, and took spiritual comfort from its services, support, and activities. It was still the spiritual glue that bound society together. Nevertheless, changes were underway that would tear Christendom apart and this would impact on the history of Christ.

Why did the Reformation occur?

Rulers were increasingly trying to curtail the involvement of the church in their societies in order to increase their own power and influence. We usually associate this with Henry VIII (ruled 1509–47) in England and Wales, but Henry was not alone in his wish to be a strong king who brought society into line with his own wishes. In central Europe the Holy Roman Emperor Charles V (ruled 1519–56) was prepared to go against the pope if he disagreed with him and strong centralizing forces were increasing in Spain under the rule of Ferdinand and Isabella, despite them being given the title "Catholic King and Queen" by Pope Alexander VI in 1494. None of this meant that these nations were about to morph into Protestant states; indeed even Henry VIII was highly "Catholic" in his personal religious outlook, apart from in the area of papal authority. However, what it did mean was that papal authority could easily be construed as papal interference in countries where a growing sense of national identity, even of what we might describe as patriotism, was occurring. In England, the Netherlands, and in some of the cities of Switzerland and Germany, the unity of Christendom was beginning to fracture.

Alongside this, leading thinkers were beginning to question excesses in the church and medieval developments in beliefs and practices which seemed at odds with New Testament Christianity. This was encouraged by a renewed interest in Greek and Roman ideas – and this included a renewed study of the Greek manuscripts of the New Testament. In Florence (Italy), Angelo Poliziano became professor of the study of Greek in 1480 and this new interest in Greek was by no means unique. In the Netherlands, Desiderius Erasmus (1469–1536) studied the New Testament in Greek and the writings of the early church fathers, and argued in favour of a new and more critical study of Christian ideas. Nineteenth-century historians called this process of change the "Renaissance" ("rebirth"), though at the time many of those engaged in these studies were described as "humanists". It was a use of the term far removed from its twenty-first-century use to describe secular and non-religious ideology and practices. To start with, these humanist scholars sought to revitalize the church and its studies – to take it back to its core scriptural beliefs and to challenge medieval accretions that seemed to obscure or distort them.

The critics of the Catholic Church

The sixteenth century was not the first time that there had been serious criticism levelled at the Catholic Church. Much earlier, Peter Waldo or Valdes (died in 1205), the founder of the Waldensians, had encouraged an emphasis on poverty in imitation of Christ, and preached a biblical message outside the control of church authorities. He eventually rejected Catholic beliefs that he felt lacked scriptural support. Jan Hus of Prague (c. 1370–1415) had called for reform of the clergy, opposed the sale of indulgences, and argued that forgiveness only came from true personal repentance. He was influenced by the writings of the Englishman John Wycliffe. Hus was burned as a heretic in 1415. Wycliffe (c. 1330–84) wrote that Scripture was the sole authority in Christian doctrine and instigated its translation into English. He believed that the bread and wine in the Eucharist remained as such (in contrast to Catholic belief in transubstantiation) and he called for reform of the clergy.

So when Martin Luther (1483–1546) nailed his Ninety-five Theses to the door of the castle church at Wittenberg, in Saxony, he was not the first to demand reform in the church. Nor was his condemnation of indulgences and of beliefs without scriptural support. His growing conviction, however, that salvation came only through faith in Christ and therefore a personal relationship with him as saviour, while not unique to him, was to prove explosive within a church where popes and clergy, saints and the Virgin Mary had come to be seen as intermediaries between the believer and God. Despite Luther's excommunication in 1521, the radical ideas spread and accelerated. What had started as a call to reform the Catholic Church became something more divisive, radical, and out of control. In 1529 the Catholic Holy Roman Emperor threatened the use of force against those in Germany who supported Luther. German princes who opposed this threat of force protested. Now both "Protestant" and "Reformation" were being added to the lexicon of the church. A new world was coming to birth.

Other leading thinkers in this accelerating situation of change included John Knox (c. 1514–72) in Scotland and Huldrych Zwingli (1484–1531) in Switzerland – where a later leader, John Calvin (1509–64), made Geneva a virtual Protestant theocracy (government by religious leaders who claim inspiration from God). Others, with a more revolutionary agenda of social change, would also take up these new ideas and take them in directions that Luther had never dreamed of. Radical Anabaptists (see chapter 12) would threaten the religious and social assumptions of their day: some by peaceful doctrines that challenged the contemporary order, others by bloody revolution that attacked the status quo and sought to build a "New Jerusalem" on earth.

These changes permanently altered the religious map of Europe and indeed of the world. But what difference did they make to the way Christ was seen?

The Reformation and Christology

When the Reformation started, it looked as if it was mostly going to divide the church over matters of ecclesiastical authority. The leading reformers were firmly in support of the classic statements about Christ's nature, found in the Nicene Creed, the Chalcedonian Definition, and the Athanasian Creed. Although they took their stand on the basis of Scripture as the sole authority in matters of faith – which is known as *sola scriptura* (Latin: "by Scripture alone") – they accepted the writings of the early church fathers and the creeds. It was not until the eighteenth-century Enlightenment that the status quo of Christology was seriously questioned.

New ideas *can* clearly be seen in the Reformation in the areas of how a believer is saved through faith in Christ; the impact of Christ on personal faith and conduct; and the implications of faith in Christ for how society should be ordered. This last point in particular sharply divided what we might call the "Conservative Reformation" from the "Radical Reformation". More of that later.

First, though, it is worth reflecting on just how the more conservative reformers expressed their ideas about Christ. Luther wrote a hymn that was inspired by how the incarnation is described in the first chapter of John:

All praise to Thee, eternal God, who clothed in garb of flesh and blood, dost take a manger for thy throne, while worlds on worlds are thine alone.[1]

His alignment with the classic statements about the nature of Christ was made clear in a number of his writings. This revealed itself in his defence of the belief that Christ was truly God. While the humanity of Christ was an issue for debate, as we have seen, in the early church, it has been his divinity that has continued to be the focus of debate in most subsequent generations. Consequently, it is not surprising that this aspect of Christ's nature attracted the attention of Luther when he wrote: "If Christ is divested of his deity, there remains no help against the wrath of God and no rescue from his judgement."[2]

Like John Calvin in Geneva, Luther was determined in his opposition to beliefs which deviated from this core belief. He was even prepared to call on secular authorities to take action against those who strayed beyond the bounds of "acceptable" beliefs. This revealed itself strikingly in Luther's opposition to the radical Thomas Müntzer, a rebel leader during the popular uprising known as the Peasants' War (1524–25). This was a series of economic and religious revolts in which peasants – protesting against high taxes and social restrictions, with their radicalization increased by a new sense of their Protestant spiritual status, of being in direct relationship with God – were often supported by radical Protestant clergy. Müntzer's theology, for example, had both mystical and End Time apocalyptic features. In common with a number of more radical interpretations of the Reformation he believed in the imminent second coming of Christ and the End of Days.

Both Catholic and Lutheran princes cooperated to crush the revolt. The defence of their mutual self-interest with regard to their economic and social status was more important than their religious differences. While Luther's ideas may have added intensity to this peasants' movement, it did not create it, and the two phenomena had their own separate causes, with the Peasants' War being primarily triggered by economic pressures and social restrictions. By its end, somewhere in the region of 100,000 of the 300,000 peasants involved had been slaughtered.

Where Luther did stand out from many Christian thinkers who had gone before him was his drive to simplify creeds. He was determined to reduce the speculative and complex expression of Christology which had dominated so many medieval debates. For Luther, what primarily mattered was that a believer had a personal and saving faith in Christ. Since it was this that led to salvation (not good works, pardons, Masses said, or indulgences) it was essential that this was understood in a straightforward way and by all. And, given the fact that Protestants thought that there was no priestly intermediary between a believer and God, it was important that ordinary people should understand on what their faith was grounded.

For Luther, like Anselm (see chapter 9), Christ's death had "satisfied" God. The Father could not ignore sin, nor deny his holy anger at sin, unless his righteous nature and holiness were satisfied. Consequently, Christ's substitution for human sinners was crucial in achieving this and, in this, his holiness as the pre-existing *Logos* and his coequality with God the Father were vital. Thus, Luther wrote:

> Christ, the Son of God, stands in our place and has taken all our sins upon his shoulders... He is the eternal satisfaction for our sin and reconciles us with God the Father.[3]

The emphasis is clear: Christ is the Son of God; Christ substitutes for humanity; Christ satisfies God; Christ reconciles, to God the Father, those who trust in him. The cross is undergone by Christ for God the Father. This is its primary function. For Luther, the victory over evil that flows from Christ's death is due to the fact that the devil no longer has a hold over humans due to their guilt and being under God's judgment. Christ has liberated humanity from this oppressed status and so from the hold of the devil. Since Luther believed in the nature and status of Christ as outlined in the Chalcedonian Definition, this cannot be simply represented as Christ saving humanity from a vengeful God, since God was in Christ and Christ was coequal with God the Father. The Holy Spirit brings regeneration to the believer who trusts in this sacrifice made by Christ. In this Trinitarian understanding of the crucifixion (and it is by no means limited to Luther) God, in Christ, takes upon himself the punishment that humanity deserves and so, as it were, squares the circle of both righteous holiness that cannot ignore sin *and* eternal compassion that desires to free sinners and restore them to loving relationship with God. It was an understanding made clear in the Augsburg Confession of 1530, which summed up Lutheran belief:

> ... the Word, that is, the Son of God, did assume the human nature in the womb of the blessed Virgin Mary, so that there are two natures, the divine and the human, inseparably enjoined in one Person, one Christ, true God and true man, who was born of the Virgin Mary, truly suffered, was crucified, dead, and buried, that He might reconcile the Father unto us, and be a sacrifice, not only for original guilt, but also for all actual sins of men.[4]

There were, though, those afterwards who felt that Luther, in his emphasis on the divine nature of Christ, had rather neglected his humanity. This is open to debate, but those who suffered in the Peasants' War and in other aspects of the Radical Reformation would perhaps have argued that a little more focus on Christ as the "Son of Man" might have made Luther rather more open to criticizing the oppressive elites who exploited his social inferiors in the peasantry. Christology, though dependent on creative tension between the two natures of Christ, does tend to find one emphasized to the detriment of the other in many periods of history. It might, therefore, be argued that Luther's lack of social radicalism to balance his religious radicalism is an example of just such a phenomenon.

For Calvin too, it was vital to assert that Christ was both truly God and truly man. In this way he came as a divinely empowered priest to deal with our sins in the tradition of the high priests of the Old Testament; only they had never been able *permanently* to make sacrifices for sins. In this, Calvin took up themes that were strongly expressed in the Letter to the Hebrews in the New Testament. Again, like Anselm, Calvin believed that the incarnation had occurred in order to redeem lost humanity through the death of the one sent to be mediator between humanity and God. As Calvin put it:

> As a pure and stainless Mediator he is by his holiness to reconcile us to God. But God's righteous curse bars our access to him, and God in his capacity as judge is angry toward us. Hence an expiation must intervene in order that Christ as priest may obtain God's favor for us and appease his wrath.[5]

Calvin, like Aquinas, described this sacrifice by Christ in words reminiscent of the penal sacrifice implied in Anselm's words. As a substitute for us, Christ had experienced the wrath of God.

In contrast to Luther, Calvin laid greater stress on Christ's humanity and insisted on the humility of Christ in order to enter into the low condition of being fully human. The human nature of Christ was truly human and did not become majestic because of the union with Christ's divine nature. He even stated that after the ascension, Christ's human body remained limited to one place, while the *Logos* was omnipresent (present everywhere). This rather suggested that Christ's two natures existed beside each other, rather than were fully united. This was never fully worked out by Calvin but the impression seemed inescapable that after the incarnation the *Logos* existed both within the human nature and beyond it. This seems more of an *association* than a full *unity* and some have accused Calvin of adopting a view not unlike the Nestorians, who believed in the independence of the divine and human natures of Christ (see chapter 8).

The alternative reformers... Christology outside the boundaries of the mainstream tradition

Neither Luther nor Calvin offered a fresh insight into the nature of Christ. Rather than rethinking their Christology from a fresh reading of the New Testament, they were generally content to re-present the medieval doctrines that were based on the creeds of the late Roman empire. This was understandable since they had to defend themselves against accusations of heresy and were determined to show that, in fact, it was their new insights into reformed Christianity that were in line with the great truths of the church, from which the Roman Catholic Church had deviated and gone astray. Nevertheless, in both their writings, there was a hint that they had not fully thought through some of the issues inherent in the belief in Christ's dual nature. This was, of course, not new since the church had always struggled to adequately express how the creator of the universe could become fully human *and* how that humanity could be comparable to the humanity experienced by other humans. And the more explicit the language and the more forensic the examination of the incarnation, the more the inadequacies of the language used prompted ever more searching questions which seemed beyond the capabilities of any formulae to adequately express.

In contrast to Luther and Calvin, though, there were those who began to rethink the nature of Christ in the context of the great

Reformation re-examination of faith. Among some Anabaptist groups this strayed towards the edges of acceptable Christology, as defined by most church authorities at the time. While some of these groups were anti-Trinitarian, others offered their own take on Christ's divinity which was within a Trinitarian context but deviated from the usual way of expressing it. Dutch Anabaptists, for example, accepted that Christ was born "out of" Mary but not "from" her. They insisted that the Holy Spirit had created Christ *ex nihilo* (from nothing) within Mary's womb but that Christ did not derive his humanity from Mary.

To both mainstream Catholics and Protestants, this belief seriously compromised the real humanity of Christ. The Dutch Anabaptists would have countered that this was how God had created Adam – and Adam was fully human. This, though, was not how the mainstream Christian community, from the Chalcedonian Definition onwards, had explained the human aspect of Christ's nature. Menno Simons (c. 1495–1561) argued, in effect, that this "heavenly flesh" of Christ was the reason why his human body was morally perfect and unaffected by the fallen nature of humanity. Caspar Schwenckfeld (1489–1561) asserted, in a way that puzzled contemporaries and later students, that "both in his humanity and in his divinity Christ was the Son of God and had God as his Father".[6] This left little to Mary other than being a conduit for Christ's birth. This wrestling with exactly how Christ's human flesh was one with his divinity and was also perfect, continued a much older debate that had earlier occupied Duns Scotus (died 1308) – who had almost but not quite reached the same conclusion as Schwenckfeld – and William of Ockham (c. 1287–1347). These medieval theologians had argued that Christ could have become incarnate in any material object, since God cannot be limited by any created object. But that is taking the argument and the conclusion in a different direction.

However controversial this sixteenth-century Anabaptist claim was, other radical Protestant thinkers (and their followers) promulgated beliefs about Christ which took them far beyond the boundaries of mainstream theology. They soon found themselves on territory that mainstream Christian communities, both Catholic and Protestant, would describe as heretical. The two thinkers most prominent in this were Michael Servetus (c. 1511–53) and Fausto Sozzini (1539–1604), better known from the Latin form of his name as Socinus. The emphasis on religious liberty and a personal response to God through a believer's own reading of the Scriptures that Luther, Calvin, and others had started was to create an unintended culture of dissent. This would lead to an ever-expanding pluralism of ideas and variations that shattered the old religious monoculture of Western Christendom. These innovations would affect all areas of Christian thinking including that of Christology, and start a process of debate and fragmentation that continues to the present day. From the start it threw up ideas that horrified the more conservative critics of the Catholic Church who had set the process in motion.

Servetus was a Spanish theologian with a wide-ranging set of intellectual interests including map-making, the study of pulmonary circulation, mathematics, astronomy, meteorology, and law. He was involved in the Protestant Reformation and developed a non-Trinitarian Christology that was consequently condemned by both Catholics and Protestants. For Servetus, Jesus was not the eternal Son of God. Influenced by Platonic philosophy, Servetus' ideas were virtually pantheistic in that they envisaged God as the essence of all things and revealed in all things. The *Logos*, for Servetus, was very different to the "person" envisaged in mainstream theology. The *Logos* only became a person at the incarnation, so Christ did not have the kind of pre-existence stated in the creeds. Before that the *Logos* was more an idea and a potential that only became personal in the conception of Christ. Nor was Christ's mission to redeem sinners but, rather, to reveal the nature of God and eternity. This was, of course, inherent in mainstream theology but he had now stripped it of its salvation character. When he used the term "Trinity" (as he sometimes did) he meant three modes in which God was revealed, not the idea of "three persons in one God" of the creeds. Similarly he could describe Christ as "divine" but only in the sense that all things revealed the divine. In his earlier writings his view of Christ had been even lower as he, at that point, wrote that Christ was only a man who was made Son of God by divine grace (a form of adoptionism). Christ, to Servetus, was different from other humans in his supernatural birth and sinless character but not in having a substantially different nature to other human beings.

Servetus clashed with Calvin. Such was the severity of their disagreement that Calvin wrote to a friend that, if Servetus came to Geneva, "If my authority is worth anything, I will never permit him to depart alive." Luther too condemned the ideas of Servetus, as did the authorities in the Swiss Protestant cantons of Basel, Bern, Schaffhausen, and Zürich. While visiting Geneva, Servetus was indeed arrested and, on 27 October 1553, he was burned at the stake outside Geneva. His last words were allegedly: "Jesus, Son of the Eternal God, have mercy on me." His writings were influential in the Unitarian communities in Poland and Transylvania (see below). In 1942 the Vichy government of France removed and melted down a plaque commemorating Servetus that had been erected in the French town of Annemasse, because he represented freedom of conscience. The reverberations of sixteenth-century controversies over Christology continued to echo into the twentieth century.

Other non-Trinitarian groups sought sanctuary in Poland where there was a more tolerant attitude towards religious dissent.

A centre for these groups was in the town of Rakow where they became known as Socinians, after Socinus. They were reputed to have over 1,000 students there and from that base their printing presses spread their ideas across Europe. When they were finally expelled from Rakow, in 1643, some settled in the Netherlands and others in England. Following their expulsion from the whole of Polish territory, in 1658, some of the Socinian Polish Brethren settled in Transylvania, where the Unitarian Church of Transylvania continues to exist, with a majority Hungarian membership. In England, a number of Presbyterian congregations came to adopt their ideas and this was the beginning of the Unitarian movement which continues in existence today.

The doctrines of the Socinians were expressed in the Racovian Catechism of 1605. It set out to examine each scriptural text used to promote mainstream Trinitarian beliefs and put forward its own counter-argument. To the Socinians, Christ's dependence on God and his empowering by the Holy Spirit both indicated that he was not, in fact, God. The Racovian Catechism states:

> The Scriptures explicitly declare that whatever of a divine nature Christ possessed, he had received as a gift from the Father... because Christ repeatedly prayed to the Father: whence it is evident that he had not in himself a nature of that kind which would have made him the supreme God.[7]

While those who believed in the nature of Christ, as outlined by the Chalcedonian Definition, would argue that this dependence on God through the Holy Spirit was consistent with the self-limiting state accepted by Christ in the incarnation, the holders of this mainstream belief had not put a great deal of effort into explaining Christ's dependence on prayer, and it was in this space that this Socinian argument grew.

Like the earlier Arians, the Socinians accorded Christ a divine status but not one on a par with the Supreme God. Unlike the Arians, however, the Socinians denied that Christ had any pre-existence. To them he came into existence in Mary's womb; he was not the eternal *Logos*, not even an exalted pre-existing created being who had been granted high divine honour. This latter, Arian, concept had always been rather difficult to integrate into a monotheistic outlook but the Socinians avoided it altogether. To them the world had not been created through Christ, whatever his status, because he had not existed before his conception. This indeed was heresy as defined by any mainstream Christian church of any persuasion, Catholic or Protestant. To the Socinians it was as the one responsible for a New Creation (the community of believers as recorded in the gospels) that Christ was Son of God. He had been adopted as such by God following his birth.

This was very hard to square with the New Testament's insistence on incarnation and on Christ as the one through whom creation came into existence. The Socinians' answer was contrived however one understands the New Testament, and insisted that what was meant there was that Christ "was the cause of God's creating the world and all things" and "the world was created with a view to the Messiah".[8] This clashes with what the writer of John's Gospel says in his opening verses, but it was how the Socinians interpreted it. For them, Christ was the *cause* of God creating the world but not the *agent* through whom it was made.

The Socinians were divided over whether prayer and worship should be addressed to Christ. In 1574 a bitter dispute divided the Unitarian Church in Transylvania over this issue. In the end it was concluded that it was appropriate to do so because God had chosen to give Christ honour as Lord over angels and people. In order to differentiate this from their worship of God the Father, the Socinians stated that "we adore and worship God as the first cause of our salvation, but Christ as the second".[9] In this action God was the "ultimate object" and Christ was the "intermediate object". Given the Socinians' denial of the true and full divinity of Christ, this was yet another example of how they were caught between the grinding millstones of their denial of Christ's ultimate divinity and the witness of Scripture. One only has to recall the declaration of Thomas, in John 20:28: "My Lord and my God!" as he meets the risen Christ or the verse, "When they saw him, they worshipped him..." (Matthew 28:17). The Socinians were well aware of this and found it another circle that they had to square, but could not.

The Socinians had clearly identified areas within mainstream belief that were difficult to adequately express and to fully understand. On the other hand, the Socinians had already decided, as a first principle, that these mainstream beliefs could not be accepted. But they still attempted to reconcile their beliefs with Scripture. In this conjunction of standpoints they placed themselves in a difficult position, although their questioning undermined faith in the Nicene Creed among a number of those who came across their doctrines. In the longer term this trend increased and, in the nineteenth century, others would take up the Socinian arguments as they too questioned the Nicene Creed which had, prior to the sixteenth century, been accepted by almost all in Western Christendom at least.

A different legacy was being prepared by other strands in the Radical Reformation that would shake the social order in the sixteenth and seventeenth centuries although it would not have as long lasting an effect. But in the two centuries after Luther, those who used the demise of Catholic authority to challenge the social order through revolutionary activity, communicated a very different Christ.

Chapter 12

"King Jesus and the Heads upon the Gate!"

Central to the Christian concept of Jesus is that, as God's anointed Son, he came to bring about a transformation of the world (indeed the cosmic) order. This idea of the messiah's new world order – in which God's rule would be fully revealed, the people of God would be vindicated, and evil defeated – was inherited from Judaism. And, like the Jewish concept, the Christian one too looked forward to a visible end of the current age and the ushering in of the Kingdom of God. This was why in Acts 1:6 the assembled disciples asked the risen Christ: "Lord, is this the time when you will restore the kingdom to Israel?" They clearly expected that they were about to witness the revealing of the kingdom in visible form. Jesus' reply revealed that this was not to occur immediately and, furthermore, that: "It is not for you to know the times or periods that the Father has set by his own authority" (Acts 1:7). However, this did not mean that the Christian community was to set aside this messianic hope. For, in the aftermath of the ascension, angelic messengers announced: "This Jesus, who has been taken up from you into heaven, will come in the same way as you saw him go into heaven" (Acts 1:11). This sums up the two fundamental characteristics of the Christian belief in the future: that Christ would come again in visible form and no human being could predict when. Certainty and mystery were combined.

As we saw in chapter 8 the study of this belief is described as eschatology. While, in its broadest scope, it covers beliefs pertaining to death, the resurrection of the dead, and heaven and hell, it is usually used specifically to refer to the second coming of Christ. This is sometimes also referred to as the *parousia*. This Greek word means "presence" and could be used in the New Testament to describe human beings without any dramatic eschatological meaning. Paul, for example, used it to refer to his physical presence among Christians in a church community (2 Corinthians 10:10 and Philippians 2:12). It was also used to refer to presence after an absence. So 1 Thessalonians declares the hope: "may he [Christ] so strengthen your hearts in holiness that you may be blameless before our God and Father at the coming of our Lord Jesus with all his saints" (1 Thessalonians 3:13). Non-Christian Greek inscriptions reveal that this Greek word was used to refer to the arrival of a ruler and also to the manifestation of a divinity (Asclepius). Therefore, it came to be used of Christ's second coming and has come to mean this in modern theological writings. Other Greek words used in the New Testament to describe this End Time event were *apokalupsis* (apocalypse), meaning "revelation" and *epiphaneia* (epiphany), meaning "manifestation". This latter word was also used to refer to the incarnation in Bethlehem. The second coming was also referred to in the New Testament in a Greek phrase that translates into modern English as "the Day of the Lord" and which itself was based on a Hebrew expression used in the Old Testament to describe the decisive act of God in a future time of judgment. Contractions of this phrase that are also found in the New Testament – but imbued with the same meaning – include: "last day" and simply "day".

So the concept was a central feature of early Christianity, a significant factor in the world view of the early church. When this did not occur it clearly caused concern. This is reflected in a passage from one of the later letters, probably written in the late first century at the earliest (some scholars argue for a second-century date of composition):

> But do not ignore this one fact, beloved, that with the Lord one day is like a thousand years, and a thousand years are like one day. The Lord is not slow about his promise, as some think of slowness, but is patient with you, not wanting any to perish, but all to come to repentance. But the day of the Lord will come like a thief, and then the heavens will pass away with a loud noise, and the elements will be dissolved with fire, and the earth and everything that is done on it will be disclosed. (2 Peter 3:8–10)

The fact that the second coming did not occur meant that, while for some Christians it remained an event imminently expected, for many others, the belief was reinterpreted. Debates over the subject have continued for the past two millennia. The questions and assertions about it are varied. It might be a spiritual metaphor for the revelation of Christ in the hearts of believers. It might refer to the transforming power of the gospel as preached by the church. It might be accelerated through the active seizure of power by those who are the most insightful of the elect. It might come secretly and surprise all. Could its coming be predicted – despite the warning given by Christ in Acts – through a careful study of biblical prophecy and analysis of the "signs of the times"? Within these discussions (and there are many more permutations) there remained a firm belief among many Christians that it *would* still be an actual future event. In this sense it remains a tenet of faith among Christians today.

The speculations concerning this looked-for future event are highly complex, derived as they are from the study of different combinations of Old and New Testament prophetic writings (with very different time periods, genres, and approaches) and, at times, the identification of certain scriptures as "End Time Prophecies" that would not be so classified by all Christians. Great differences can be discerned among those who attempt to construct the sequence of events that will lead to the second coming. Very different schools of thought can be identified among different Christians over the past 2,000 years.

Despite this being a frequently debated matter of faith, twenty-first-century Christians can be divided into those for whom the second coming is a belief that is not central to their day-to-day Christian lives and those for whom its detailed study and cross-referencing of scriptures alongside analysis of contemporary events is a central feature of their Christian experience. These latter Christians draw on an ancient tradition that has experienced hot spots of activity at various times in history. We have seen how the belief influenced the early church and the outlook of some eleventh- and twelfth-century crusaders. Other medieval groups too proclaimed millenarian beliefs, such as the Secret Flagellants of Thuringia in the 1360s. The Bohemian Taborites, a radical section of the Hussite Movement (a forerunner of the Protestant Reformation) until their defeat in battle in 1434, preached the imminence of the second coming of Christ and the establishment of the Millennium. The belief again became prevalent among sixteenth- and seventeenth-century radical Protestant groups (as well as among not so radical ones too) and has become high profile at certain points since then. Given the "mark of the beast" (666) in Revelation 13:18, it is not surprising that the year 1666 caused a burst of millenarian activity. As early as 1597 an English writer, Thomas Lupton, in a publication entitled *Babylon is Fallen*, named that year as the date of the second coming. He followed this with a second work, *A Prophesie That Hath Lyen Hid, Above These 2000 Years*, in 1610. In 1593, John Napier calculated that the key date was, instead, 1688, in his book, *A Plaine Discovery of the Whole Revelation*.

In the second half of the twentieth century, the establishment of the State of Israel (in 1948) prompted another upsurge of interest in millenarian prophetic interpretation among some Christians, particularly influenced by writers from the USA but by no means limited to there. The existence of a Jewish community in the Middle East is central to many Old Testament prophecies of the End Times and this has been drawn on by some Christians as evidence that the world is now in the Last Days.

But to return to the Reformation period: radical Christians drawn from the Protestant wing of the church burst dramatically on the scene in the sixteenth and seventeenth centuries. Their world view was delineated by their belief in the End Times and the idea that the *parousia* was at hand – and indeed that they would play a major part in its implementation on earth. Their outlook was encouraged, as the Reformation had both removed papal authority – allowing an uncontrolled explosion of radical ideas – and created such vicious infighting within fragmenting Christendom (with each side accusing the other of being the Antichrist) that it seemed as if the known world was coming to an end. Furthermore, the Reformation's emphasis on a personal relationship with God and free access to interpret the Scriptures had the unintended consequence of encouraging some interpretations which were far outside mainstream Christianity, among some who were now utterly convinced of the rightness of their personal spiritual insight and authority. These included serious students of Scripture, uncontrolled but well-meaning enthusiasts, and hard-line radicals on a collision course with all that they dismissed as worldly. Into the mix came the brutally unscrupulous and some who, in any society, would have been judged seriously mentally unbalanced. As a consequence, it is difficult to generalize about the groups who were swept along in this torrent of millenarian enthusiasm.

One group which attracted considerable attention in the sixteenth and seventeenth centuries were the Anabaptists (meaning "baptized again"). This group rejected the validity of infant baptism and, instead, insisted that the only valid form of baptism was adult believers' baptism. This was radical both because it challenged centuries of church tradition and control over the rite, and also because it emphasized the believer's ability to have a personal relationship with God and to *choose* to be baptized (something missing from infant baptism, where the faith of parents and church played a part). If one could *choose* to be baptized, then one could also decide on a whole range of religious and, indeed, political issues. Not for nothing has it been commented that in this period the word "Anabaptist" had a similar connotation to the term "Red" during the twentieth century's Cold War! In England, during the Civil Wars, Cromwell was often accused of harbouring Anabaptists in his regiments, although he usually denied this or asserted that it was irrelevant, given the quality of a particular soldier being so accused.

Over time, many Anabaptist communities simply developed into the independent Baptist churches whose descendants still exist today. These Christians (although once controversial due to their rejection of infant baptism) were and are thoroughly mainstream in their Christology. Others among the amorphous mass of groups labelled "Anabaptist" in the sixteenth and seventeenth centuries were anything but!

In Germany, in 1534, a serious incident occurred at Munster in Westphalia, that reverberated over the next century to either inspire or horrify depending on outlook. John Mathias or Matthys of Haarlem (Netherlands), John Buckhold or Bockelson of Leiden (Netherlands), and a group of extreme Anabaptists seized control of the city. Things soon got out of hand. The social order was inverted, a reign of terror instituted, and polygamy established; the latter to justify the sexual excesses of those in leadership. John Buckhold – remembered as "Jan of Leyden" – took the title "King of Justice, King of the New Jerusalem".

There were precedents for this in the previous century, and in each case, in the absence of the returning Christ, a leader of a minority cult declared that he himself was Jesus or a substitute for him. Thus in Bohemia in the 1460s a renegade Franciscan claimed that he was the "Anointed Saviour" and was supported by two brothers – Janko and Livin – from Wirsberg, in Bavaria. The doctrine they preached was that the messiah of Old Testament prophecy was not in fact Christ but the "true Son of Man" who would represent the Trinity on earth. In short: the ex-Franciscan in question. The movement was crushed. In 1476 the so-called "Drummer of Niklashausen" (near Würzburg, in Franconia, Germany), Hans Böhm, announced messages from the Virgin Mary, which included denunciations of the clergy and the arrival of the New Jerusalem focused on Niklashausen. Some of those who flocked to him declared him to be the "Man of God, sent from heaven", a title with clear messianic features. Although he was not ascribed Christlike status, the titles were straying dangerously close. When arrested, he was said to be preaching in a tavern, naked, in symbolic reference to the new state of innocence that he was proclaiming. He was burned at the stake on the orders of the bishop of Würzburg. In the early sixteenth century the so-called *Bundschuh* (peasants' clog) risings lacked the millenarian features of these earlier revolts but still offered the hope of a God-sanctioned overturning of the social order.

It was against such a background that Thomas Müntzer (1489–1525) began preaching in Zwickau, in Saxony, in the 1520s. Müntzer's message was that the *parousia* was at hand but first there would be a period of terrible upheaval. After this the elect would rise up and destroy the godless. These "elect" were those who received "the living Christ", whom Müntzer differentiated from the historic Christ. Born in the individual soul, "the living Christ" brought salvation to the minority elect who would be so inspired and transformed that they would, in Müntzer's words, be capable of "becoming God". For Müntzer his own role was that of "Christ's Messenger" and, as he faced increasing opposition, so the focus of his mission changed to that of destroying the rich elites on behalf of the poor. In 1525 he was executed by an alliance of German princes who had annihilated his peasant army and crushed all opposition in the Peasants' War.

Back to Munster. It was against this background of millenarian enthusiasm and popular uprisings that some Anabaptists seized control of Munster in 1534. Lutherans and Catholics were driven from the city, which was soon besieged by the bishop of Munster. Claiming status as prophets, Mathias and his supporters began a reign of terror against critics. All money, gold, and silver were seized and held communally and books were destroyed. In March 1534, Mathias, convinced that he had been ordered to do so by God, took a small force out of the city to break the siege, and was killed. He was replaced by John Buckhold, who soon proclaimed a policy of polygamy and took fifteen wives. Women who refused to be given in marriage were executed. Soon all sexual order was breaking down.

Then, in August 1534, came the final and dramatic break with any recognizable form of Christian orthodoxy. John declared that he, not Christ, was "Messiah of the Last Days". He was to rule the world as a descendant of King David. It was John, so it was proclaimed, who fulfilled Old Testament prophecies of the messiah. His coinage declared: "The Word has become Flesh and dwells in us"; it was clear that this referred to King John. A richly endowed court was established around him, while the city starved. He explained that this was not sinful because he was dead to the world. In 1535, the besiegers gained entry to the town and slaughtered the Anabaptists; in 1536 John himself was tortured to death with red-hot irons. The nightmare of Munster was finally over but echoes continued. In 1567, a cobbler named Jan Willemsen set up another "New Jerusalem" in Westphalia with himself as messiah. Finally, he and his supporters were captured and executed. Willemsen himself was burned at Cleves in 1580. But later seventeenth-century millenarians looked back to the events at Munster and claimed that the stories of its horror were inventions of its enemies. For such later millenarians, the *parousia* was still imminent.

In England during the period of the Civil Wars and the later Protectorate of Oliver Cromwell, a group called the Fifth Monarchy Men continued this trend of millenarian expectation which looked to the imminent second coming of Christ. Compared to the Anabaptists of Leiden, they were thoroughly mainstream in their Christology but their focus on the *parousia* was striking. Indeed, they took their name from a reading of the Old Testament book of Daniel and the New Testament book of Revelation. From a combined analysis of these prophetic books, they concluded that four world empires were referred to and that the fourth was the Roman empire. From this fourth empire would arise the "beast" or the Antichrist in a second phase of this fourth kingdom. The second coming of Christ would overthrow this evil empire and inaugurate a millennium of peace and justice:

the "Fifth Monarchy". After this would come the full and final transformation of the cosmic order.

The question was: when would this Fifth Monarchy appear? And was it necessary for the "saints" (usually defined as those in agreement with a particular radical, puritan programme) to actively bring it in? And where did that leave allegiances to contemporary rulers? When the Fifth Monarchist, Vavasour Powell, cried: "Lord, wilt thou have Oliver Cromwell or Jesus Christ to reign over us?"[1] it was not simply dramatic rhetoric. He meant it. The choice for Powell was between what he considered to be a worldly government or a theocracy – and a theocracy dependent on the imminent revealing of Christ on earth. Oliver Cromwell knew exactly what such people meant and countered with a theology that pictured the revealing of Christ as occurring *within the heart* of the believer: "A notion I hope we all honour, and wait and hope for: that Jesus Christ will have a time to set up his reign in our hearts."[2]

In 1661, a small group of Fifth Monarchy Men caused panic in London, in the ill-fated Venner's Revolt, with their battle-cry of "King Jesus and the heads upon the gate!" After this failure they faded away, although during the equally ill-fated Monmouth Rebellion of 1685, contemporaries noted that, among the more radical of his followers, there were those who wore the sea-green ribbons of Civil War radical groups, and others who looked for "the coming of Christ". The Duke of Monmouth, it should be noted, was definitely not of this persuasion. It was though in the 1640s and 1650s that this group was particularly prominent. They interpreted their role as being forerunners of Christ, who would prepare the way for his kingdom being finally revealed on earth. This preparation would take the form of seizing power and instituting a godly regime of the "saints". The Fifth Monarchy Men's millenarian zeal was uncompromising and prepared to countenance violence. Indeed, their declaration of 1656 resolutely declared: "God's people must be a bloody people."[3] They believed that the *parousia* was imminent. They did, though, adopt a version of millenarianism called "post-millennialism", in which it was thought that first the godly would seize power and then Christ would later appear. They also interpreted the poverty and suffering of Christ as evidence for his opposition to the rich and powerful. As a result, one Fifth Monarchist, Mary Cary, wrote of her hatred for the rich and how she longed to: "murther [murder] and destroy them", in a book entitled *The Little Horn's Doom and Downfall* (1651) – a title prompted by the prophecy of Daniel.

The Fifth Monarchy Men had a Christology that was mainstream but some contemporaries developed one that was not. In some areas this was less controversial. In the 1650s, the early Quaker, James Naylor, wrote that after the resurrection, Christ's body was "not carnal but spiritual". This touched on the complex area of exactly how Christ's humanity continued after his ascension into heaven, which was clearly accompanied by glorification and transformation in the New Testament. The New Testament is silent on this detail but earlier Protestant writers, such as the Swiss theologian Huldrych Zwingli, had argued in the opposite direction that, after his ascension, Christ's human body is present in a particular location in heaven while his spiritual presence is unlimited. This very literalistic view had caused a falling out between him and Luther (who accused him of advocating Nestorian ideas – see chapter 8). But both would have fallen out with Naylor in his later career. Naylor's theology of the nature of Christ being present in all believers developed into a perfectionism common to a number of early Quakers. His personal union with Christ, so his followers maintained, was such that the two had become indistinguishable. This soon mixed End Time hopes with a Christology that broke the bounds of Christian faith in the uniqueness of Christ. One of Naylor's followers wrote: "Thy name shall no longer be James but Jesus." Another called Naylor: "Thou lamb of God." This was to apply the language of Christology to someone other than Christ. Naylor and his followers were on a collision course with mainstream Christianity. In 1656, Naylor entered Bristol in imitation of Christ's entry into Jerusalem. For this he was arrested, tried, and whipped, had "B" for Blasphemy branded on his forehead, and his tongue was bored through with a hot iron.

Bristol was a long way from Munster and Naylor's actions were a long way from the violent messianic claims of "King John of Munster". Nevertheless, there was a thread which connected them. In seizing hold of language normally only applied to Christ, they had distorted belief in the second coming so that, in their construction, they stood in the place reserved for Christ in mainstream belief. They were, of course, as exceptional as they were extreme. And most Christians of their time maintained faith in the second coming alongside Christology that had been standard in the church for over 1,000 years. Nevertheless, one can understand why, in the aftermath of such events, enthusiastic support for millenarian belief was treated with great suspicion by church authorities. It was not inevitable that such belief would lead to theological excesses – but it had an alarming track record of so doing. All in all, the sixteenth and seventeenth centuries had constituted an extreme period in the history of Christ. In the so-called "Enlightenment", which followed in the next century, some very different conclusions would be drawn by some who contemplated the person of Christ.

CHAPTER 13

Christ in the Age of the Enlightenment and Western Imperialism

Between 1750 and 1914 the world underwent a dramatic transformation which started in Europe and spread outwards. The driving force behind this change was industrialization, accompanied by an intellectual revolution later called the "Enlightenment". While the roots of this process can be traced back into the so-called Early Modern Period of the sixteenth and seventeenth centuries, it is undeniable that it was the eighteenth century which witnessed both a challenge to age-old patterns of thought, and also huge changes in how goods are produced and how people communicate and live. This then accelerated in the nineteenth and early twentieth centuries, before the course of development was significantly changed by the cataclysm of the First World War.

Industrial and imperial transformation

Beginning in the eighteenth century, in western Europe, the means used to produce goods changed beyond all recognition from what had gone before, through the increasing use of machines in factories that were themselves powered first by water and then by coal (producing steam). This, in a relatively short space of time, led to a fall in the price of products as they were produced in numbers that would have been unimaginable in the previous era of muscle-powered production and more limited use of other power sources. In this we can see the beginning of a mass-production culture that would eventually – in the twentieth century – lead to a consumer society.

At the same time as this occurred, the world population soared as huge numbers migrated to increasingly urbanized centres, where factory production was located. To give some idea of what this means: in 1750 the world population was somewhere in the region of 700 million; by 1850 it stood at about 1.2 billion; by 1900 it reached about 1.6 billion. This upward trajectory has continued to accelerate. In 1950 it had reached 2.55 billion. In 2015, by comparison, it was in the region of 7,298,977,000 and rising. These are astonishing statistics, when one thinks that as recently as 1500 it was no more than 450 million.[1]

Since this process of industrialization began in western Europe and North America, it gave huge advantages to these regions and their ability to dominate the rest of the world. This too had roots that extended back into the late fifteenth-century age of European exploration. As a consequence, the search for raw materials, competition between states for prestige, and the desire to control world trade routes meant that the age of industrial expansion soon became synonymous with the age of Western imperialism. European and European-related culture in the USA became a dominant force and influence across the world; it was imposed or imitated in various proportions in different places at different times.

Since Christianity had been the dominant cultural characteristic of Europe for over 1,000 years, this expansion of

European imperial power had huge implications for the spread of Christianity across the globe. As imperialists and indigenous peoples mixed (in varied combinations of conflict and cooperation), ideas about Christ were shared with, imposed on, and developed by this cultural interaction. It was a process which reverberates into the twenty-first century as we will see in later chapters. And, while imperial power initially accompanied this worldwide spread of Christianity, it should not be assumed that it was only a white person's idea of Christ that would eventually be found in the colonies and – latterly – ex-colonies of the European powers. Indigenous people who converted to Christianity soon added their own take on the way in which Christ was and is communicated and this too continues as a lively dialogue into the modern world. The great "conversation about Christ", originally dominated by Aramaic and Greek, has now become a multilingual discussion across huge numbers of cultures and experiences. The history of Christ has entered into a worldwide phase that continues to this day. We will explore more of this in chapter 16.

The fall-out from the Enlightenment and the growth of scientific method

At the same time that industrial growth was changing and challenging Europe, an intellectual shift that is known today as the Enlightenment occurred. The Enlightenment was a formative period in the modern history of Western thought and culture; it began in the 1650s and ran throughout the eighteenth century. It had a huge impact on science, philosophy, how we understand society, and on politics. As it occurred it destroyed the medieval world-view which was dominated by religious outlook (Christian in Europe) and replaced it with what we now see as a modern and

Western way of understanding the world. This did not, of course, sweep away religious faith or a spiritual way of interpreting life. It did, however, put an end to this being the dominant way by which the world was understood. And it put forward another way of exercising this understanding, based on religious freedom, and increasingly on social equality, human reason, and scientific method. This scientific method has been applied to human experience and ways of discerning the world, the relationship between humans and the natural world and, in time, the whole nature of the cosmos and time itself. It is a process that has changed how we view the universe. For many, it replaced religious concepts and outlook with a rationalist, secular way of explaining life. And for many in western Europe and North America this has meant the abandonment of Christianity in a way that would have been unimaginable in, say, 1600.

For the very many who have continued in faith in Christ since the Enlightenment, it is undeniable that their faith and mental outlook are different to what they would have been, if this earthquake in intellectual thought and practice had not occurred. An outlook has developed in which faith and scientific understanding coexist (a little uneasily for a minority). It has involved a critical examination of the origins of the New Testament, and a greater awareness of both its cultural context and the process by which it and the faith it documents came into existence. It has – for some – challenged the belief in the miraculous that was taken for granted in medieval Europe. As modern people have explored more closely the nature of what it means to be human so this, in turn, has affected how we explore and understand the humanity of Christ. In such a context it is not surprising that many old "certainties" have been questioned and, for some believers, these have been replaced by different ways of explaining old mysteries. In short, the same tensions and stresses that pulled apart European society have deeply affected the church and its theology and Christology. We will explore more of the ramifications of this in chapters 14 and 19. But, for now, we will consider how the history of Christ was affected by the whirlwind of change that started in the mid-eighteenth century.

The search for the "historical Jesus"... but where does this leave Christ?

We have seen that, having broken the monopoly on theological debate that was enjoyed by the Catholic Church, the Protestant Reformation led, unintentionally, to a fragmentation of medieval Christendom (at least in western Europe and ultimately in its North American colonies). It was as if one centrally controlled debate had disintegrated into a multitude of conflicting and violent arguments. In this process a kind of status quo that had existed for a thousand years (and which accepted the Creed of Nicaea and the Chalcedonian Definition) was shattered. This was not immediately apparent because most of those in mainstream Protestantism adhered to an outlook regarding Christ which was in line with these late Roman statements of faith. But the potential for radically different Christologies and ideas that had long been regarded as heretical revealed itself at Munster, Rakow, and in the writings of Servetus. When combined with a more critical scholarly study of biblical texts by humanist scholars and then with the more scientific scrutiny of these same texts (and faith itself) during the Enlightenment, ideas appeared which were major departures from historic Christianity. With the controls over intellectual debate loosened, those who continued to hold that the traditional ways of explaining Christ were still relevant in the new context found themselves sharing the platform with others who drew very different conclusions.

One aspect of this was seen in a non-supernatural attempt to explain Christ and his significance. Some who took part in this "search for the historical Jesus" did so within a framework of Christian faith; others did not, including Hermann Reimarus (1694–1768). In his book, *The Aims of Jesus and His Disciples*, he argued that Jesus stood in the long Jewish messianic tradition but in a way shorn of all divine aspects. Jesus, according to Reimarus, believed in the messianic message, but did not experience its manifestation in his own life. Instead, he went to Jerusalem intending to force a confrontation which would lead to his proclamation as messiah and the eventual inauguration of the Kingdom of God which would then follow. But the hoped-for messianic uprising did not occur. Jesus was arrested and executed and his followers dispersed. These same followers finally reacted to the collapse of their hopes by stealing his body and proclaiming that he had been raised from death and had ascended to heaven. In contrast to Jesus' own Jewish understanding of the messiah, these followers then developed a belief system which reinvented Jesus as "the Christ" in a way that was incompatible with Judaism. Christ's divinity, the concept of the Trinity, the idea of Christ as saviour, the longed-for second coming were all inventions of the early church and distortions of the actual message of Jesus. For Reimarus, the gospels were therefore constructed with this distortion in mind but he claimed that, by stripping them of all that was miraculous or Christological, it was possible to discover a core of Jesus' sayings and deeds which pointed to his "true intentions". This was a secular Jesus for a non-believing age of scepticism: a Jesus who was not Christ.

Over the next century many German Protestant biblical scholars and theologians adopted aspects of Reimarus' method. This was rooted in a rationalist examination of the key texts of the New Testament in a way that was not guided by previous ideas about Christ. These scholars were sceptical about the conclusions that earlier Christians had reached and this included those who had authored the gospels and letters of the New Testament. It was as if the beliefs of earlier writers had actually been an obstacle to their reliable recording of events. All was to be subjected to what was regarded as "historical-criticism", in which the miraculous and supernatural were excluded. Some of those who carried out this reappraisal were antagonistic to Christian faith, such as David Friedrich Strauss who wrote *On Christian Doctrine* (1840–41) and *The Life of Jesus, Critically Examined* (1846). The Earl of Shaftesbury called the former book: "the most pestilential book ever vomited out of the jaws of hell". Strauss applied to the gospels the rationalism of the Enlightenment in such a way as to dismiss all the miraculous events as inventions of the early church, constructed so that Jesus fulfilled all the messianic expectations of Judaism. For Strauss, his characterization of Jesus' "Christ-credentials" as "mythical" accompanied a rejection of Christian faith. In fact, he separated the "Jesus of history" (about whom he assumed that only a little could be said) entirely from the "Christ of faith" (who for Strauss dominated the accounts compiled by the early church). Just why the early Christian community came into existence, with its dramatic and vibrant message and claims about Jesus the Christ, is rather difficult to envisage from the very sketchy picture of the "historical Jesus" put forward by Strauss. Everything of "impact" is relegated to being a product of the myth-construction project of the early church.

Nevertheless, many later Christian writers have been influenced by Strauss and his use of the term "myth" to explain the significance of the miraculous in the gospels – "myth" being an explanation of perceived truth that is not historically accurate but is not the same as falsehood either. These later writers – and this tradition is widespread, though by no means universal, in twenty-first-century theology – would argue that it was and is possible to hold onto Christian faith, while no longer accepting the complete historical veracity of the gospel accounts of Christ's life. This would be hotly argued by more conservative evangelical students of the New Testament but serves to show how influential Strauss has been in the developing Christology of the last two centuries. Albert Schweitzer (1875–1965), in his book, *The Quest of the Historical Jesus* (1906), went so far as to state that, in the search for the "historical Jesus", there existed only two broad periods: "the period before David Strauss and the period after David Strauss". It must, though, be made clear that many contemporary theologians who use the concept of myth as a tool to deconstruct (or decode) the gospels do so as part and parcel of a personal Christian faith. The use of the term "myth" in their analysis should not be taken to mean lack of faith. But it does indicate an approach to the miraculous, as seen in the gospel accounts of the life of Christ, that stands in contrast to many previous centuries of Christian thought and analysis regarding these features of the gospel accounts.

Returning to Albert Schweitzer; as a medical missionary in Africa, who was also famous for his historical work on Jesus, he straddles the world of imperialism, the global expansion of Christian influence, and the search for the "historical Jesus" that so influenced intellectual ideas about Christ in the nineteenth and twentieth centuries. Schweitzer differed from Reimarus in the way that he took seriously Jesus' self-conscious belief in his own significance as the one through whom God would bring in the Kingdom. But for Schweitzer Jesus' mission was not focused on a preoccupation with political change but, instead, was a determinedly eschatological venture. Schweitzer's Jesus considered himself as the embodiment of the "Son of Man" foretold by the prophet Daniel in the Old Testament. Where

Schweitzer was similar to Reimarus was in the way that he thought that Jesus' life could be fully explained through rational analysis without recourse to supernatural activity. As a consequence, the Christ, as revealed by Jesus, was a heroic but tragic figure. As Schweitzer graphically put it, Jesus:

> ... in the knowledge that He is the coming Son of Man lays hold of the wheel of the world to set it moving on that last revolution which is to bring all ordinary history to a close. It refuses to turn, and He throws Himself upon it. Then it does turn; and crushes Him. Instead of bringing in the eschatological conditions, He has destroyed them.[2]

Schweitzer believed that the "messianic secret" (Jesus telling others not to proclaim him as the Christ) can be explained by the fact that only Jesus understood his own messianic status but that this had undergone a severe shift during the three years of his earthly ministry. At first, Schweitzer argued, Jesus thought that when he sent out his disciples to preach, they would face great tribulations and that God would establish the coming Kingdom through him before their mission was complete. Then, when this did not occur, he came to realize that he alone would drink the cup of suffering on behalf of others and that only then would the Kingdom come. This was only revealed to the inner core of his followers. When Jesus went to his death he did so alone, as the Christ whose death would initiate the cosmic transformation foretold in Old Testament prophecy. But it did not occur. And it was this that the church was left trying to explain over the next 2,000 years. In this way the great question of Christianity is the puzzle over the Christ who, at the moment of his sacrifice, failed to see the great act of God occur that he had confidently laid down his life to bring about. For

Schweitzer, "The historical Jesus will be to our time a stranger and an enigma."[3]

This view of Christ stands in stark contrast with the proclaimed faith of the church over the centuries. Yet Schweitzer proposed it from the position of one who considered himself in sympathy with the Christian community and its message. He was no Reimarus. Yet, for all that, all that Schweitzer was left with was the hope that from Jesus "a mighty spiritual force streams forth from Him and flows through our time also".[4] With no resurrection, no vindication of his status as Christ, no ascension, and no eternal triumph (all central features of the mainstream Christology of the church) it is rather hard to see exactly what Schweitzer found to be so positive about. His writings had created a strange and barren meeting place for the idea that Jesus could be fully understood only through Enlightenment rational analysis and the claim that Jesus did, in fact, believe himself to be the Christ – but whose hopes disintegrated on the cross. This is not to say that an analysis of the human thinking of Jesus – set within a particular historical context – cannot or should not be attempted. Indeed, the great battles within the church to establish faith in the reality of Christ's humanity (as well as his divinity) mean that such an enterprise is certainly appropriate and necessary. Rather, it reminds us that, once we remove from the equation all talk of divinity and supernatural agency, we are left with an image of Christ that sits awkwardly (if it can be made to sit at all) with what has been claimed about him from the very first generation of Christians onwards.

And yet the Enlightenment preoccupation with rational analysis would not go away. Some theologians, such as the German, Friedrich Schleiermacher (1768–1834), had already begun to try to express an understanding of what constituted Christ-ness in Jesus, on the basis of: "His God-consciousness, which was a veritable existence of God in Him."[5] Yet, while this allowed for psychological analysis and was strongly allied to the study of human spirituality in response to God, Schleiermacher's approach was devoid of attention to the work of the Holy Spirit both in the relationship of Father and Son and as a way of explaining how and why believers respond to Christ in faith. In addition, he was more concerned with exploring religious feeling than with belief in the revealed truth of Scripture.

Other theologians would approach the task of exploring the nature of Christ in different ways but, from the nineteenth century onwards, the preoccupation of Christian theologians has been how to talk about Christ's divinity and the power and influence of supernatural agency in the prevailing language of the post-Enlightenment world. The challenge continues.

Like Schleiermacher, other theologians of the nineteenth century explored Christology through a refocusing on humanity. This was not only through exploring the human sense of the divine in order to understand Christ, as Schleiermacher had done. Others, such as the German theologian Albrecht Ritschl (1822–89), looked at the way in which Christ revealed perfect morality; those who followed him were spreading his good works throughout the world. Ritschl's approach recognized the limits to reason, since faith, he said, came from value-judgments. This is sometimes described as "functional Christology" because, for the believer, Christ functions as God because he reveals the highest form of morality.

The direction of this way of thinking about Christ, as exemplified by the ideas of yet another German theologian, Adolf von Harnack (1851–1930), led away from Trinitarian concepts. Harnack presented Jesus as a teacher of righteousness but rejected belief in the Trinity and regarded it as an invention imposed on God by people. For von Harnack, all the supernatural features of Christ in the New Testament and early Christianity were mythological inventions projected onto a historical Jesus, and owed more to first-century Jewish eschatological hopes and Greek philosophy than reality.

This division between the "Jesus of history" and the "Christ of faith" was emphasized by the writings of Martin Kähler (1835–1912). This was exemplified in the title of an essay that he wrote in 1892: *The So-called Historical Jesus and the Historic Biblical Christ*. For Kähler, it was impossible to reconstruct a "historic life of Jesus", since the gospels were made up of statements of faith by the early Christian community and did not contain any material through which the actual life of Jesus could be discerned. In short: the image of Christ had completely obscured the person of Jesus; Christian faith was focused on the idea of the risen Christ as divine presence and had no relationship with historical events.

A similar rejection of the value of attempting to explore any historical evidence regarding Christ can be found in the work of the earlier Danish philosopher, Søren Kierkegaard (1813–55). He argued that no historical study was capable of revealing the real Christ; this was only possible through a leap of faith in him as the incarnate Saviour who saved humankind from sin though his death and resurrection. This rejected the reductionist trend among nineteenth-century liberal German theologians which reduced Jesus to the wise teacher, the supreme example of morality, and the one supremely conscious of God. And yet the problem of Kierkegaard's approach, it can be argued, is that – while accepting that, in Christ, God broke into time and space – it assumes that nothing survives of this in the extant historical record. All in all, the legacy of the nineteenth century was going to be complex in terms of debates about Christ in the twentieth century.

Christ in the empires of Europe

While the Christian church in Europe was wrestling with how to understand Christ through the rational thought processes and language of the Enlightenment, it was a much more traditional view of Christ that missionaries were taking out into the rapidly expanding empires of the European colonial powers. This view was rooted in evangelical commitment to conversion and a mainstream presentation of Christ and the Trinity. This is revealed in evidence such as the writings of the Indian, Rammohun Roy (1772–1833), who rejected the miracles of Jesus as featured both in the gospels and in missionary teaching, which he described as "heathenish doctrines and absurd notions".

In contrast, it was the Europeanization of Christ that the Indian, Keshub Chunder Sen, objected to in 1904:

> It seems that the Christ that has come to us is an Englishman, with English manners and customs about him, and with the temper and spirit of an Englishman in him... But why should you Hindus go to England to learn Jesus Christ? Is not his native land nearer to India than England?[6]

The question was a fair one to ask since, while the Christology of the missionaries tended to be in line with historic Christianity (in contrast to many of the conclusions of the German Protestant theologians we considered above), the person of their Christ was racially white and very European. Any images of a Middle Eastern Jesus, let alone that of a colonially oppressed Jew executed by an imperial power, were banished. Almost every illustrated Bible in the empires of the European powers contained a white Christ, who appeared as God's stamp of approval on white supremacy. Yet in the twentieth century, as European imperial power disintegrated, Christ was rediscovered and communicated in a radically different way among those whose ancestors had converted to Christianity in imperial times, but whose children and grandchildren discovered an Afro-Asiatic Jewish Christ (see chapter 16) whose message was of liberation for the oppressed (see chapter 15).

CHAPTER 14

Christ in the Age of Total War and the Search for a "Modern Christology"

If the nineteenth century tested the resilience of a centuries-old Christology – even as it saw Christianity become a global faith across the colonies of the European imperial powers – then the twentieth century challenged faith even further. In a century of Total War and vast numbers of deaths through fighting, genocide, and neglect, many would question the reality of the existence of God. These questions were seared on the consciousness of many through the horrors of the First and Second World Wars. As if this was not enough, the arrival of nuclear weapons in 1945 threatened the very existence of advanced life forms on the planet. The rise of atheistic Marxism in the Soviet Union, China, and their allies both in the developing world and within the intellectual circles of the West, offered yet another threat to religious faith of all kinds. Then, in the second half of the century, rising Western consumerism and the arrival of the so-called "permissive society" of the 1960s led to challenges to both traditional spirituality and traditional morality at the same time. At first glance this might seem something of a perfect storm through which faith battled its way, with its hatches battened down and its sails shredded as it was driven before the force of the gale. And yet, as we shall see in later chapters, Christianity has continued to grow dramatically in the developing world even as its membership has reduced in the West. And even there – as well as in the developing world – a renewed belief in personal empowerment by the Holy Spirit has led to a dramatic growth in certain areas of the church, even as more traditional areas have experienced decline. So a century that at one time looked like it was going to witness the withering away of Christian faith, ended with the faith still being the largest religion on the planet and increasing in size. Nevertheless, in such a situation of turmoil, it is not surprising that ideas about Christ have continued to change and develop as many theologians have felt the need to create a more modern Christology that meshes with contemporary language and ways of expressing Christian faith in Christ. In the history of Christ, the twentieth century witnessed significant developments in Christology, even while many believers remained committed to a faith that would have been instantly recognizable to those present at the Council of Nicaea in 325.

Ideas of Christ in an age of world wars

What might be described as the moral self-confidence of Europe, at least, was torn apart by the First World War. Old certainties and confidence in the established social order (that were already being challenged by socialism and Marxism from the late nineteenth century) were severely damaged by the carnage of war. When Rupert Brooke (1887–1915) wrote (in the poem "The Soldier") of "hearts at peace, under an English heaven", he expressed a quiet, idealistic, and vague spirituality that blended patriotism with the concept of personal sacrifice. But Brooke died, from an infected mosquito bite, on his way to the landing at Gallipoli, and before the war had descended into its most brutal period of industrialized killing. And indeed before he had seen any fighting. He never went to the western front in Belgium or France. Nevertheless, in the early stages of the war he was not alone in his positive appraisal of the conflict. Many in 1914 felt, in the words of Harold Begbie's poem, "Fall-in", that: "England's call is God's!" It was this kind of patriotic Christian confidence that led to the myth of the Angels of Mons who were said to have been fighting a celestial battle on behalf of the retreating British Expeditionary Force in the autumn of 1914. It should also be noted that German soldiers went into battle with the words *Gott mit uns* (God with us) on their belt buckles. The bitter irony of the (ostensibly) Christian nations of Europe slaughtering each other added to the disillusionment of many. A later myth (never satisfactorily substantiated) that German soldiers crucified a captured Canadian soldier reveals the way that Christian imagery and war-mythology changed as the bitterness of the conflict intensified. As it did so, some would abandon faith, while others would see in Christ's suffering a vivid picture of the suffering of the soldiers around them. Siegfried Sassoon used Christ as a metaphor for the common solder when he described a man carrying planks along a trench, in a manner reminiscent of Christ carrying his cross.[1]

Christ's suffering has become a metaphor for the suffering of the war. And yet the futility of the war means that this suffering does not add to our understanding of Christ since, by back-projection, it could equally be concluded that Christ's suffering too was futile. There is nothing of the triumph of the cross – or of faith – in such poetry. Rather, the Christ-imagery simply serves to shock religious sensibilities and religious complacency. We may presume that this was why Sassoon chose to give this poem the provocative title: "The Redeemer". But there is nothing of redemption in the Christ of the poem. It says more about the Christlike suffering of the soldiers than it does about the significance of the suffering of Christ. The, now less well-known, poet Robert Nichols wrote of: "the soldier's cup of anguish, blood and gall", whose feet, hands, and side "Must soon be torn, pierced, crucified" ("Battery Moving Up to a New Position from Rest Camp: Dawn").[2]

In a similar way, Sassoon's poem "Christ and the Soldier" has an exhausted soldier fall before a statue of the crucified Christ but receive little consolation.[3]

It was mining a similar vein of irony that caused Wilfred Owen to write, in a letter to Osbert Sitwell:

For 14 hours yesterday, I was at work – teaching Christ to lift his cross by numbers, and how to adjust his crown; and not to imagine he thirst till after the last halt; I attended his Supper to see that there were no complaints; and inspected his feet to see that they should be worthy of the nails. I see to it that he is dumb and stands to attention before his accusers. With a piece of silver I buy him every day, and with maps I make him familiar with the topography of Golgotha.[4]

Not everyone, though, looked on the cross of Christ in such bleak terms. P. T. Forsyth, the Scottish Congregationalist theologian, was one of many whose vivid awareness of the desperate fallen state of the human condition (as exemplified by the horrors of the First World War) led him to a greater emphasis on the grace of God which, in Christ, breaks into human history, society, and culture. Such a Christ was much more than a noble moral example for citizens of a self-confident nation and empire. Instead, he was the only remedy for a desperate condition. Forsyth put it memorably when he remarked that his theological outlook had shifted from being a "lover of love" to being "an object of grace". It is significant that it was in 1917 that he wrote *The Justification of God*, in which he urged his readers to understand Christ as the supreme act of God, by which disobedient humanity could be saved from the catastrophic state into which it had fallen. Written in the same year as the slaughter of Passchendaele, it was a clear example of the conjunction of history with Christology. Other books by Forsyth included: *The Person and Place of Jesus Christ* (1909), *The Work of Christ* (1910) and, in the context of this discussion, the very appropriately titled *The Cruciality of the Cross* (1910). In his work he developed the theme of the self-giving of God in Christ. This self-giving was expressed in the Greek term *kenosis* which comes from the word *kenoo*, translated in modern English as "emptied". This "*Kenosis* [or *Kenotic*] Christology" drew on New Testament passages such as Philippians 2:6–8 which describes Christ:

who, though he was in the form of God,
did not regard equality with God
as something to be exploited,
but emptied [kenoo] himself,
taking the form of a slave,
being born in human likeness.
And being found in human form,
he humbled himself
and became obedient to the point of death –
even death on a cross.

Another Scottish theologian, James Denney (1856–1917), also emphasized the nature of sin and the work of reconciliation with God that was only made possible through Christ's death (the atonement).

All of this meshed with the terrible suffering of the trenches in a way that gave a new urgency and depth to Christology and the suffering of Christ, unknown in the poems of Sassoon and Owen. A Christian poet, the army chaplain G. A. Studdert Kennedy (1883–1929), known to the soldiers as "Woodbine Willie" from the cigarettes he gave them, drew on his experiences of the suffering of war to illustrate the terrible suffering of Christ to redeem a fallen world. In 1923 he wrote:

> The Father Whom we worship is revealed in Christ crucified as well as in Christ risen, and Christ ascending, and in that revelation there is no sign of what I call, for lack of a better term, "easy omnipotence".[5]

Cross-centred Christology

Later theologians, also working in the context of war or the aftermath of war, continued to explore this new-found resurgence of cross-centred theology. For the German theologian Dietrich Bonhoeffer (executed by the Nazis in 1945) the cross was central, not only to an understanding of reconciliation with God but also as the way by which Christians are truly motivated to live out the Christian life in the world:

> The Christian… like Christ himself… must drink the earthly cup to the dregs, and only in his doing so is the crucified and risen Lord with him, and he is crucified and risen with Christ.[6]

Christ is crucified to the world and the world to Christ. And therefore, for the believer, faith in such a Christ cannot be limited to personal salvation only, nor only to hope beyond death. Rather it leads to a sacrificial commitment to live out the Christian faith in a way that transforms the world in the here-and-now too. The Christian must take the world and its liberation as seriously as Christ did. As Bonhoeffer put it:

> The cross of atonement is the setting free for life before God in the midst of the godless world; it is the setting free for life in genuine worldliness.[7]

A real engagement with the world – what Bonhoeffer provocatively called "genuine worldliness" – is only possible because of Christ's cross and living life according to its values of sacrificial love. In Bonhoeffer's words this was also the only way that a person could truly fulfil their nature because only in union with Christ was the potential of an individual's humanity fully achieved and experienced:

> Only in the cross of Christ, that is, as those upon whom sentence has been executed, do men achieve their true form.[8]

This is a striking understanding of what it means to be members of the church. It makes of this group a radical and revolutionary community with outrageous claims regarding modelling what love lived to the full should look like. No Christian community can remain unchallenged by such a view of the union of the church and the crucified Christ. Again, to return to the words of Bonhoeffer:

> It is in her [the Church] that Jesus realizes His form in the midst of the world. That is why the Church alone can be the place of personal and collective rebirth and renewal.[9]

This echoes themes found in the New Testament that emphasize the demands of following Christ through total identification with him, and the way in which Christ acts through the church in order to communicate the gospel. In the gospels we read: "Then Jesus told his disciples, 'If any want to become my followers, let them deny themselves and take up their cross and follow me' " (Matthew 16:24). Paul took up the themes of Christian intimate unity with Christ *and* acting as Christ's agents through the empowerment that this brought, when he wrote of the church:

> For as in one body we have many members, and not all the members have the same function, so we, who are many, are one body in Christ, and individually we are members one of another. We have gifts that differ according to the grace given to us. (Romans 12:4–6)

This cross-centred concept drove Bonhoeffer's theology, and it is moving, because Bonhoeffer, the Christian intellectual and scholar, was hanged in a stark execution room at Flossenbürg concentration camp for his opposition to the evil of Nazism. He died at dawn on 9 April 1945. It was two weeks before US soldiers liberated the camp and a month before Nazi Germany surrendered.

Bonhoeffer's exploration of the power of the cross of Christ was developed by Jürgen Moltmann (born 1926) in the book *The Crucified God* (1972). For Moltmann, suffering could become an active and life-affirming experience, and the concept of the crucified God challenged the political and social structures of the world, as well as its religious expectations. As Moltmann succinctly put it: "For the crucified Messiah to become a present reality amongst slaves is as dangerous to their masters as their reading of the Bible in general."[10] In this idea, Christology was returning to its shocking and radical first-century roots and overthrowing centuries of church collaboration with the powerful in the current human world order. In an age of genocide and world wars, the theology of Moltmann, and those like him, engaged seriously with the dark side of the human condition and argued for the liberating hope of redemption, which could only be achieved through the agony and suffering of Christ. And since Christology claims that "God was in Christ" this gives rise to the assertion of the identification of God with suffering reflected in the book's provocative title. For, while this raises all of the 2,000-year-old questions of how God can experience pain, death, suffering, and limitation, the irreducible core of New Testament teaching is that he did, in Christ.

Moltmann's emphasis has been taken up by proponents of liberation theology (see chapter 15). But Moltmann and theologians such as the Croatian Protestant theologian, Miroslav Volf (born 1956), and John Zizioulas (born 1931), the Eastern Orthodox Metropolitan of Pergamon, are also noteworthy for a theology that has been described as the "Social Trinity". While by no means unique to their writings, this approach to the traditional belief in the Trinity emphasizes how the Trinity consists of three persons whose unity is that of a loving relationship. In short, since God is a social being, the Trinity provides a model for all relationships of love, as well as explaining what God is like. Worthwhile human unity is patterned on this supreme expression of divine unity.

Christ and the "demythologizing" debate

Much of the Christology and indeed the whole question of how to read the New Testament in the twentieth century was affected by the debate over the "demythologizing" of the gospel accounts. In some ways this continued a line of enquiry that had been clear in writings of what might be termed more liberal theologians in the nineteenth century. One of those who continued and developed this approach was, like them, a German: Rudolf Bultmann (1884–1976). Bultmann was a German Lutheran theologian and also professor of New Testament at the University of Marburg. One of the major figures of early- to mid-twentieth-century biblical studies, he was also prominent within liberal Christianity. Essentially, he argued that the accounts of Christ's resurrection were not accounts of an objective historical event. Instead, they were faith-statements designed to communicate the need to die to self (as Jesus did) and to experience the triumph of faith; but this was not rooted in an actual bodily resurrection of Christ. In Bultmann's view, the New Testament was essentially a compilation of preaching materials. It was the "*kerygma* [message/proclamation] of the cross" as preached by the early church, but not a historical record. It was designed to encourage faith and needed to be demythologized in order to be truly understood. In 1941 he presented much of this view in his lecture "New Testament and Mythology: The Problem of Demythologizing the New Testament Message". This view gained wider circulation in the English-speaking world after the end of the Second World War when the book *Kerygma and Myth: A Theological Debate* was translated into English in 1948. What mattered, to Bultmann, was the "thatness", not the "whatness", of Jesus. There was, in fact, no "historical Jesus" to study and analyse.

This position was hotly contested by more conservative and evangelical theologians and continues to be so. They would point to the insistence of Paul that "if Christ has not been raised, then our proclamation has been in vain and your faith has been in vain" (1 Corinthians 15:14) and to the gospel accounts of an empty tomb, to counter-argue that, regardless of the difficulty this poses to some modern readers (and those wishing for a non-supernatural basis for Christianity), it *is* a core value *and* a core feature of the New Testament and the early church whether some modern Christians like it or not. The battle lines continue to divide more liberal and more conservative Christians. To this conservative defence, more liberal scholars would retort that many cultures contain mythological literature and traditions which are used to define their significance and values without being regarded by modern students as historical accounts, so why should Christianity's early literature be any different? The debate/argument continues in the twenty-first century.

The Swiss Reformed theologian, Karl Barth (1886–1968), had a career that steered a middle course between the more liberal and conservative extremes of Christian theology. While not arguing for the Bible as a historically or scientifically accurate document and rejecting many aspects of conservative theology, Barth nevertheless emphasized the sovereignty of God, the sinfulness of humanity, the knowledge of the Trinitarian God gained only through God's revelation of himself, and the simultaneous rejection of human sin and the election of humans to salvation through Christ. All this also distanced Barth from many liberal Christian theologians. The consequences of Christ's act of saving power, in Barth's view, meant that eternal salvation for everyone (including those who reject God) is a possibility. More conservative theologians accused this theology of straying close to "universalism" (the belief in the salvation of everyone rather than those holding faith). Nevertheless, Barth's outlook was still Christ-centred, even if some of his conclusions were contested. His ideas influenced Moltmann and the concept of the "crucified God".

History and the resurrection of Christ

What is the role of the events of history in the revelation of God to humanity? Wolfhart Pannenberg (1928–2014) – like the late eighteenth/early nineteenth-century German philosopher Hegel – believed that history is an unfolding process through which spiritual understanding and freedom are revealed. He was also heavily influenced by Barth's concept of revelation occurring "vertically from above" and dependent on the action of God in self-revelation.

For Pannenberg, while only at the end point of history will this be complete, the resurrection of Christ provides a kind of flash-forward which makes sense of (and reveals) the real nature of this unfolding series of events. In this sense, the end of the world has already begun. Perhaps his most famous work was *Jesus – God and Man* (1968) in which he strove to create a Christology "from below". In this book, he drew his conclusions about the nature of Christ from a study of his life and, in particular, his resurrection. While he believed in the historical reality of this event, he laid more stress on the impact of the risen Christ – and faith in him – as experienced by the early church. In this he stood apart from the attitude towards the resurrection found in the writings of more liberal twentieth-century theologians.

He was, though, unwilling to accept the traditional view of Jesus as the incarnation of the *Logos*. The whole language and imagery of descent and ascent was for Pannenberg:

> ... the mythical element of the incarnational Christology; it conceptually divides the eternal Son of God and the earthly, human appearance of Jesus, which together constitute the concrete existence of Jesus, into two separate beings.[11]

Pannenberg objected principally to what he considered to be the Greek "mythological" language and concepts used in the creeds to describe the incarnation, and to the description of Jesus as the union of two distinct persons. Instead, he proposed that Christ's divinity was apparent in three main ways: firstly, what he termed the "Christ event" is the revelation that begins the end of all things; secondly, this self-revelation by God can only be understood as a single revelation – and that is Christ; and thirdly, God who self-reveals and the Revealer are identical. This revelation is supremely seen in Christ's resurrection. Jesus is God because of this event. To those who might accuse Pannenberg of advocating a form of "adoptionism" (long rejected as a heresy) he would argue that, in fact:

> Jesus did not simply become [at the resurrection] something that he previously had not been, but his pre-Easter claim was confirmed by God.[12]

The language used by Pannenberg (like the early church) borrows language and concepts. In his case, they come from the German philosopher Hegel and from Barth. Without commenting specifically on Pannenberg's conclusions, even a theologically conservative Christian would admit that the creeds are not Scripture and represent an attempt to explain the inexpressible in the language of the Greek-speaking late Roman empire. Consequently, it is not inadmissible to question how well they do that task and to ask whether other words and phrases could do it better. We shall return to this when we consider aspects of Indian Christology (see chapter 16). Whether Pannenberg succeeded, though, will continue to be a subject of debate. Many would argue that, by abandoning the traditional concept and language of the incarnation of the pre-existing *Logos*, too much else in the theological structure begins to collapse or, at least, becomes unstable. Perhaps the answer lies in a different approach to expressing "incarnation" rather than in replacing it? This debate will, no doubt, occupy areas of the church in the twenty-first century.

This debate will not be the only one. In the final quarter of the twentieth century traditional Christology has been addressed and challenged by radical feminists; proponents of Jesus as an eastern sage; creation-Christology; and a concept of divine empathy that almost removes effective power from divinity, to name but a few. We will return to these in the final chapter, as we look forward to the next century of debate. But before that, we need to address other themes that emerged strongly in the twentieth century: liberation Christology, the Christology of the "developing world", and then Christ and the Charismatic movement.

CHAPTER 15

Christ with a Kalashnikov?

Liberation theology is a radical Christian movement that developed in the Catholic Church in South America, in the 1970s, although it has also influenced thinking in a number of "developing countries" in other areas of the world. Essentially, it stated that the church should actively involve itself in movements to bring about social change. In order to do this, it should ally itself with working-class organizations and with political groups geared to challenging the social order as a way of bringing about justice for the poor. This often meant working with or in association with Marxist groups, though not exclusively so. In some areas this took the form of social projects aimed at bringing about improvements in the living conditions of the poor; in other situations it involved active alliances with groups (trade unions and political parties) who were regarded by some in authority as revolutionaries. Often it saw church leaders speaking out against examples of injustice, exploitation, and inequality; in more extreme situations it might even involve radical church members getting involved in revolutionary agitation. In a number of South American countries, priests and nuns demonstrated their solidarity with the poor by relocating to the poorest neighbourhoods and living among those in the deepest poverty and need.

One of the most high profile of the clergy associated with liberation theology was the Archbishop of San Salvador (in El Salvador), Óscar Romero (1917–80). He spoke out on behalf of the poor and oppressed in an increasingly violent situation, while remaining an exponent of non-violence. In El Salvador, in the late 1970s, executions, kidnappings, and torture were being used against both the rural poor and activists who opposed El Salvador's right-wing government. Right-wing death squads terrorized those whom they regarded as threats and did so in the name of anti-communism. The government was backed by the USA as part of its policy of opposing left-wing movements during the Cold War. In 1980, Óscar Romero was gunned down while celebrating Mass. No one has ever been brought to justice for his murder. In May 2015, Romero was officially beatified by the Catholic Church, a key step towards being declared a saint.

Exponents of liberation theology claimed that the church only had legitimacy when it both took social justice seriously and also rooted itself in the poorest members of the community. Furthermore, the Bible should always be read from the perspective of the poor. The basis of this claim was threefold. Firstly, the Bible has many examples in which God is presented as being on the side of justice and the poor. Secondly, the doctrine of the Trinity envisages God having a collegiate nature, in which the members of the Godhead are united in mutual love. This sets a pattern for human relationships and communities. Christian-inspired communities should effectively be Trinitarian in terms of mutual love, care, and self-giving. Thirdly, the example of Christ was presented as one who was poor, homeless, and persecuted by the rich and powerful and, therefore, challenged the norms and expectations of the world.

It is this third feature that is of the most interest to us in this exploration of the history of Christ, as it presented a set of beliefs that we can call "liberation Christology". Based on a radical appraisal of the nature and life of Christ, it is argued that Christianity (if it is emulating Christ) is set on a collision course with the current world order in all its forms. And this includes its economic and political ideologies, expectations, controls, values, and demands. The church is a revolutionary movement whose agenda includes radical social and economic change. This is the logical outcome of "liberation Christology".

Pope John Paul II (pope 1978–2005) opposed the movement. He was particularly concerned at what he saw as a highly politicized form of the movement which seemed to be fusing Christianity with aspects of Marxism. He felt that it was overly focused on social justice, to the detriment of the church's spiritual message of personal transformation. To John Paul II, it looked as if the church in some areas was turning into a secular and political institution. He believed (and many agreed) that, for all the radical lifestyle of Jesus, he was never a political revolutionary and should not be presented as such. A number of those closely involved with liberation theology found themselves in trouble. The Brazilian theologian, Leonardo Boff (born 1938), was banned from teaching. Other theologians, who were advisers to the various conferences of bishops around the world, were punished or lost their official licence to teach. The Jesuits too found themselves under increasing papal control as a result of their involvement in politics and liberation theology. The alternative papal message was that the church *should* be the voice of the poor and *should* champion the poor *but* in a way that was not politically partisan and did not espouse revolutionary violence. The aim of the church was to bring about the Kingdom of God. It was not to work for a Marxist society, nor to adopt strategies of violence or class conflict. Given the pope's previous experience of Marxist oppression of the Catholic Church in his native Poland, it is perhaps not surprising that he was alarmed at what he saw as a Catholic–Marxist alliance in South America. To John Paul II, those who argued for liberation theology – regardless of their sincerity – were distorting Christianity and Christology.

In 1984, the Congregation for the Doctrine of the Faith issued the *Instruction on Certain Aspects of the "Theology of Liberation"*. This detailed document, while committing the Catholic Church to social justice and opposition to exploitation and inequality, included these telling points:

> Faced with the urgency of sharing bread, some are tempted to put evangelization into parentheses, as it were, and postpone it until tomorrow: first the bread, then the Word of the Lord…
>
> In giving such priority to the political dimension, one is led to deny the "radical newness" of the New Testament and above all to misunderstand the person of Our Lord Jesus Christ, true God and true man, and thus the specific character of the salvation he gave us, that is above all liberation from sin, which is the source of all evils.[1]

Presiding over this meeting was Joseph, Cardinal Ratzinger, later to become Pope Benedict XVI (pope from 2005 until his resignation in 2013).

What is the nature of "liberation Christology"?

What we can call "liberation Christology" tends to focus on two main themes. Firstly, it asks how do the nature and purpose of Christ impact on the lives of the poor? Secondly, and as an outworking of this, it explores the nature of the Kingdom of God as defined by Jesus and revealed in his life, and how this liberates humanity from those structures that constrain them. It is an example of the type of belief that is sometimes called "Christology from below". Rather than starting from reflecting on the glorified Christ (sometimes referred to as "the Christ of faith") it, instead, starts from reflecting on the experience and outlook revealed in the life of Jesus – what we might call "the Jesus of history".

This focus has been accused of relying too much on contextualizing faith, of looking too much at the life of Jesus in a social context, rather than exploring belief in his eternal nature and significance, the focus of much traditional Christology. It is charged with concentrating too much on "Jesus the man" and not enough (or even not at all) on "Jesus the Son of God, the Christ". It might, at times, even run the risk of not being "Christology" at all. This certainly would be the view of its severest critics. Furthermore – and arising from this – it has also been accused of an overemphasis on the impact of Christ on the present, on socio-economic themes and, thus, underestimating or even ignoring the nature of spiritual bondage and sin which, traditional Christianity teaches, lies at the root of all wrong human behaviour and which needs to be dealt with more fundamentally than just transforming social and economic systems (as important as that is). Allied to this, its eschatology may, at times, seem divorced from the traditional cosmic concept of (literally) universal transformation at the ending of the current world order and, instead, asserts a belief in a reduced eschatology which sees social and political change as the essence of the implementation of the Kingdom of God. More traditional Christians, who see the salvation of Christ as a once-for-all-time event in the past that impacts on the present and future, may also feel that liberation Christology is overly preoccupied with what has been called "historicized salvation". This conceives of salvation as an ongoing process that is only achieved through being liberated from the oppression of the particular system in which people live. As such, it may never be definitively achieved, since the struggle itself is ongoing.

To these charges, the exponents of liberation Christology would argue that too much traditional Christology is concerned with speculation over spiritual details of otherworldly aspects of divine existence and is too little concerned with the radical impact of Christian values on this world's structures. They would add that Jesus in the gospels is directly concerned with challenging this world's social order. He meets with tax collectors and prostitutes, the objects of others' contempt. He confronts religious hypocrisy and the self-satisfied outlook of the rich and powerful. He persistently models the character of the Son of Man. Even this preferred title (while carrying strong connotations of Old Testament images of God's world-transforming agent) also has the meaning of being an Everyman, one who identifies with the totality of humanity in order to liberate it. In the view of liberation Christology, there is little of Christ *Pantocrator* in the gospels and much of the Son of Man, impoverished and persecuted. Too much of Greek-language speculations and End Time preoccupations, they might argue, has obscured the figure of Jesus and the kind of Christ that he represents.

The problem for this approach is that this preoccupation started very early on in the history of Christ and can be argued to be fundamental to it. Consequently, it might be asserted that to remove it hollows out the nature of Christianity and Christology itself. Those who argue to the contrary seem to be suggesting that the whole history of the church and its speculation about Christ went astray from the middle of the first century until it was corrected in the 1970s. This debate will roll on as it goes to the heart of exactly who Jesus is and what he changes in people's lives. It also impacts on the status of the traditional church creeds when measured against the Jesus of the gospels.

Liberation Christology and the incarnation

Liberation Christology challenges Christians to rethink implications of the incarnation. According to the Peruvian liberation theologian, Gustavo Gutiérrez Merino (born 1928), all liberation in history occurs because of the incarnation of God in Jesus Christ. Just as God lived in Christ, so the Holy Spirit lives in the lives of ordinary people and directly interacts with their particular circumstances. Christian action towards others consequently causes them to interact with God. This is why justice for the poor is an integral part of God's salvation plan and of salvation history. Since God draws people to participate in the divine nature as a direct consequence of the existence of Christ in history, it follows that he wills neither poverty nor oppression and is set against it. So human beings need to confront such affronts to the will of God. This is why liberation Christology leads to liberation theology, and in turn leads to political and economic liberation. It is rooted in the incarnation.

Sin, in this approach, is supremely seen in the systematic subjection of others to poverty and suffering. It is contrary to God's will for creation. Gutiérrez Merino has been specific in where he sees such sin and its origins:

> ... domination exercised by the great capitalist countries, and especially by the most powerful, the United States of America.[2]

His Christology of incarnation and its effects directly leads to explicit political statements regarding the current world order.

222

One can begin to see why liberation Christology, in practice, is such a controversial set of beliefs.

For a liberation theologian such as Jon Sobrino (see below), this Kingdom of God as revealed in Christ is fundamentally about the "liberation of the poor" and is committed to "transforming reality". All that is contrary to this he has termed "the Anti-Reign, the world of sin". The reign of God is fundamentally "the Reign of the poor".[3] We are back to the idea of incarnation proposed by Gutiérrez Merino. In present society, God is incarnated in the poor and the oppressed, as in the first century he was incarnated in Christ. In this sense the suffering poverty of Jesus and the suffering poverty of today's poor become the dominant lens through which all ideas about God and his purposes are understood. In Sobrino's book, *The True Church and the Poor* (1984), he argued that the core principle of the community of Christ – the church – lies not in it being *for* the poor but consisting *of* the poor. For Sobrino, this was more than just a way of describing the inclusivity of the ideal Christian community. Instead, he would argue that this is a statement as much about Christ as about his people. Since Christ surrounded himself with the poor, the ongoing church must be rooted in the poor if it is to truly be the church, the Body of Christ. Not for nothing was a later book of his provocatively called *No Salvation Outside the Poor: Prophetic-Utopian Essays* (2008). Furthermore, he saw the suffering poor in contemporary society as representing Christ's suffering in modern terms. This was more than simply a striking comparison. It was rather how Christ was to be seen and understood by modern people in their own context. Hence the title of one of his books: *The Principle of Mercy: Taking the Crucified People from the Cross* (1994).

For proponents of liberation Christology, the life of Jesus of Nazareth is more important than what they would describe as abstract exploration (even speculation) about his status before and after his earthly ministry. Indeed, they would no doubt accuse many mainstream concepts of "Christ" as having very little connection with "Jesus of Nazareth". And even *if* the New Testament sources do not convey the actual words and actions of Jesus (as is claimed by those involved in the quest for the historical Jesus), what matters most for liberation Christology is what they reveal about the impact of Jesus and how he affected those who reflected on him. For, they would argue, what matters *today* is the latest expression of that impact. This means that some theologians of liberation Christology are much less concerned with sieving the New Testament in order to discover the authentic voice of Jesus than are many other theologians. This process is much less important to them than the radical reapplication of such a significance (whatever its historical accuracy and authenticity) to present-day circumstances and economic and social structures. As Leonardo Boff put it in his book, *Jesus Christ Liberator: Critical Christology for Our Time* (1978), every generation constructs their understanding of Jesus in the context of their contemporary community. Therefore, all Christology is, in his words: "clarification done by the community afterwards".[4]

If understood this way, liberation Christology is no different, as it defines Christ in the context of the struggle against injustice. For Boff, it was the experience of God in Jesus (in his down-to-earth teachings, combined with his deeds) that led his contemporaries to exclaim: "Only a God could be so human!"[5] In Jesus' healings of those without hope and casting out of demons, liberation both was demonstrated and directly impacted on those living in bondage. In the same way, exponents of liberation Christology would argue, it is only in the experience of current economic liberation through the inspiration of Jesus, that modern individuals find themselves engaging with Christ and the power of God.

The impact of liberation Christology can be seen beyond the boundaries of those South American Catholics usually associated with it. Others, from very different theological backgrounds, have also engaged with its ideas of Christ's poverty and what this says both about Christ and about the church itself. Pentecostal (see chapter 17) Hispanics in the USA have also been influenced by a liberation Christology that has spoken both to their personal experiences of Christ through the Holy Spirit in "Spirit Christology" and to their cultural context of often being socially marginalized as Jesus was. This expresses itself in the concept of *El Divino Companero* (the Divine Companion) who identifies with the dispossessed, while also filling them with the Holy Spirit. As Sammy G. Alfaro has put it, Christ is: "the one who walks with them in midst of pain and struggle, and makes provision for their needs through his Spirit".[6] In addition, Alfaro asserted that: "A Hispanic Pentecostal Christology, then, focuses on the liberating presence and praxis [practice, as distinguished from theory] of Jesus' mission in the Spirit."[7]

In geographical terms, too, it has spread beyond its heartlands in South America and has influenced thinking in a number of developing countries, where Christians have sought to explore their understanding of the impact of Christ in LEDCs (Less Economically Developed Countries).

A future for liberation theology?

In 2007, Pope Benedict XVI continued the emphasis of John Paul II when he criticized the Christology of one of the leading proponents of liberation theology. This was Father Jon Sobrino (born 1938), who lived in El Salvador, although he was originally a Basque, from Spain. Benedict XVI accused him of focusing too much on the humanity of Jesus to the detriment of his divinity, and being insufficiently clear over whether this was taught in the New Testament. Father Sobrino had described Jesus as "our brother in relation to God". In addition, Sobrino was accused of making "the church of the poor" (as Sobrino described it) the central context for theology, rather than the apostolic traditions of the church and the early church councils. Clearly, the Vatican doubted his commitment both to the creeds and to the historic teachings of the church, beyond a narrow emphasis on the poor and their experiences.

He was also accused of teaching "assumptionism"; that is, treating the Jesus of history as a figure distinct from God, who was "assumed" by the divine Son of God into union with God. In addition, it was felt that he was insufficiently clear about Jesus' self-consciousness of his status as Christ and as Son of God and that he reduced the cross of Christ to the status of a moral example. Sobrino rejected these representations of his theology. The Vatican's concerns, though, were clear: too much emphasis on social liberation and not enough on spiritual liberation; too much emphasis on Jesus' humanity and not enough on his divinity. It is significant that Christology was very much at the core of the Vatican's concerns, alongside misgivings over strategy, church tradition, and political emphasis. The disagreement (however others may assess the accuracy of the concerns) was over Christ, as much as over politics.

In contrast to these earlier stances on liberation theology by Popes John Paul II and Benedict XVI, some have suggested that under Pope Francis (pope since 2013) the movement, in a new form, is now back on the agenda of the Catholic Church – at the highest level. In 2014, he condemned global inequality and those ideologies which defend the supremacy of market forces and financial speculation. Radical economic thinking is now at the heart of Vatican pronouncements. This is not, however, a return to anything approaching a Catholic–Marxist alliance (despite accusations of this) but is, instead, an emphasis on New Testament Christian radicalism, that has featured in other periods of Christian history. It is significant that Jorge Mario Bergoglio took the papal-name of Francis, after Francis of Assisi, famous for his commitment to the poor. And it is a radicalism rooted in a very traditional view of a fully divine Christ who is, nevertheless, allied with the poor through his humanity, humility, and poverty, rather than Christ with a Kalashnikov. But it is a belief with a cutting edge when it comes to twenty-first-century problems.

Later in 2014, in a speech to the plenary of the European Parliament, meeting in Strasbourg, Pope Francis emphasized the importance of "the promotion of human rights" and "the dignity of the person". He also urged the need to defend Europe from "multinational interests" and to "restore dignity to labour by ensuring proper working conditions".[8] This was in addition to the need for active respect for the environment and showing compassion towards immigrants. For Pope Francis, these concerns were rooted in Christ.

In his first homily as pope in 2013, Francis had stressed – in terms that would be recognized and accepted by mainstream Christians, whether Protestant Evangelicals or traditional Catholics – the centrality of Christ to the mission of the Christian church:

> … if we do not profess Jesus Christ, things go wrong. We may become a charitable NGO, but not the Church, the Bride of the Lord… when we profess Christ without the Cross, we are not disciples of the Lord, we are worldly.[9]

CHAPTER 16

Christ in the Developing World: Some African and Asian Christologies

For centuries one of the dominant images of Christ was as he was envisaged in western Europe. This portrayed him very much as a white European and loaded the image with the cultural characteristics of Europe. In this way the Christ of the early Middle Ages dressed in a mixture of styles inherited from the Mediterranean world and western and northern Europe. Guards at the crucifixion might look like Anglo-Saxon or Frankish warriors. A crucified Christ from Scandinavia included features reminiscent of pagan Viking art. Throughout the Middle Ages, and beyond, this continued; the houses of Bethlehem or Nazareth came to resemble those of medieval, Renaissance, or early modern European societies. When Pieter Bruegel the Elder (1525–69) painted *The Adoration of the Kings* in 1564, the costumes of civilians and soldiers are those of the mid-sixteenth century, and baby Jesus, on Mary's lap, is white. When Henry Holman Hunt painted one of the most famous paintings in Christian art history

– *The Light of the World* – in 1851–53, the scene is a European woodland and Christ is European. It was this image of Christ that travelled the world with nineteenth-century missionaries.

All this is very understandable. Since Christian Christology proclaims Christ as being human as well as divine, it is to be expected that human beings will visualize him as one like themselves. Thus the humanity of Christ transcends cultures and is capable of adopting many different forms. The problem comes when the image gets "fixed" and for many of European descent this has occurred. But beyond this particular image of Christ, a set of alternative, equally valid images have emerged.

As a Middle Eastern first-century Jew, the historic Jesus would have had an appearance very different to many modern stereotypes; although this is beginning to be reflected in more culturally accurate representations of him in modern art and cinema. This would have come as a particular shock to those Europeans and Americans of the recent past who even consciously attempted to strip Christ of his Jewish and Middle Eastern identity, such as Houston Stewart Chamberlain (1855–1927) who believed Jesus was of Germanic extraction, Madison Grant (1865–1937) who thought him "Nordic", and the Nazis who claimed – in the face of all reason and evidence – that Jesus was Aryan and not Jewish at all.

The emergence of more culturally accurate images of Christ is striking. Recent examples include a 2001 project sponsored by the BBC, France 3, and the Discovery Channel, to produce an image of Jesus that was more likely to represent the actual appearance of a first-century Galilean Jewish male.[1] The result was certainly not a "white Christ". However, this is by no means new. In the medieval Ethiopian church, in post-colonial Africa, in Asia and South America, especially since gaining independence from European rule, responses to Christ have explored different ways of portraying and understanding him. Indigenous Christians have looked at Christ in ways that resonate with their indigenous culture. We have already examined the South American theme of liberation theology, and while that is not the only South American contribution to Christology, in this chapter we will restrict our focus to themes affecting Africa and Asia. We will only succeed in giving an outline of these dynamic issues but, in so doing, we will examine one of the most important developments in the history of Christ that has occurred in the twentieth and twenty-first centuries.

Christ in Africa

In forming their own views and expressions of Christ, Africans have had to overcome centuries of white European dominance which imposed a Eurocentric view of Christ and dictated that Africans were not the deciders of their own destinies. In answer to this, Africans have asserted their own legitimacy in deciding how they communicate Christ in a number of ways. Since Christ lived in the Middle East and early Christians were soon active in Egypt and Ethiopia, the historic incarnation was a non-European event, and Christianity was in Africa before the nineteenth-century missionaries. Furthermore, since the pre-existing *Logos* is the expression of God, it is reasonable, African theologians have argued, to look for examples of God's communication to humanity in aspects of pre-Christian cultures. Also, the power of the resurrection has liberated Christ from all worldly constraints and so we should not try to reconstrain him in the structures and approaches of one particular culture or form of expression. Christ is everywhere through his Holy Spirit and that includes in Africa.

Writers such as the Catholic Tanzanian, Charles Nyamiti (born 1931), have argued that aspects of African historic culture can be used in order to express ideas about Christ. These include the concepts of Christ as the Chief, Christ as the Healer, and Christ as our Ancestor. The concept of Christ as our Ancestor, which gave rise to Nyamiti's 1984 book of that title, is clearly one that engages with many aspects of African culture, and has been investigated by a number of African theologians from different church backgrounds. In 1979, the Protestant Ghanaian, John Pobee, wrote:

> Our approach would be to look on Jesus as the Great and Greatest Ancestor – in Akan language *Nana*. With that will go the power and authority to judge the deeds of men, rewarding the good, punishing the evil. [However,] he is superior to the other ancestors by virtue of being closest to God and as God.[2]

In 1984, the Methodist Ghanaian, Kwesi Dickson (1929–2005), also expressed this Christology in a way that meshed with African traditional concepts of ancestors as those who define the identity of their descendant communities:

> Christ was the perfect victim; by his death he merits, to use an African image, to be looked upon as Ancestor, the greatest of ancestors, who never ceases to be one of the "living-dead," because there always will be people alive who *knew* him, whose lives were irreversibly affected by his life and work.[3]

The matter, though, is complex as it affects ordinary believers, for while it uses the language of traditional society it does so by, arguably, using it in a different way. A similar issue faces Indian Christians in their use of traditional Hindu terms, such as *avatar* and *guru*, to describe Christ and communicate ideas about his nature and role, as we shall shortly see.

A survey conducted in 2004 among eighty students at the Theological College of Northern Nigeria highlighted some of the complications. One student wrote:

> Christ lived and died without having biological children, so that disqualifies him as an ancestor in Bura culture. He died at the age of 33 years which to Bura people is a tender age, so that proves that his age is not fit for him to be qualified as an ancestor.

Another wrote:

> Christ is never an ancestor in Taroh land due to the fact that (i) he died a shameful death ...; (ii) had no wife nor children (male) ...; (iii) he is never a member of any clan in Taroh land ...; (iv) had no compound nor history in Taroh land.

A large number of others also drew attention to Christ not being married and not having children as meaning that he did not fit into traditional definitions of being an "Ancestor".[4]

Even allowing for the interpretation that these students may have been responding through a very literal definition of "Ancestor" as they were used to the term, compared with a more elastic and flexible handling of the term as used by Pobee, Dickson, Nyamiti, and many others, it nevertheless does remind us of the complexities that can arise from the coining of new Christological terms, especially when these terms still have widespread currency and are still understood in particular ways within a culture. Other critics of the use of the term have identified problems in using a tribal/clan term for a universal saviour, and yet others have feared that its use might appear to condone ancestor-cults in which ancestors might variously be seen as revengers, bringers of disease, or objects of fear. Some have asserted that the very nature of the resurrection puts Jesus on a different plane to dead ancestors, however their continued influence is felt to be significant.

No doubt the term will continue to be used but these reservations do give some pause for thought. However, it might be asserted that terms such as *Logos* were borrowed from existing cultures, and eventually became so imbued with a new meaning that they became technical Christian Christological terms, so only time will tell whether these African terms have a long or short future in the language of the African church.

Anselme Sanon (born 1937) has added a further category of Christ as the Master of Initiation. In addition, François Kabasele (born 1947) has included the idea of Christ as son of the Great Chief (God) and, therefore, the Elder Brother of believers who is able to act as a Mediator between them and God. This is a relationship also explored by Nyamiti. All of these terms are drawn from pre-Christian African culture but each can be used to communicate something of the nature of Christ, and in a way that resonates with African society. This approach is known as "inculturation" and so this "Inculturation Christology" is a way of finding the tools and images to convey understanding about Christ within one's own existing culture.

African Christology, although difficult to succinctly describe, nevertheless does possess certain distinctive features. It certainly exemplifies "theology from below": understanding Christ from the experiences of believers and his impact on life. And in this the life of Christ resonates with many Africans, mirroring the "practical realities of poverty, illiteracy, ethnic tensions, colonialism, dictatorship, illness, disenfranchisement, and suffering".[5] This emphasis on the suffering Christ who understands and is immediately understood by people is rooted in incarnation beliefs. It seeks, as we have seen, to integrate belief and expression into existing language and culture. It also takes very seriously the belief of Christ as continuing to bring supernatural healing in a way that is still accepted by theologically conservative Christians globally but downplayed by more liberal Western approaches.

Christ in India

The Indian subcontinent has seen other distinctive and intriguing explorations of what Christology means to modern people in a developing setting.

The first of these is the *Ashram* Movement. The Christian Ashram movement started in 1921 with the founding of the Protestant *Ashram Christukula* (Family of Christ). These ashrams were influenced both by the contemplative experiences of ancient Hindu ashrams and by the modern ashrams of the nationalist Gandhian movement. Post-independence, Roman Catholic ashrams were founded by monastics who sought a different fulfilment compared to traditional monasticism. While Protestant and Roman Catholic ashrams differed in emphasis (Protestant ashrams are more orientated to social action, Catholic ashrams more monastic-orientated) they all shared one aim: to explore Christianity in a way that resonated with Indian traditions. The central understanding of Christ, based on the Hindu ashram community structure, is constructed around an authoritative *guru* (teacher), and views Jesus as a *sadhu*, a holy man, devoted to God, teaching divine truth and serving others. This supposes that if Christ had been incarnated in India then he would have been a *sannyasa* (one completely renouncing the world and rejecting society). This idea then relates directly to belief in the incarnation and how best to express it in ways that contemporaries can understand. This aspect of a *sadhu-guru*-Christ figure has scriptural foundations, as sixty of the ninety direct addresses to Jesus in the gospels are to him as "teacher". However, in contrast to a culture which emphasizes the existence of many gurus, the Ashram movement emphasizes that Christ is the supreme guru, maintaining the uniqueness of Jesus. This understanding of Christ involves the bringing together of Christian monasticism and Hindu mystic traditions in the community structure, as Christ is the unique teacher who reveals the divine. It attempts to find pointers towards Christian faith in Indian traditions. As the Indian theologian and proponent of the Ashram movement, Savarirayan Jesudason (1882–1969), wrote:

> poets and prophets of this land have abundantly proved their experience of the *eternal* Christ (though strangers to the *historic* Christ) through their lives, teachings and songs.[6]

This raises the question of how far Christians can borrow from existing cultures in order to express the uniqueness of Christ. The question is not a new one. As we have seen, John innovatively used the terminology of the Greeks, *Logos*, to describe the incarnation of Christ. Jesudason compared use of the pre-existing Greek word *logos* with the Hindu holy syllable *OM*, and argued that these two concepts are so similar that John, if writing in the present day, would have no qualms using *OM* of Christ. Not all Christians would agree, but it raises an important question since almost all theological and Christological terms are borrowed, and existed before being deployed by Christians. However, *logos* has long come under the control of the Christian pattern of thought, whereas with *OM*, Hindu connotations and not Christ are the first reference. It is a question of which fundamental image is in control and this will cause disquiet among many Christians.

The second approach, from the Indian Protestant theologian Vengal Chakkarai (1880–1958), rather than adapting Christianity to a Hindu institution, instead used Hindu terminology to express Christ in an Indian context. Chakkarai, a member of the "Rethinking Christianity" group, promoted the urgent need for a rethinking of Christ within a Hindu setting as part of the "Indianization of Christianity". His 1926 book encapsulated this aim in its title: *Jesus the Avatar*. How then does this approach present Christ? Chakkarai explains the incarnation of Jesus in Hindu terms: Jesus, as an *avatar*, is the full, final, transcendent, human manifestation of God (expressed in the Hindu term *Brahman*) on earth. Yet, Chakkarai himself was aware that "*avatar*" and "incarnation" are different, not interchangeable. *Avatar* is the temporary presence of God with a recurring nature who cannot assume human weakness, becoming man. This is not the traditional Christian understanding of the incarnation of an eternally united humanity and divinity in the person of Christ.

Chakkarai argued, however, that one avoided the confusion of assuming a Hindu Christ, comparable to Krishna or Rama, through clear definition of meaning and context, and biblical reference to assist definition of terms. For Chakkarai, both *avatar* and Jesus acquire new meanings once applied to each other. Furthermore, as Chakkarai has emphasized, Christians believe that Christ was not just temporarily incarnated as a man in the first century, but that his Spirit continues to live in believers. Therefore, while the term *avatar* clearly has no biblical basis, Chakkarai argued that such a definition (of the Spirit of Christ eternally reincarnated in man) finds a basis in John 14:16: "he [God] will give you another Advocate, to be with you for ever". In this way "Advocate" (the Holy Spirit) may be used alongside the Indian term "*antaryamin*", the "indwelling experience of his devotees", as in Galatians 2:20, "Christ who lives in me." In this way Chakkarai would have argued that his use of Hindu terminology has not compromised his Christology. The challenge, of course, lies in the question of whether it is really possible to use and redefine a term that is so imbedded in Indian culture and continues to be used within Hinduism?

Other – visual – images are more easily assimilated, even if they surprise Western viewers. In November 2014, *The Times of India* carried a report on the opening of the Indian Christian Art Exhibition, at Our Lady of Mount Carmel Archiepiscopal palace chapel, Se Cathedral, Old Goa. The exhibition had as its highlights work by the late Goan artists Angelo da Fonseca (1902–67) and Angela Trindade (1909–80) among others. These artists in particular used their art as a bridge between Christian belief and Asia (especially Indian culture). Trindade's paintings included Mary wearing a sari and Jesus dressed in orange robes as a guru accompanied by similarly dressed disciples. Da Fonseca's depiction of the Trinity portrayed Father and Son sitting cross-legged on the roots of an inverted tree, whose branches (below them) embraced the world. The Father is robed in white and the Son in orange robes reminiscent of an Indian holy man. Between them the Holy Spirit, in the form of a dove, hovers before the cross.

Another Indian artist, Frank Wesley (1923–2002), in his painting *Home in Nazareth*, depicted Christ with Mary and Joseph, as a blue-skinned infant, evoking the image of the Hindu god Krishna, who is often depicted in his child form. Wesley demonstrated how not only language but Hindu iconography can be transferred to Christ. In this particular painting, there is a curious fusion of Asian art since the perspective is Japanese and is based on a print by the Japanese graphic artist Hiroshige. Wesley lived for five years in Japan, studying art, which helps explain this surprising influence. More alien to Western depictions and more controversial was Wesley's painting, *Before Abraham Was I Am*.

It clearly draws on both Hindu and Buddhist iconography and depicts deity in a female form. Her right hand holds a lotus bud and conveys the meaning that deity has not yet achieved human form (that is, the *Logos* has not yet been born as Jesus Christ). This image of the *Logos* before the incarnation deliberately and provocatively starts within Hindu imagery as its first point of reference, in order to communicate the Christian concept about the pre-existing Christ.

A very different approach to expressing Christ has emerged in India in what has been called "Dalit Theology". The Christian Dalit movement (formed between 1975 and 1986) addresses the issue of poverty experienced by those within the Hindu caste system, who are categorized as the polluting "untouchables", outside the hierarchy of religious purity. In the 1970s, Christian Dalits adopted this name (in Sanskrit meaning "broken") as an expression of their oppressed status within Indian society and even within the Indian minority Christian community. Dalit Christology offers hope for their own liberation. Firstly, Jesus himself is presented as a Dalit born into poverty. Indeed, "his dalitness is the key to the mystery of his divine human unity".[7] In the incarnation, Christ became "Dalit, oppressed and despised", identifying with Dalit struggles.[8] They find New Testament evidence of this in the very beginning of the gospel accounts, since the genealogy at the start of the Gospel of Matthew lists, along with Jesus' Jewish ancestors, four names of non-Jewish women, which provides evidence that Jesus was, in Dalit terms, of mixed caste, a Dalit characteristic.

While a strict reading of the text would lead one to question whether the gospel writer intended such a deduction when placed alongside Jesus' descent from King David, nevertheless this humanness does find scriptural basis in the Son of Man sayings in the gospels. As the Son of Man, Christ experienced rejection and death, mirroring Dalit brokenness. The humiliation of the cross is the supreme representation of Christ's Dalitness and at the same time, in its combination of suffering humanity and divinity, offers the hope that those who now share in suffering will, in Christ, also share in the victory of his divinity.

Susheila Williams, president of the Indian Christian Art Association, has encapsulated much of what is understood in this view of the crucifixion in her painting, *The Man on a Village Tree*. Christ is crucified on a tree outside a South Indian village. In the middle distance a woman, holding a baby, looks questioningly at the sight, with the thatched village beyond. The picture demonstrates how Christ was not only alongside the poor and oppressed of his day, as recorded in the gospels, but suffers with low-caste impoverished villagers in the rural areas of India today. As the so-called "Dalits Creed" movingly expresses it:

Our cries for liberation from harsh caste-bondage
Were heard by God, who came to us in Jesus Christ...
Jesus Christ is our Lord, Saviour and Liberator.[9]

Other Asian insights

The startling use of indigenous imagery, that we saw used by Frank Wesley, has been deployed by other artists from different cultures but with the same intention. In Bali (Indonesia) the artist Nyoman Darsane (born 1939) communicates Christian concepts through Hindu-Balinese art forms. In his 1978 painting, *He Came Down*, the female worshipper prays with a lotus blossom between her fingers and adopts a pose that is typically Balinese. Christ descends, bare-chested, garlanded, and with flowing hair, like a dancer; light shines from him and drives the demons away. Darsane has summed up his approach in this way: "Bali is my tradition. Christ is my life."[10]

Choan-Seng Song (born 1929), distinguished professor emeritus of theology and Asian cultures at the Pacific School of Religion (California), has criticized what he sees as the Western-centric nature of Christian theology. In his view it presents an overly individualistic gospel with insufficient reference to community life, family, and group identity, and this disengages non-Western converts from their original cultures. Given the way Asia has been exploited by non-Asian powers, this can also create an identity crisis for Asian Christians and a sense of disloyalty to their local culture. Influenced by South American liberation theology, he has argued that Asian Christology must start from the identification of Christ with the poor and what this reveals about both his nature and his relevance to people. More controversially, he has stated that God united with Jesus at his baptism (a belief traditionally rejected as "adoptionism") and that the cross was not part of God's or Jesus' intention, since "the God of Jesus is not a murderous God".[11] God's silence at Jesus' death, he has argued, was the silence of grief and compassion with which the suffering people of today can engage. This adoptionist approach constitutes a rejection of traditional ideas about the atonement.

Other Asian Christians, influenced by Hindu beliefs in multiple incarnations of the divine alongside Buddhist teachings, have suggested that God has become one with humanity in many ways and times and not exclusively through Jesus. This, though, abandons the uniqueness of Christ's incarnation that is central to traditional Christology.

What unites the alternative Christologies of South America, Africa, and Asia is the assertion by people in these societies that Christ can be imagined as one of them; it is not necessary to be constrained by inherited Western language and images. As C. S. Song has put it, unless this is done, "Christianity will always remain a stranger."[12] It must, though, be noted that many other Asian

Christians in Korea, China, and elsewhere are part of churches whose Christology (and theology generally) is thoroughly mainstream, and in line with the historic creed-statements and images of the church, whether Catholic or Protestant. Clearly, not all believers are looking to express Christ in indigenous terms. The belief in Christ in Asia, as elsewhere, is complex.

CHAPTER 17

Christ and the Power of the Holy Spirit

Some years ago, when one of the authors was training for a preaching role in a traditional, mainstream Christian church in the United Kingdom, an elderly mentor made a very intriguing remark. "When I was a young girl," she said with some puzzlement, "if a person felt called to go abroad as a missionary they would say: 'Jesus told me to do this.' But today they say: 'The Holy Spirit told me to do this.'" It was an interesting point and the change, though by no means universal, had been sufficient for her to both notice it and not fully understand what was going on. In subsequent conversation, there was even a hint of concern on her part. It was as if the central role of Jesus Christ in these Christians' spiritual lives and their ways of expressing their relationship with God had been replaced by the third person of the Trinity, the Holy Spirit. What was going on? Had something changed in the Christology of the church? What does this reveal about the history of Christ?

To some people reading this chapter that elderly mentor's puzzlement will seem very strange indeed, since they are completely comfortable with the phraseology that she spotted and did not, herself, fully grasp. Other readers may share something of her questioning regarding this matter and may wonder what is going on in the phraseology and experience of some Christians, while others may frankly wonder what this discussion is all about. To help us explore this a little further, some very basic aspects of this spiritual landscape may need establishing. This will come nowhere near explaining the nature and importance of this area of Christian faith but it may, at the very least, help us see the wood for the trees.

Father... Son... Holy Spirit...

To put it very simply indeed, the first of the first-century followers of Jesus were Jews who believed that there was only one God who could not be seen, described, or imagined but whose character and holiness could be sufficiently understood to have faith in him and to respond to his demands on life because he *chose* to reveal sufficient of himself to human beings (supremely to the Jewish people and through their history). Then they met Jesus. Over time – and especially in the aftermath of the resurrection which they proclaimed had followed his execution – they came to the understanding that in this real man, God had again revealed himself but this time in a way unique in history. More than this, they came to believe that, in a way impossible to fully describe, God was in this person. Indeed, that this person was God; not the totality of the substance of God (as if God was not also in heaven during the earthly life of Jesus) but nevertheless God. This Jesus, they proclaimed, was "the Christ" and even more than that, he was "the Son of God". This was, at its simplest, the implication of the Christian belief in the incarnation: that the pre-existing *Logos* of God had become "flesh", as John put it in his Gospel. Because later Christians were Greeks, with a complex philosophical language at their disposal, and because the Christian community soon became embroiled in bitter arguments over the exact nature of this God-man Christ, there followed four centuries of debates which eventually led to the formation of the creeds.

However, this was not the end of the matter. For the followers of Jesus soon began to say that, although he was no longer among them, he was still present in their lives and in their actions. The unseen – but personally experienced – power of Jesus was living in their lives and in their communities, and this was made possible, they claimed, because God had poured out his Holy Spirit on the individual members of the Christian community. This had started at Pentecost, as recorded in Acts (although a preliminary giving of the Spirit is stated in the Gospel of John, as recorded in John 20:22, before Jesus' ascension), but was ongoing whenever a person came to faith in Christ. The Holy Spirit was not an impersonal force, nor were Christians dependent only on the principles and guidelines that had been left by Jesus. Instead, they claimed that Jesus the Christ was alive and living in them. Something of the invisible nature and power of God – that they had intimately experienced in their relationship with Jesus – was now even more intimately living in them and uniting them with God. This empowerment was not the work of a thing but of a person: the Holy Spirit of God. Doing "theology on their feet" they were, in effect, constructing in outline the doctrine of the Trinity. Paul pointed out some of the key features of this belief when he wrote:

> If the Spirit of him who raised Jesus from the dead dwells
> in you, he who raised Christ from the dead will give life to
> your mortal bodies also through his Spirit that dwells in you.
> (Romans 8:11)

Here can be seen some of the key features of belief in this new Spirit-filled life: firstly, the Spirit is from God the Father and indeed is *his* Spirit; secondly, the action of the Spirit is intimately connected with the fact that Jesus had been raised from the dead; thirdly, this experience is accompanied by the Spirit living in the believer in an ongoing way; fourthly, the consequence of this indwelling of the Spirit is that believers gain a new empowering of their life. Other passages would talk of a Christian being "a temple of the Holy Spirit" (1 Corinthians 6:19) and receiving gifts to enable them to carry out the tasks that God has for them to do, to build up his church. Some of these gifts, as identified in the New Testament, clearly implied supernatural knowledge and discernment by way of words of prophecy and inspired teaching; others were more like supernaturally charged natural abilities such as administration. Another, the gift of tongues, engaged the believer in a joyful experience of power that transcended earthly speech, but could also be translated by those appropriately gifted as a way of communicating a message from God to the assembled Christians.

The Holy Spirit and Christ

The passage quoted above clearly identified the Holy Spirit as coming from God the Father.

This can be seen in many other New Testament passages too. For example, in a comparable one, Paul wrote:

> … you were washed, you were sanctified, you were justified in the name of the Lord Jesus Christ and in the Spirit of our God. (1 Corinthians 6:11)

And again, but in a way that emphasizes the threefold but complementary roles of Father, Son, and Holy Spirit in the life of a Christian:

> The grace of the Lord Jesus Christ, the love of God, and the communion of the Holy Spirit be with all of you.
> (2 Corinthians 13:13)

However, terminology could be a little more complex and give rise to questions over the exact nature and origin of the Holy Spirit. At one point, while recounting a decision over what route to follow on a missionary journey in Asia Minor (modern Turkey), Acts says:

> When they had come opposite Mysia, they attempted to go into Bithynia, but the Spirit of Jesus did not allow them…
> (Acts 16:7)

Yet one verse earlier we are told that they had been "forbidden by the Holy Spirit to speak the word in Asia" (Acts 16:6). The term used to describe the Spirit who directs them varies over two adjacent verses. In a different context, when talking about assistance from God we are told:

> I know that through your prayers and the help of the Spirit of Jesus Christ this will result in my deliverance. (Philippians 1:19)

These are interesting passages. Clearly, we would be completely wrong to assume that the New Testament teaches that there is "the Holy Spirit from God the Father" and, in addition, "the Spirit of Jesus". This would go against the whole grain of the belief system that was emerging through these documents, as the early church thought through its understanding of the nature of God. So, how are we to understand this difference in terms?

The most obvious answer is that these early Christians were quite relaxed in their terminology. At times they wrote of

Father, Son, and Holy Spirit in a distinct way. At other times they wrote of God the Father working through the Holy Spirit. At yet other times, they so associated the Spirit-filled experience with the presence and personality of Christ that they used the term "the Spirit of Jesus". In a similar way, a revelation from God, which in a different context might be described as being communicated by the Holy Spirit, might be directly attributed to Christ, as when Paul wrote concerning the authority of his own knowledge and teaching:

> I did not receive it from a human source, nor was I taught it, but I received it through a revelation of Jesus Christ. (Galatians 1:12)

It should be remembered that Paul never met Jesus during his earthly ministry. Did Paul mean that Christ *himself* appeared to him in a vision or that the *message* from Christ was revealed to him? If the latter, then in other circumstances this might be attributed to the Holy Spirit. In a clearer example we find:

> Now may our God and Father himself and our Lord Jesus direct our way to you. (1 Thessalonians 3:11)

At other times such a "direction" might be attributed to the actions of the Holy Spirit. When the leaders of the Jerusalem church were clarifying how non-Jewish Christians should behave it was through advice that "seemed good to the Holy Spirit and to us…" (Acts 15:28).

This varied emphasis has, though, caused tension in the later Christian church as it formulated the creeds and attempted to precisely define the nature of the Spirit's origin in God. As a consequence the Nicene Creed reads:

> We believe in the Holy Spirit, the Lord, the giver of life,
> who proceeds from the Father [and the Son].
> With the Father and the Son
> he is worshipped and glorified.[1]

The earliest form of this creed simply stated that the Holy Spirit is from ("proceeds from") God the Father. However, in the Western church the words shown in brackets above were added to communicate the belief that the Holy Spirit comes from *both* Father *and* Son. This is the famous *Filioque*-Clause that we considered earlier. It remains an area of contention between Western Christians and Eastern Orthodox Christians.

Most Western Christians and those whose origins are derived from Western traditions are heirs to the *Filioque* belief, even if they are not aware of it. As a result, it is this form of the belief that has gained global use due to the actions and influence of Western European missionaries in the nineteenth and twentieth centuries and as a result of missionaries and church-plants from US evangelical Protestant churches in the twentieth and twenty-first centuries. This means that a terminology that variously uses the terms "Holy Spirit", "Spirit of God", and "Spirit of Jesus" has developed and ordinary Christians (not given to complex theological internal debates on Trinitarian and Christological emphases each time they speak and pray) might find themselves moving unconsciously from one phrase to the other. Or they may simply say "Jesus", "Christ", the "Holy Spirit", or "God" has spoken to them or revealed something to them, without their choice of terms being code for any profound theological difference when compared to the last time they used a *different* term.

But there have been trends in Christian faith and experience over the last century which explain why some terms are now used more frequently in a number of Christian communities (but not all) and it is undoubtedly this that confused that elderly mentor we met at the start of this chapter. It can confuse other Christians too. And it can certainly confuse non-Christians.

Charismatic Christians today

So-called "Charismatic Christianity", also sometimes known as "Spirit-filled Christianity" or "Renewed Christianity", places significant emphasis on the work of the Holy Spirit in the life of a believer, in the continued existence and use of spiritual gifts, and on miracles and "signs and wonders". The word "charismatic" comes from the Greek word *charismata*, meaning "grace (spiritual) gifts".

Some Christian denominations, such as the Pentecostals, have a theology and practice with a major focus on spiritual gifts as part of a personal experience of Christ as saviour. Growing out of the "Holiness Movement", Pentecostal churches took on a distinct character from the early twentieth century. The stimulus to this included the Azusa Street Revival (in Los Angeles, USA), which started in 1906 and lasted for three years. This was at a time when many mainstream churches taught that the spiritual gifts seen in Acts and referred to in the letters of Paul were no longer to be found in the church. Pentecostals, in contrast, believe that this is not the case and that Christians still experience these in their daily lives.

Associated with what is called the "baptism in the Holy Spirit" or "filling with the Holy Spirit", this experience of empowerment may be associated with initial conversion or experienced as a second phase of deepening experience after conversion. It may, or may not, be associated with the laying on of hands. Some charismatic Christians differentiate between the two terms, with "baptism" being used to describe the initial encounter with the

Holy Spirit and "filling" being used for subsequent experiences of additional renewal. As a number of Christian writers have put it, Christians are "leaky vessels"[2] and so more than one "filling" may be needed. As a result of this belief, it *may* be stated that Christians who do not exhibit these "grace-gifts" have not experienced the "baptism" or "filling" with the Holy Spirit. This claim, of course, is controversial. There is no hard and fast rule as to how these terms are used and different Christian individuals and groups may use them differently.

From the 1960s, these ideas began to spread through a number of the mainstream denominations, both Protestant and Catholic. As a result, it is now possible to find both individuals and churches whose beliefs and practices would be described as charismatic while still being part of a wider church network (e.g. the Church of England, the Roman Catholic Church, the Baptist Church, etc.) which is not of this persuasion overall. This widespread phenomenon is often referred to as the Charismatic Movement. While sharing many characteristics with Pentecostals there may be less emphasis on speaking in tongues as a definite sign of Spirit baptism (something emphasized in Pentecostalism), but this varies.

While this phenomenon has affected all Protestant denominations and the Roman Catholic Church, there seems rather less evidence of it within Eastern Orthodoxy. However, this last point needs qualifying a little. In North America, there is some evidence of conversion to Orthodoxy involving a small but noticeable number of Christians coming out of a charismatic background. They want the personal and emotional "experience" of Christ but also the historical roots and validity that they see in a church rooted in the rulings of the early ecumenical councils. In this way, very different traditions – that both offer experiential forms of Christianity – may at times combine.

Another group of churches are sometimes referred to as "Neo-charismatic" churches or "Third Wave", referring to three great moves of the Holy Spirit: the first in the early twentieth century leading to Pentecostalism, the second in the 1960s leading to the Charismatic Movement, and the third from the 1980s onwards leading to the growth of these churches. A widespread example of such Christian communities would be the Vineyard churches.

While there is no such thing as a definitive charismatic church service, due to the large number of traditions represented, there are nevertheless certain characteristics that occur across a number of church communities. These include a fairly high degree of informality; extended times of worship, often using contemporary musical styles and worship bands; Bible-based preaching, although in some churches the teaching can be based rather more on personal spiritual experience than on detailed scriptural exposition; and congregational participation through shared words of knowledge, prophecies (inspired messages from God), and "pictures" (shared images which illustrate a spiritual message). There can also be a fairly high profile for women since charismatic inspiration (for example in prophecy or words of knowledge) is not bound by social and gender norms or expectations. This can circumvent male-orientated authority and teaching structures by giving increased opportunity for the female voice within churches.

The movement is global and can be experienced in US and European churches of many types, South Korean mega-churches, Chinese house churches (often meeting without official government agreement), independent African churches, and in South America.

As might be imagined, there are no clear boundaries between these churches and many enjoy good relations with each other. Members – much less conscious of "denomination" than in previous periods of history – may move from one to another with relative ease. It has been estimated that charismatic Christians number somewhere in the region of 500 million people, or 25 per cent of the Christian population of the world. "It is widely regarded as the fastest growing element of Christianity and as a consequence it is reshaping the demography of Christianity".[3] This is because there has been an explosion of charismatic churches in the southern hemisphere.

Is there such a thing as a distinctive "charismatic Christology"?

The short answer to this question might seem to be "No." This is because charismatic Christians tend to be theologically conservative, Bible-based, and very much within the traditional creedal mainstream of Christianity. As a result, emphases on the deity of Christ, the reality of the incarnation, the harm caused by sin and the need for repentance, atonement through the cross, and the bodily resurrection of Christ all underscore the traditional theological and creedal nature of this broad movement. There may also be an emphasis on eschatology and the second coming of Christ but, again, this is a current that has always flowed within the Christian mainstream:

> In contrast to what many outsiders think, these movements are not centered on the Holy Spirit more than on Christ, even though their spirituality is charismatic and spiritualistic.[4]

So, to return to the anecdote that began this chapter, the puzzled elderly mentor was reacting to a change in terminology that occurred after the middle years of the twentieth century, not a change in Christology.

On reflection, though, the answer to the question "Is there such a thing as a distinctive charismatic Christology?" could be "Maybe." This is not due to any redefinition of the nature and role of Christ, but rather a rethinking of the relationship of the believer with Christ and expectations of Christ.

A *relationship* is a key feature of charismatic Christology: the idea that the believer can experience a personal connection with Christ, a sense of unity with him, and an immediacy of divine Christ-presence through the experiential aspects of charismatic worship and the exercise of spiritual gifts. Periods of extended worship tend to focus on an exaltation of Christ, along with a personal and sometimes emotional response on the part of the believer. While this has been criticized as over-subjective and even overemotional – with a love relationship being expressed that, at times, might seem to border on romantic – it should be remembered that such intensity of emotional engagement with Christ is as old as Teresa of Avila, and romantic language in spirituality is as old as the Old Testament book, Song of Songs. No doubt the issue is really about emotional/intellectual, subjective/ objective *balance*.

The other issue is expectation. charismatic Christians expect Christ to act. With an emphasis on inspired messages, healing, and deliverance from spiritual bondage, this is a Christology of an active and liberating Christ. In addition, Christ is central to the whole charismatic experience, since the Holy Spirit only comes to the believer due to faith in Christ and it is Christ through whom the baptism with the Spirit and the reception of the gifts of the Spirit are possible. This, then, is a Christ-centred spirituality, which actually emphasizes "the centrality of Christ (not the Holy Spirit) and the unique instrumentality of faith in him".[5]

In addition, it could be argued that charismatic Christians place less emphasis on the Passion of Christ (his suffering) than has been done in traditional Catholicism and also in many Protestant churches. While accepting completely the atoning nature of Christ's death on the cross, it could be argued that within the newest charismatic churches, there is less emphasis on Christ's suffering and more on his triumph. This is simply a matter of emphasis but, arguably, it is discernible.

What charismatic Christology also does is draw our attention firmly to the part played by the Holy Spirit in the earthly ministry of Jesus. If we envisage the Trinity as Father and Son eternally united in love through the Holy Spirit, then the part played by the Spirit becomes a crucial way by which Christians can understand how Christ was, in his humanity, utterly dependent on God and, in his divinity, fully united with his Father throughout the years of his time on earth. As a result, Christ was born of the Holy Spirit in the incarnation and was continually one with the Father through the same indwelling Holy Spirit. He was anointed and empowered for his ministry when the Spirit descended on him at his baptism. This then sets a pattern for the life of the believer: born again through the work of the Holy Spirit for salvation and empowered by the Spirit for active service. This twofold experience, mirroring that of Christ, may occur simultaneously, or the empowering for ministry may occur after initial conversion and may happen more than once. In the same way, Jesus' earthly emphasis on prayer, dedication to God, and expectancy that God will act, are crucial aspects of his incarnate existence, giving insight into how that operated, and also providing a pattern for Christian believers. In their experience, charismatic Christians would say the Holy Spirit is the dynamic power that transforms them, bearing witness to Christ, and through this (as through the earthly life of Christ) the Father is glorified. Far from neglecting Christ, charismatic Christology is both Christ-centred and thoroughly Trinitarian.

CHAPTER 18

Christ in Other Religions

Christ is, of course, the central character of Christianity but this major and controversial figure affects other world religions too. Here we will look at how Jesus is understood in four of the major world religions. To make this more manageable we will look specifically at these religions in the context of Christian claims that he is the messiah and Son of God; the nature of Old Testament prophecies and Jesus' birth; and his death and resurrection. We will begin with the two other Abrahamic faiths, Judaism and Islam, before exploring Hindu and Sikh interpretations of Jesus the Christ.

Christ in Judaism

Many Christians believe that Jesus fulfils forty-four Old Testament prophecies about the coming of the messiah, the Christ. For example, Micah 5:2 foretells that the messiah shall be born in Bethlehem; Isaiah 7:14 foretells that he shall be born of a virgin (in the Greek translation of Hebrew "young woman"); Psalm 69:8–9 and Isaiah 53:3 foretell that he will be rejected by his own people; and Psalm 22:16 foretells that his hands and feet shall be pierced (he will be crucified). However, many Jews believe that Jesus did not fulfil all of the prophecies that concern the messiah, for example that all the Jews would be returned to Israel (Isaiah 11:11–12; Jeremiah 23:8); that there would be an end to all wrongdoing (Zephaniah 3:13); and that the third Temple would be rebuilt (implied in Jeremiah 33:18; Ezekiel 40–47).[1] Therefore, Jews are still awaiting the coming of the messiah who is prophesied about in the Old Testament and believe that he will come at the End Times. Consequently, they do not believe that this messiah was Jesus.

This Jewish rejection of Christian beliefs about Jesus (principally belief in his divinity and in the Trinity) is as old as the later first century and was the cause of the split between early Christians and Judaism. Today there is no official or consistent Jewish thought on Jesus as a person; overall he is not really considered a significant figure within Judaism, so there is no set Jewish teaching about him. Centuries of persecution of Jewish communities by Christian authorities have done nothing to assist Judaism to engage positively with Christian beliefs.

Consequently, while Jews do not have a collective "position" on Jesus, it is generally perceived that Christianity came about after Jesus. Some Jews would argue that Jesus was a religious radical within his Jewish context which, after his death, led to his followers accepting Gentile members, which led to the formation of Christianity; yet he did not see himself as a leader of a new religion separate from Judaism. Some Jews believe that Jesus himself did not claim to be the Son of God, but that this claim came about through misunderstanding by later Christians. Most Jews would consider Jesus a teacher, but of no greater significance than his first-century contemporaries.

Many Jews would also agree with some of the teachings of Jesus that are also found in the Old Testament. For example, Jesus' teaching "You shall love your neighbour as yourself" (Mark 12:31) is also found in Leviticus 19:18: "You shall not take vengeance or bear a grudge against any of your people, but you shall love your neighbour as yourself: I am the Lord." However, Jews will reject the Christian belief that Jesus fulfilled the Old Testament Law and established a new covenant with God. In short, while Judaism may engage with Jesus the Jew, it does not engage with Jesus the Christ.

When it comes to Jesus' death, many Jews would agree with the gospel accounts that Jesus was crucified, arguing that there is historical evidence for Jesus dying on the cross. Jesus was seen as a revolutionary within Judaism at the time, however he was also seen as dangerous by the Romans as he was attracting attention and support which they feared could lead to unrest, regardless of whether Jesus believed this to be his mission. Judaism does not accept the gospel accounts of Jesus' resurrection that are so central to Christianity.

Christ in Islam: *Isa al-Masih*

Jesus, or Prophet *Isa* as he is known in Islam, is believed by many Muslims to be one messenger in a line of messengers bringing God's message to humanity. Many Muslims argue that God (*Allah* in Arabic) sent a messenger for every nation, and that Jesus was the messenger to the House of Israel (Jews) because they had turned away from God and were not living life in the way that God had intended. Muslims will say "peace be upon him" after saying the name of *Isa* as a sign of respect and the Qur'an compliments Jesus as a prophet: "We sent Jesus, son of Mary: We gave him the Gospel and put compassion and mercy into the hearts of his followers" (Qur'an 57:27).[2] However, Muslims believe that the final revelation was revealed to Muhammad;

Muhammad is the "seal of the prophets". This is not to say that Muslims believe Jesus was a false prophet or that his message was wrong. The Qur'an states that Jesus brought the same perfect message as Muhammad and taught the word of God (as did previous prophets), but humans distorted this message and wrongly recorded it. Therefore, Moses brought the Torah and Jesus brought the gospel; however, they believe that Muhammad was the only prophet whose revelation was recorded correctly. This distortion by humanity is not necessarily deliberate but due to human error.

It is because of this understanding about Jesus and the importance of his message that one of the titles given to Christians and Jews is "the People of the Book". The Qur'an declares that Christians believe in the same God: "[Believers], argue only in the best way with the People of the Book, except with those of them who act unjustly. Say, 'We believe in what was revealed to us and in what was revealed to you; our God and your God is one [and the same]; we are devoted to Him'" (Qur'an 29:46). Therefore, some believe that Christians will be allowed entrance into heaven: "The [Muslim] believers, the Jews, the Christians, and the Sabians – all those who believe in God and the Last Day and do good – will have their rewards with their Lord. No fear for them, nor will they grieve" (Qur'an 2:62). Some Sabians lived in what today is Iraq, and spoke their own language.

However, while sharing belief in the importance of Jesus' message, Muslims deny the main Christian belief that Jesus is the Son of God: "Those who say, 'God is the Messiah, the son of Mary,' are defying the truth" (Qur'an 5:17). The Qur'an mentions specifically that God does not have a son: "It [Scripture] warns those people who assert, 'God has offspring.' They have no knowledge about this, nor did their forefathers – it is a monstrous assertion that comes out of their mouths: what they say is nothing but lies" (Qur'an 18:4–5);[3] "God has never had a child. Nor is there any god beside Him" (Qur'an 23:91); "The Jews said, 'Ezra is the son of God,' and the Christians said, 'The Messiah is the son of God': they said this with their own mouths, repeating what earlier disbelievers had said. May God thwart them! How far astray they have been led! They take their rabbis and their monks as lords beside God, as well as Christ, the son of Mary. But they were commanded to serve only one God: there is no god but Him; He is far above whatever they set up as His partners!" (Qur'an 9:30–31). Muslims believe that Jesus is a creation of God and does not share in his sovereignty.

The Qur'an teaches specifically that God cannot be described as a Trinity: "People of the Book, do not go to excess in your religion, and do not say anything about God except the truth: the Messiah, Jesus, son of Mary, was nothing more than a messenger of God, His word directed to Mary, and a spirit from Him. So believe in God and his messengers and do not speak of a 'three' – stop [this], that is better for you – God is only one God, He is far above having a son, everything in the heavens and earth belongs to Him and He is the best one to trust" (Qur'an 4:171). And: "Those who say, 'God is the Messiah, son of Mary,' have defied God" (Qur'an 5:72). This statement is followed by another specific rejection of the belief in the Trinity: "Those people who say that God is the third of three are defying [the truth]: there is only One God. If they do not stop what they are saying, a painful punishment will afflict those of them who persist" (Qur'an 5:73).

Such teachings are a clear reaction to the Christian belief that God is Father, Son, and Holy Spirit. Therefore, because of this tension between believing that Jesus' message was important as one of God's messengers, yet proclaiming that the Christian belief in Jesus as the Son of God is a blasphemous act that can only lead to punishment, the Qur'an portrays a spectrum of opinions from very positive to very negative about some Christians and their fate.

Where Christianity and Islam do agree is on the virgin birth of Jesus to Mary; similar to the gospel accounts Qur'an 3:45–51, Qur'an 19:16–21, and Qur'an 21:91 state that Mary, a virgin, received the angelic message and submitted to God after initial shock. However, the birth of Jesus is different, as Qur'an 19:22–33 tells how Mary gave birth to Jesus on her own, while holding onto the trunk of a palm tree. Furthermore, the story is even more miraculous than the gospel accounts, as during the birth, baby Jesus spoke to Mary and afterwards to those who accused her of wrongdoing. At this point Jesus, as a baby, explicitly and miraculously said that he was a prophet. In contrast, the gospel accounts state that his first miracle was not performed until he began his ministry, roughly thirty years later.

Regarding the death of Jesus, some Muslims argue that before his arrest, when Jesus was pleading with God to save him from the fate of death,[4] he was submitting to God's will, thus declaring his *Islam* (surrender to God). Islam teaches that Jesus was not in fact crucified but was taken up to heaven after his death, which was not caused by crucifixion: "[The People of the Book][5] said, 'We have killed the Messiah, Jesus, son of Mary, the Messenger of God.' (They did not kill him, nor did they crucify him, though it was made to appear like that to them; those that disagreed about him are full of doubt, with no knowledge to follow, only supposition: they certainly did not kill him – No! God raised him up to Himself. God is almighty and wise…)" (Qur'an 4:157–158). While Christians agree that Jesus ascended to heaven, they believe that this only happened after his death and resurrection, not before. Some Muslims, guided by the *hadith* (sayings of the Prophet Muhammad), believe that God changed the face of Judas, Jesus' betrayer, so that he looked like Jesus. Judas was then crucified in Jesus' place; it was only made to appear that Jesus was crucified. These Muslims believe that the cross is not a sign of the cleansing of human sin through the sacrifice and resurrection of Jesus, but a sign of justice: Jesus' betrayer was given the punishment that he deserved for such a deed.

The reason why Islam teaches that Jesus was not crucified is because this death (worthy of a criminal) would be insulting for this prophet, but mainly to show that God is the best of planners. The people had planned in detail to kill Jesus; however, God is more powerful than humanity so their plan did not come to fruition. Therefore, Muslims do not believe that Jesus was resurrected, nor that the Holy Spirit guides his followers after his ascension into heaven. Some Muslims interpret John 16:12–13, "I still have many things to say to you, but you cannot bear them now. When the Spirit of truth comes, he will guide you into all the truth; for he will not speak on his own, but will speak whatever he hears, and he will declare to you the things that are to come", as a prophecy of the Prophet Muhammad who would continue and complete the message.

Yet, Jesus' role has not finished and many Muslims believe that Prophet *Isa* will return on the Day of Judgment with the *Madhi* (the awaited soldier of God) to restore justice and peace on earth. Therefore, Jesus is not just an important figure in Islamic history, but also has a part to play in the eschatological future of Islam and its people. His Arabic title, found in the Qur'an, is a form of the word that gave rise to the titles "messiah" in Hebrew and "Christ" in Greek. In Arabic he is described as *Isa al-Masih* (the Anointed/Anointer), variously understood as describing either Jesus' appointment by God as a blessed prophet, his lack of a permanent abode, his role as a healer, or divine anointing at his birth. What is clear is that Muslims do not mean by this term what Christians understand by their use of the term "Christ".

Christ in Hinduism

Before beginning the investigation of how Jesus is spoken of in Hinduism, it must be understood that there is not a singular set of Hindu beliefs and no Hindu "church", unlike the central institution in Christianity. Each Hindu will therefore have their own personal beliefs and, arguably more importantly, their own bodily, mental, and spiritual practices or *sadhana*.[6] It is through such practices that a person is freed from the bondage that they were born into. Therefore, if someone's spirituality is seen by their practices, to understand Jesus from one Hindu perspective is to look at his practices while on earth. It is through personal practices that one becomes God-conscious; therefore when Jesus said "I and the Father are one" in John, perhaps he was recognizing his awareness of God rather than claiming to be part of God.

Some Hindus will refer to Jesus as Saint *Ishu* who taught a universal message that "You shall love the Lord your God with all your heart, and with all your soul, and with all your strength, and with all your mind; and your neighbour as yourself" (Luke 10:27).[7] In this sense some Hindus would argue that Jesus was a holy man or teacher, known in Hinduism as a *sadhu*, demonstrated by his compassionate behaviour and teachings of non-violence: "Blessed are the peacemakers, for they will be called children of God" (Matthew 5:9). He was a guru and guide to all humans who wanted a true spiritual relationship with God. *Ishu* is not seen to be a figure of Christianity alone, but a figure who is also significant in Hinduism and not to be constrained to specific religions. The humble origins of Jesus, the Epiphany story (visitation from the wise men), Jesus' miracles, and the Sermon on the Mount are elements of Jesus' life which are also known in the Hindu religion. Christ's life, how he was tempted and suffered and overcame such trials, can then act as an example to Hindus of how to live a good spiritual life. The Sanskrit word *acharya* means "one who teaches by example" and so the life of Jesus, his humility, sincerity, and trust and love of God, can be influential for the practices of those outside Christianity too. It is the message of selfless love and the example of Jesus that are important to some Hindus rather than the man himself; what he did during his life is the focus, other aspects are minor or irrelevant. Arguably, his *message* alone can save humanity – his death and resurrection are not then believed to be necessary for salvation.

A different Hindu understanding of Christ is based upon the Hindu belief that the highest Ultimate Reality, who causes everything, is Brahman, and all Hindu deities are a form of Brahman. The many gods are therefore representations of the many aspects of God, as God is not one-dimensional. Therefore, Brahman has appeared to humanity in many forms throughout history, known as *avatars*, the bodily incarnation of a deity on the earth. The purpose of an *avatar* is to re-establish *dharma*, which is righteousness in the social and cosmic order.[8]

Therefore, some Hindus would argue that Jesus was indeed a revelation of God, as he was an *avatar*, an empowered incarnation, who was sent by God to earth with a particular purpose and mission. This purpose was to bring people back to God as they had become preoccupied with material possessions. Jesus' teachings, his challenge to the Jewish hierarchical religious system, and his supposed threat to society led to his death. Believing Jesus is an *avatar*, a form of God on earth, some Hindus will have images of Jesus in their homes or temples and will pray to him. Some Hindus also argue that Hindus should not be discouraged from attending church either. Hindus accept that Jesus was crucified, and many Hindus believe that such a death was a good thing as it probably led to another reincarnation. Some Hindus believe that after Jesus' death he became enlightened and merged with Brahman, the creator of all.

Overall, unlike Christianity which argues that Jesus is the singular representation of God on earth in history, some Hindus would argue that Jesus is one of many manifestations of God on earth in history alongside, for example, Vishnu. In contrast, for Christians it is the uniqueness of Christ's incarnation which is central to traditional Christology.

Christ in Sikhism

In a similar way to Islam and Judaism, Sikhism teaches that there is one God:

> God is One.
> He is the Supreme Truth.
> He the Creator, is without fear and without hate.
> He is immortal.
> He is neither born and nor does He die.
> By Guru's grace shall He be met.
> Chant And Meditate on His Name.
> In the beginning, He was the Truth.
> Throughout the ages, He has been the Truth.
> He is the Truth now and He shall be the Truth forever.[9]

From this perspective, Jesus cannot be God as he was a historical figure and a human being of flesh and blood who walked this earth; he was born and he died.

However, while Sikhs would not accept that he is God, Jesus as a prophet can be accepted as being one with God; this is supported by one of the sayings of Jesus in John 10:30 which states, "The Father and I are one." Many Sikhs believe that the gurus, the line of God-sent teachers throughout Sikh history, the first of whom was Guru Nanak, are also one with God. An analogy that might be used by some Sikhs is that of a drop in the ocean: the drop is part of the ocean but is not the same as the ocean.[10]

Many Sikhs would point to the fact that Jesus himself did not specifically claim to be God; they would argue that it is human misinterpretation and mistranslation that have led to the belief that Jesus is God. They believe that all humans have a part of God in them due to the fact that God created humans with a soul; however this does not make humans divine but children of God. Arguably, all good acts are done because humans have a soul; this is what it means to be made in God's image. When Jesus taught the disciples to pray the Lord's Prayer, he was teaching them to pray to God and not to himself, and thus not claiming to be God. Jesus also referred to God as "Father", indicating that he was sent from God, one who is higher. For Sikhs, Jesus might be described as a "son of God" sent to earth from God to enlighten people, but not "the Son of God" being understood as God himself. He represents God but is not God; a man who delivers God's word therefore is in the presence of God but is not divine.

Additionally, a central teaching in Sikhism is that all humans are equal; this is why many Sikh men will take the name "Singh" and Sikh women will take the name "Kaur" as a reaction to the Hindu caste system whereby surname and family background determine societal rank. In the Bible Jesus was ridiculed for mixing with "tax-collectors and sinners" (Matthew 9:10) and breaking societal norms as he taught, "Those who are well have no need of a physician, but those who are sick; I have come to call not the righteous but sinners" (Mark 2:17). There are numerous accounts of Jesus associating with women who would have been marginalized at that time: he is anointed by "a woman... who was a sinner" (Luke 7:36–38); he heals a woman who had been bleeding for twelve years, and so was deemed unclean (Mark 5:25–34); and he shows kindness and preaches God's word to a Samaritan woman who had had five husbands and was currently living with a man who was not her husband (John 4:1–42).11 Therefore, many Sikhs would agree with Jesus' teachings that God's message and a relationship with God are for everyone regardless of background, and not just for the richest or those society deems are the "holiest" or "best" people.

Sikhism also agrees with the biblical account that Jesus did die, but Sikhs do not believe that he was resurrected. In this sense, Jesus did not die to take away human sin, but died for his religion. Throughout Sikh history gurus (for example the fifth and ninth gurus) and other Sikhs have died for the right to practise their religion; the story of the *Panj Pyare* where five volunteers began the Sikh community (*the khalsa*) despite belief that this would lead to imminent death is particularly significant for Sikhs. Therefore, many Sikhs will argue that Jesus' death is a sacrifice; yet not a sacrifice for sin, but a sacrifice for worshipping One God, and teaching God's true word. Therefore, many Sikhs would argue that Jesus is to be revered as a significant martyr and messenger of God and is an important historical figure but not the divine Christ of Christian faith.

Can common ground be established regarding beliefs about Christ?

Given the little attention accorded to Christ in Judaism, it is difficult to establish a great deal of common ground between Jews and Christians beyond that which explores his first-century Jewish context as a teacher. Christ is the point in history which led to the departure of some Jews from traditional Jewish teachings, and it is at this point – when Jesus is claimed to be the messiah (Christ) and Son of God – that common ground ceases to exist.

Overall, Islam, Hinduism, and Sikhism all agree that Christ is a significant figure and that his teachings are highly influential. Therefore, related beliefs to those held by Christians, centred upon certain aspects of Jesus – as a perfect messenger or a manifestation of God whose love-filled teachings might affect our decisions and actions – can be identified within all these world religions. However, Christian beliefs about the uniqueness of Christ's divine characteristics and incarnation are to be found in Christian belief alone. Therefore it is at this point, when Christ becomes, for Christians, God's one and only Son, who is of the same substance as God and with God from the beginning of creation, that the major world faiths must inevitably agree to disagree.

CHAPTER 19

Postmodern Christ?

Where is Christology going in the twenty-first century? Is it possible to identify directions and chart possible trajectories?

The short answer is that there is no one direction that Christology is taking. This is not surprising. Debate has characterized this core area of Christianity since the Roman period. At the Reformation, as we have seen, a fairly clear consensus – at least in western Europe – over Christ, which held to the Nicene Creed and the Chalcedonian Definition, began to fragment. The intellectual challenge of the Enlightenment, the nineteenth-century "search for the historical Jesus", and the so-called demythologizing approach towards the New Testament accelerated this into the twentieth century. The disintegration of consensus received a further boost from the turmoil of an age of Total War, followed by the emergence of a liberal (and even "permissive") attitude towards what some saw as traditional ways of thinking, morality, and conduct. This could leave us concluding that now we really do have a "postmodern Christ", concerning whom there is no longer an all-encompassing set of commonly held beliefs. All is relative. Everyone's view is as valid as everyone else's. There is no overarching narrative or unit of measurement. What matters now is only how we variously and individually see things. The twenty-first century is the heir of this situation of fragmentation.

All of this is very important but it should not be overstated. Indeed, there is a danger of projecting the angst and uncertainty of the "postmodern" developed world (where allegiance to Christianity has experienced decline) onto the global church. In reality it is clear that for many Christians across the globe there is still a belief in Christ that sits well within the mainstream Christology of the church that has existed for much of the past 2,000 years. Among what we might call theologically conservative, evangelical, Bible-believing Christians (whether charismatic or not) can be found a Christology that is consistent with the faith-statements of much of the church for much of its history since the late Roman empire. Among million of Christians on all continents but especially in the developing world there is no ambiguity or reservation when they recite (if they do recite) the historic creeds. Their Christology is similarly orthodox, even if their worship, style, and organization vary enormously; and even if these differences sometimes trigger anxieties in more traditional believers.

Within the Western Christian church too, theologians such as N. T. Wright (bishop of Durham 2003–2010) have argued strongly that, for the apostle Paul, Christ fulfilled all the Old Testament promises of God and that, within a generation of the life of Jesus, Christians accepted a view of Christ that ranked him alongside the God of Israel. It is this Christ who is at the heart of Christian belief. This reminds us that faith in an exalted Christ is still very much a feature of twenty-first-century Christian debate.[1]

Some challenges to traditional Christology

In contrast to what has been said above, though, there are strands of belief that certainly challenge this more traditional outlook. In very liberal interpretations of his life and significance,[2] a

Jesus emerges who has little connection with his Jewish context or with the faith-statements of the early Christian church; he is without End Time teaching; he cannot reliably be found in the four gospels; and, at times, he is presented as an inspired sage and certainly not the incarnate Son of God. There is nothing supernatural in the Christ who emerges from these deliberations.

A different challenge to historical Christology (indeed to all Christian theology) comes from what is called process theology. This maintains that God is changing as is the universe. Subscribers to this approach deny the absolutes both of God's immutability (unchangeability) and of truth. From this perspective God must have been changed by the experience of the incarnation, even if the abstract features of God (for example, goodness, wisdom) remained constant. From this perspective, Christ was not only revealing God but changing God as God went through the process of being a human being. Furthermore, God in Christ can be understood as representing a powerless divinity; but one who was in total empathy with the plight of the suffering facing the human race. Some process theologians, such as C. Robert Mesle, would argue that Jesus is not singularly or essentially God. Instead, he was perfectly synchronized to God throughout his life.[3] Christ can therefore be described as the divine Word in human form – but not in the sense of being the unique union of divinity and humanity, since God is incarnate in any person when they do his will. More orthodox believers (while accepting the idea of the indwelling of God) would object that this conclusion is at odds with the belief in Christ as the supreme and unrepeatable revelation of God in human form.

That form, of course, was that of a man. This is a matter that has divided modern feminist theologians. For some, there is a reluctance to accept a male saviour who represents and acts for women. Some would even argue that it is the maleness inherent in concepts such as "Father" and "Son", and salvation through a son sacrificed to his father (rectifying the fall that started with Eve), that has underpinned the Christian sexual hierarchy over 2,000 years. What is needed, Mary Daly has provocatively and shockingly argued, is the "castration" of God and of Christianity because the myths of sin and salvation scapegoat both women and Jesus.[4] Other feminist theologians, though, would take the line that, although Christ's maleness was a crucial part of his incarnate being, the nature of deity transcends gender and is not limited to maleness. In this approach, the maleness of New Testament (and Old Testament) language reflects its cultural context rather than the fundamental nature of God and Christ. Yet others would point to the radical impact of Christ on women and the way his acceptance of women (including their role as primary witnesses of his resurrection) challenges gender restrictions. Christ was a male unlike other males of his time; his message and actions were greater than his gender; his maleness need therefore be no barrier to basing feminist Christology on his person.

What of an ecological Christ, a "Green Christ"? The belief in caring for creation is often neglected by proponents of different understandings of Christ. But the New Testament stridently proclaims that, not only does Christ offer individuals the possibility of becoming a "new creation" (2 Corinthians 5:17 and Galatians 6:15), but his ultimate revealing in his second coming will bring about the healing and transformation of the whole created order as well as bringing vindication and victory for those who believe in him:

> For the creation waits with eager longing for the revealing of the children of God; for the creation was subjected to futility, not of its own will but by the will of the one who subjected it, in hope that the creation itself will be set free from its

bondage to decay and will obtain the freedom of the glory of the children of God. (Romans 8:19–21)

If God in Christ plans the restoration of all creation through Christ, then this should also be built into Christology, as also into a general attitude of Christian love and care towards the created order (which longs for such restoration). Christology in the twenty-first century will, no doubt, be increasingly challenged to take this into account.

Back to the future...

However all these currents of thought eventually move and combine, what is clear is that for most Christians the radical nature of their Christ-faith will remain rooted in an engagement with the New Testament. And however much they debate and disagree about how best to read it, it is this set of documents and the person they describe that have been at the heart of the Christian community for 2,000 years and will continue to be so. It is appropriate, therefore, to end where we began, with the radical and controversial teachings of this first-century group who had known Jesus, whom they had come to believe was and is the Christ.

Acts contains some of the oldest faith-statements in the history of Christianity. Known to theologians as the *Petrine kerygma* (proclamation of Peter) or *Jerusalem kerygma* (the earliest preaching of the Jerusalem church), we can see preserved in these passages the earliest strata of Christology. Earlier than the gospels and the earliest of Paul's letters and composed long before the formation of the later creeds, there is a directness to these statements which reveals a (still Jewish) church expressing what it believed about Jesus the Christ. After the trauma of the crucifixion, the dramatic claims about the resurrection, and the experience of filling with the Holy Spirit at Pentecost, the whole of Jesus' life was now viewed by looking backwards through the lenses of these events. Already we can discern the themes that would dominate Christian debate over the centuries; that would define the history of "Christ: The First 2,000 Years..."

To his Jewish listeners, the ex-fisherman Peter explained the radical beliefs that would soon explode beyond the boundaries of Judaism and eventually grow to be the largest religion in the world:

> This Jesus God raised up, and of that all of us are witnesses. Being therefore exalted at the right hand of God, and having received from the Father the promise of the Holy Spirit, he has poured out this that you both see and hear...
>
> Therefore let the entire house of Israel know with certainty that God has made him both Lord and Messiah [Christ], this Jesus whom you crucified. (Acts 2:32–33, 36)

Picturing Christ

A number of the pictures referred to in this book can be viewed online. Below are examples of web addresses where some of these can be viewed.

Chapter 5: Portraying Christ

Reconstruction of the church at Dura Europos: http://archive.archaeology. org/online/features/dura_europos/

Catacomb of Callixtus, Good Shepherd: http://diglib.library.vanderbilt.edu/ act-imagelink.pl?RC=54382

Catacomb of Domitilla, Christ among his disciples: https://www.oneonta. edu/faculty/farberas/arth/smarthistory/early_christianity_smarthistory.html

Cástulo glass plate, clean-shaven Christ: http://www.theguardian.com/ world/2014/oct/05/spain-christian-history-challenged-discovery-4th-century-glass-plate

Catacomb of Commodilla, bearded Christ: http://orthodoxwiki.org/Catacombs

Hinton St Mary, Christ and Chi-Rho: http://www.bbc.co.uk/programmes/ b00shkn4

Ravenna, mosaic of Christ's baptism: http://www.soniahalliday.com/category-view3.php?pri=IT31-5-10.jpg

Sistine Chapel, clean-shaven Christ: http://www.italian-renaissance-art.com/ Last-Judgement.html

Chapter 6: Imperial Christ

Harbaville Triptych: http://www.icon-art.info/masterpiece.php?lng=en&mst_ id=2557

Christ crowning Emperor Romanos and Empress Eudokia: https://www. oneonta.edu/faculty/farberas/arth/Images/arth212images/ottonian/byz_imp_ ivory.jpg

Catacomb of Domitilla, sarcophagus of Junius Bassus: https://neweyesonart. files.wordpress.com/2014/03/full.jpg

St Peter's, "Mausoleum M" mosaic: http://www.villairlandaroma.com/useful-information/vatican-catacombs/

Lullingstone Roman villa, Chi-Rho symbol: https://heritagefutures.wordpress.com/2014/08/30/guides-to-lullingstone-roman-villa/

Missorium of Theodosius: http://www.shafe.co.uk/mis_sorium_of_theodosius_madrid-_ac-_de_ia_historia/

San Vitale in Ravenna, Justinian carries the bread of the Eucharist to Christ: https://www.khanacademy.org/humanities/medieval-world/byzantine1/venice-ravenna/a/justinian-mosaic-san-vitale

Histamenon nomisma of Emperor Nicephorus II: http://coins.www.collectors-society.com/usercontent/images/article_images/86001180.jpg

Christ crowning the German Emperor Otto II: https://mybyzantine.files.wordpress.com/2010/11/otto-and-theo.jpg

Chapter 7: **Christ of the Barbarians**

Landelinus plate-buckle: https://twitter.com/caitlinrgreen/status/556193607737421825/photo/1

Franks Casket, Adoration of Christ by the *magi:* http://www.christianiconography.info/3001course/franksCasket.jpg

New Minster *Liber Vitae*, King Cnut and Queen Emma donate a cross: http://britishlibrary.typepad.co.uk/.a/6a00d8341c464853ef01538f0462d1970b-500wi

Agnus Dei coin of Æthelred II, the Unready: http://www.fitzmuseum.cam.ac.uk/dept/coins/exhibitions/CoinOfTheMoment/images/AgnusDei_tn.jpg

Ethiopian Christ: http://imageweb-cdn.magnoliasoft.net/britishlibrary/supersize/061534.jpg | https://vmfa.museum/pressroom/wp-content/uploads/sites/3/2014/11/VMFA-Triptych-2014-226-v1TF201408.jpg

Royal memorial stone at Jelling: https://sites.google.com/site/infoartefactartiklar/_/rsrc/1324118832981/artikel-59/jellingC.jpg?height=302&width=250 | http://www.worldheritagesite.org/profiles/fotoos/9622.jpg

Gosforth Cross: http://www.britainexpress.com/images/attractions/editor/Gosforth-0023.jpg

Kirk Andreas Cross: https://s-media-cache-ak0.pinimg.com/736x/ab/4a/f5/ab4af5 f90ddb4454937c29a71 ecf1b4b.jpg

Chapter 8: **Christ of the Crusaders**

Queen Mary Apocalypse, Christ as a crusader: http://www.wwnorton.com/college/english/nael/images/middle/christ.jpg

Hyghalmen Roll, Christ as a knight: https://upload.wikimedia.org/wikipedia/commons/a/a1/Jesus_Coat_of_Arms_1.jpg

Chapter 9: **Christ of the Middle Ages**

The Ecstasy of Saint Teresa, by Bernini: http://www.learner.org/courses/globalart/assets/non_flash_386/work_098.jpg

Chapter 10: **Reigning from the Cross or Suffering on the Cross?**

"Alexamenos worships his god": http://s280.photobucket.com/user/eva243/media/Picture1.jpg.html

Cross of Otto and Mathilda: http://www.historyfiles.co.uk/images/Europe/Germany/Swabia_OttoI_01_full.jpg

Cimabue's distemper on wood painting, *Crucifix*: http://41.media.tumblr.com/tumblr_mde9stpu4Y1rpvjjio1_r2_1280.jpg

Man of Sorrows, by Geertgen van Haarlem: https://classconnection.s3.amazonaws.com/332/flashcards/2751332/jpg/c15_north331363732896207.jpg

Chapter 16: **Christ in the Developing World**

The Adoration of the Kings, by Bruegel the Elder: http://www.italian-renaissance-art.com/images/Bruegel-adoration-kings.jpg

The Light of the World, by Henry Holman Hunt: https://londonbygaslight.files.wordpress.com/2013/08/light-ofthe-world-by-willia.jpg

The Trinity, depicted by Angelo da Fonseca: http://www.artway.eu/userfiles/Angelo%20da%20Fonseca(1).jpg

Home in Nazareth, by Frank Wesley: https://jesusinhinduchristianart.files.wordpress.com/2013/05/ck14-lifenazareth.jpg

Before Abraham was I am, by Frank Wesley: http://mattstone.blogs.com/.a/6a00d8341bffb053ef01156f93b2cb970c-pi

He Came Down, by Nyoman Darsane: https://thejesusquestion.files.wordpress.com/2012/03/nyoman-darsane_hecamedown.jpg?w=640

References

Introduction

1. *The Holy Bible*, New Revised Standard Version (Anglicized Edition), Oxford: Oxford University Press, 1995.

Chapter 1: **What is a Christ?**

1. All Bible quotations are from *The Holy Bible*, New Revised Standard Version (Anglicized Edition), published by Oxford University Press, 1995. Where quotations refer to, for example, John 1:1 this means John, chapter 1, verse 1.

Chapter 2: **Christ in Acts and the Early Letters**

1. Psalm 110:1 reads "The Lord says to my lord, 'Sit at my right hand until I make your enemies your footstool.'"

Chapter 4: **Getting it "Right"… Getting it "Wrong"…Christ of the Creeds**

1. Kelly, J. N. D., *Early Christian Creeds*, Abingdon: Routledge, 2014, pp. 215–16.

2. Price, R., M. Gaddis, *The Acts of the Council of Chalcedon, Volume 1*, Liverpool: Liverpool University Press, 2005, p. 59.

Chapter 5: **Now You See Him, Now You Don't… Portraying Christ.**

1. *Chambers English Dictionary*, Edinburgh: W&R Chambers Ltd, 1990, p. 705.

2. Lutz, C. E., "The Letter of Lentulus Describing Christ", *The Yale University Gazette*, Vol. 50, Issue 2, 1975, pp. 91–97.

Chapter 6: **Imperial Christ**

1. The word barbarian was first used by Greeks to describe non-Greek-speakers. It was condescending and implied that their speech was unintelligible. Romans later used the term to describe non-Latin-, as well as non-Greek-speakers. It

became a term used to describe tribes living beyond the boundaries of the Roman empire and so indicated uncivilized "others" (seen from a Roman perspective). As the empire became Christian, it could also be used to describe non-Christian tribes living beyond or invading Roman territory.

Chapter 7: Christ of the Barbarians... Beyond the Mediterranean Heartlands

1. Cain, A., N. Emmanuel Lenski, *The Power of Religion in Late Antiquity*, Farnham: Ashgate Publishing Ltd., 2009, pp. 351–53.

2. Bede, *A History of the English Church and People*, L. Sherley-Price (trans.), revised by R. E. Latham, London: Penguin, 1968, p. 130.

3. Alexander, M. (trans.), *The Earliest English Poems*, London: Penguin Classics, 1977, p. 107.

4. We are grateful to the cathedral staff in Brussels for allowing us a private viewing of the reliquary, even though the treasury was shut. It was a moving and memorable experience.

5. Whitelock, D. (ed.), *English Historical Documents, Volume I, c.500–1042*, London: Eyre Methuen, 1979, p. 190.

6. Parry, K. (ed.), *The Blackwell Companion to Eastern Christianity*, Oxford: Blackwell, 2010, p. 126.

Chapter 8: Christ of the Crusaders

1. Lamoreaux, J. C., in J. V. Tolan, *Medieval Christian Perceptions of Islam: A Book of Essays*, Abingdon: Routledge, 2013, p. 4.

2. Child, J., N. Kelly, M. Whittock, *The Crusades*, Oxford: Heinemann, 1992, p. 13.

3. Kleiner, F., *Gardner's Art through the Ages: The Western Perspective*, Volume 1, Boston, MA: Cengage Learning, 2009, p. 320.

4. Johns, J., in J. McManners (ed.), *The Oxford Illustrated History of Christianity*, Oxford: Oxford University Press, 1990, pp. 179–80.

Chapter 9: The Many-sided Christ of the Middle Ages

1. Quoted in: Schwarz, H., *Christology*, Grand Rapids, MI: Wm. B. Eerdmans Publishing, 1998, p. 161.

2. Quoted in: Schwarz, H., *Christology*, p. 166.

3. Hudson, J. A., " 'God our Mother': The Feminine Cosmology of Julian of Norwich and Hildegard of Bingen", http://www.sfsu.edu/~medieval/ Volume%201/Hudson.html (accessed February 2015). See also: Innes-Parker,

C., *Anchoritism in the Middle Ages: Texts and Traditions*, Cardiff: University of Wales Press, 2013, p. 66.

4. Weinandy, T., *In the Likeness of Sinful Flesh*, London: A&C Black, 2006, p. 39.

5. Quoted in: Newman, E., *Attending the Wounds on Christ's Body: Teresa's Scriptural Vision*, Cambridge: James Clarke & Co., 2013, p. 150.

Chapter 10: **Reigning from the Cross or Suffering on the Cross?**

1. Quoted in: Viladesau, R., *The Beauty of the Cross: The Passion of Christ in Theology and the Arts*, from the Catacombs to the Eve of the Renaissance, Oxford: Oxford University Press, 2008, p. 11.

2. Quoted in: Pocknee, C. E., *Cross and Crucifix in Christian Worship and Devotion*, London: Mowbray, 1962, p. 41.

3. Quoted in: Van Os, H., *Art of Devotion in the Late Middle Ages in Europe 1300–1500*, London: Merrell Holberton in association with Rijksmuseum, Amsterdam, 1994, p. 157.

4. Quoted in: Derbes, A., *Picturing the Passion in Late Medieval Italy*, Cambridge: Cambridge University Press, 1998, p. 156.

5. Quoted in: Every, G., *Christian Mythology*, London: Hamlyn, 1970, p. 73.

6. Quoted in: Fernandes, J., *Rejoice in the Lord*, Bandra: St Pauls BYB, 2008, p. 104.

7. Quoted in: Van Os, H., *Art of Devotion*, p. 128.

8. Quoted in: Viladesau, R., *The Beauty of the Cross*, p. 157.

Chapter 11: **"Reformed" Church… "Reformed" Ideas About Christ?**

1. Quoted in: Ban, J. D., *The Christological Foundation for Contemporary Theological Education*, Macon, GA: Mercer University Press, 1988, p. 122.

2. Ban, J. D., *The Christological Foundation*, p. 122.

3. Ban, J. D., *The Christological Foundation*, p. 123.

4. http://www.iclnet.org/pub/resources/text/wittenberg/concord/web/augs-003.html (accessed March 2015).

5. Ban, J. D., *The Christological Foundation*, p. 126.

6. Quoted in: Webb, S., *Jesus Christ, Eternal God: Heavenly Flesh and the Metaphysics of Matter*, Oxford: Oxford University Press, 2012, p. 155.

7. Quoted in: Spence, A., *Christology: A Guide for the Perplexed*, London: Bloomsbury, 2013, p. 79.

8. Spence, A., *Christology: A Guide*, p. 81.

9. Spence, A., *Christology: A Guide*, p. 82.

Chapter 12: "King Jesus and the Heads upon the Gate!"

1. Quoted in: Firth, C. H., *Cromwell's Army*, London: Methuen, 1921 (3rd edition), p. 338.

2. Firth, C. H., *Cromwell's Army*.

3. This and other quotes from Fifth Monarchy Men pamphlets, now held in the British Library, London, are from Whittock, M., *"The Sword Drawne": Christian Dissent and Politics 1649–1666, Particularly in the Fields of Millenarianism and Antinomianism*, unpublished undergraduate dissertation, University of Bristol, 1980.

Chapter 13: Christ in the Age of the Enlightenment and Western Imperialism

1. http://geography.about.com/od/obtainpopulationdata/a/worldpopulation.htm (accessed April 2015).

2. Schweitzer, A., *The Quest of the Historical Jesus: A Critical Study of its Progress from Reimarus to Wrede*, London: SCM Press Ltd, 1954, pp. 368–69.

3. Schweitzer, A., *The Quest*, p. 397.

4. Schweitzer, A., *The Quest*, p. 397.

5. Schleiermacher, F., *The Christian Faith*, Edinburgh: T&T Clark, 1976, p. 385.

6. Quoted in: Sugirtharajah, R. S., "The Magi from Bengal and Their Jesus: Indian Construals of Christ during Colonial Times", in S. E. Porter, M. A. Hayes, D. Tombs (eds), *Images of Christ*, London: Bloomsbury, 2004, p. 147.

Chapter 14: Christ in the Age of Total War and the Search for a "Modern Christology"

1. See Sassoon, S., *War Poems of Siegfried Sassoon*, North Chelmsford, MA: Courier Corporation, 2004, p. 11.

2. Quoted in: Campbell, P., *Siegfried Sassoon: A Study of the War Poetry*, Jefferson, NC: McFarland, 1999, p. 90.

3. See: Lemon, R., E. Mason, J. Roberts, C. Rowland, *The Blackwell Companion to the Bible in English Literature*, Hoboken, NJ: John Wiley & Sons, 2012, p. 689.

4. Quoted in: Stallworthy, J., *Wilfred Owen*, London: Random House, 2013, p. 265.

5. Studdert Kennedy, G. A., *The Wicket Gate or Plain Bread*, New York, NY: George H. Doran Company, 1923, p. 48.

6. Quoted in: de Gruchy, J. W., *The Cambridge Companion to Dietrich Bonhoeffer*, Cambridge: Cambridge University Press, 1999, p. 149.

7. Bonhoeffer, D., *Ethics*, London: SCM Press Ltd, 1955, p. 263.

8. Bonhoeffer, D., *Ethics*, p. 59.

9. Bonhoeffer, D., *Ethics*, p. 90.

10. Quoted in: Blackburn, V., *Dietrich Bonhoeffer and Simone Weil: A Study in Christian Responsiveness*, New York: Peter Lang, 2004, p. 235.

11. Pannenberg, W., *Jesus – God and Man*, London: SCM Press, 1985, p. 154.

12. Pannenberg, W., *Jesus – God and Man*, p. 135.

Chapter 15: **Christ with a Kalashnikov?**

1. http://www.vatican.va/roman_curia/congregations/cfaith/documents/rc_con_cfaith_doc_19840806_theology-liberation_en.html (accessed July 2015).

2. Quoted in: Bohache, T., *Christology from the Margins*, London: Hymns Ancient and Modern Ltd, 2008, p. 86.

3. Bohache, T., *Christology from the Margins*, pp. 86–87.

4. Boff, L., *Jesus Christ Liberator: Critical Christology for Our Time*, Maryknoll, NY: Orbis Books, 1978, p. 13.

5. Boff, L., *Jesus Christ Liberator*, p. 178.

6. Alfaro, S. G., *Foundations for a Hispanic Pentecostal Christology: A Constructive and Liberative Approach*, Eugene, OR: Pickwick Publications, 2008, p. 155.

7. Alfaro, S. G., *Foundations*, p. 157.

8. http://www.europarl.europa.eu/news/en/news-room/content/20141121IPR79832/ html/Pope-Francis-delivers-a-message-in-Parliament-to-all-the-citizens-of-Europe (accessed April 2015).

9. http://w2.vatican.va/content/francesco/en/homilies/2013/documents/papa-francesco_20130314_omelia-cardinali.html (accessed July 2015).

Chapter 16: **Christ in the Developing World: Some African and Asian Christologies**

1. For an accessible overview of the results see: Wells, M., (27 March 2001), "Is this the real face of Jesus Christ?" *The Guardian* (London: Guardian).

2. Quoted in: Palmer, T., "Is Jesus Christ Our Ancestor?", p. 1. http://www.tcnn.org/articles/RB42_Palmer.pdf (accessed April 2015).

3. Palmer, T., "Is Jesus Christ", p. 2.

4. Palmer, T., "Is Jesus Christ", pp. 4–6.

5. Tennent, T., *Theology in the Context of World Christianity: How the Global Church Is Influencing the Way We Think About and Discuss Theology*, Grand Rapids, MI: Zondervan, 2007, p. 113.

6. Jesudason, S., *Unique Christ and Indigenous Christianity*, Bangalore: Christian Institute for the Study of Religion and Society, 1966, p. 41.

7. Nirmal, A. P., "Towards a Christian Dalit Theology", in A. P. Nirmal (ed.), *A Reader in Dalit Theology*, Madras: Gurukul Lutheran Theological College and Research Institute, 1991, p. 65.

8. "Dalit Liberation" (2005), http://cpiarticles.blogspot.co.uk/2005/02/dalit-liberation-theology-interview.html (accessed September 2015).

9. Quoted in: Prabhakar, M. E., "Christology in Dalit Perspective", in V. Devasahayam (ed.), *Frontiers of Dalit Theology*, Delhi: I.S.P.C.K., 1997, pp. 419–20.

10. http://www.omsc.org/art-at-omsc/darsane/darsane-intro.html (accessed April 2015).

11. Song, C. S., *Jesus, the Crucified People*, Minneapolis, MN: Fortress Press, 1990, pp. 82–84.

12. Song, C. S., *Third-Eye Theology: Theology in Formation in Asian Settings*, Maryknoll, NY: Orbis Books, 1979, p. 8.

Chapter 17: **Christ and the Power of the Holy Spirit**

1. Johnson, P. R., http://www.spurgeon.org/~phil/creeds/nicene.htm – using the wording of The Interdenominational Committee on Liturgical Texts (accessed May 2015).

2. For example, D. L. Moody, quoted in: Miller, S., *D. L. Moody on Spiritual Leadership*, Chicago, IL: Moody Publishers, 2008, p. 103.

3. Miller, D. E., K. H. Sargeant, R. Flory, *Spirit and Power: The Growth and Global Impact of Pentecostalism*, Oxford: Oxford University Press, 2013, p. 9.

4. Kärkkäinen, V.-M., *Christology: A Global Introduction*, Grand Rapids, MI: Baker Academic, 2003, p. 16.

5. Elwell, W. A. (ed.), *Evangelical Dictionary of Theology*, Grand Rapids, MI: Baker Academic, 2001, p. 221.

Chapter 18: **Christ in Other Religions**

1. Many Christians would argue that the sacrifice of Christ was a once-and-for-all sacrifice for human sin, eradicating the need for further animal sacrifice which would be reintroduced by the "third Temple".

2. The Qur'an is divided into 114 chapters or *surah* and each *surah* is subdivided into verses (*ayat*). Qur'an 57:27, for example, means *surah* 57, verse

27. All quotes from the Qur'an are from: The Qur'an, M. A. S. Abdel Haleem (trans.), Oxford: Oxford University Press, 2010.

3. It is possible that this particular verse is not a reference to Christian beliefs, since the classical Arabic word *walad* can mean male, female, singular, and plural. Consequently, this verse may be a reference to Meccan claims that angels were daughters of God, The Qur'an, Abdel Haleem (trans.), p. 183, note a.

4. Matthew 26:39, Mark 14:36, and Luke 22:42 all include variations on the phrase "not my will, but your will be done".

5. In this context: Jews.

6. Klostermaier, K. K., *A Survey of Hinduism* (3rd edition), Albany, NY: State University of New York Press, 2007, p. 37.

7. Das, S. R., *Saint Jesus, Jesus in Hinduism* (2009), http://www.bbc.co.uk/religion/religions/hinduism/beliefs/jesus_1.shtml (accessed August 2015).

8. Chokoisky, S., *The Five Dharma Types: Vedic Wisdom for Discovering Your Purpose and Destiny*, Rochester, VT: Destiny Books, 2014.

9. *Guru Granth Sahib* Ji, 1. http://www.realsikhism.com/gurbani/popup.php?pagenumber=1_(accessed September 2015).

10. Beversluis, J. D., *Sourcebook of the World's Religions: An Interfaith Guide to Religion and Spirituality*, Novato, CA: New World Library, 2000, p. 93.

11. As well as associating himself with a woman who would have been marginalized due to her marital history and cohabiting while being unmarried which at the time would have been scandalous, Jews and Samaritans did not mix and definitely did not talk to each other so this event was even more shocking to Jesus' disciples.

Chapter 19: **Postmodern Christ?**

1. See: Byassee, J., "Surprised by N.T. Wright", http://www.christianitytoday.com/ct/2014/april/surprised-by-n-t-wright.html, April 2014 (accessed September 2015).

2. For example, the so-called "Jesus Seminar". Sponsored by the Westar Institute, California, and organized by a New Testament scholar, Robert Funk, it aimed to determine the "authentic words" of Jesus. It operated in the 1980s and 1990s and, as the short-lived "Jesus Project", was active again between 2008 and 2009. It was very controversial, rejecting the authenticity of most of the teachings of Jesus and its critics have accused it of being too North American, disproportionately representing the radical fringes of New Testament scholarship, and being focused on attempting to undermine the credibility of more traditional conservative scholarship.

3. Mesle, C. R., *Process Theology: A Basic Introduction*, St Louis, MO: Chalice Press, 1993, p. 106.

4. Daly, M., *Beyond God the Father: Towards a Philosophy of Women's Liberation*, London: Women's Press, 1986, pp. 71–72.

Index